FLOATING PALACES OF THE GREAT LAKES

A History of Passenger Steamships on the Inland Seas

Joel Stone

University of Michigan Press

Ann Arbor

Copyright © 2015 by Joel Stone
All rights reserved

This book may not be reproduced, in whole or in part, including illustrations,
in any form (beyond that copying permitted by Sections 107 and 108 of the
U.S. Copyright Law and except by reviewers for the public press), without
written permission from the publisher.

Published in the United States of America by the
University of Michigan Press
Manufactured in the United States of America
⊚ Printed on acid-free paper

2018   2017   2016   2015   4   3   2   1

A CIP catalog record for this book is available from the British Library.

Library of Congress Cataloging-in-Publication Data

Stone, Joel (Joel Lagrou)
    Floating palaces of the Great Lakes : a history of passenger steamships
on the inland seas / Joel Stone.
        pages   cm
    Includes bibliographical references and index.
    ISBN 978-0-472-02831-3 (ebook) — ISBN 978-0-472-05175-5 (pbk. : alk.
paper) — ISBN 978-0-472-07175-3 (hardcover : alk. paper)
    1. Passenger ships—Great Lakes (North America)—History.   2. Lake
steamers—Great Lakes (North America)—History.   3. Steam-navigation—
Great Lakes (North America)—History.   I. Title.
VM381.S76   2015
386'.22430977—dc23
                                                        2015008713

Preface and Acknowledgments

There is a romanticism associated with the steamboat era on the Mississippi River that flows through the American consciousness. Be it the popularity of Mark Twain's beloved literature or the grandeur of the lush Broadway musical *Showboat,* there is little doubt that "steamboat gothic" conjures visions of antebellum riverboats and an elegant and relaxed form of travel.

Across North America this romantic sentiment has not translated to an equally iconic steamboat era on the Great Lakes. Yet, by nearly every measure, steamboats that plied the lakes were the true passenger palaces of North America's maritime. There were commercial similarities among the western competitors, but Great Lakes vessels were more versatile and robust than riverboats, designed to operate well on open waters as well as in river currents. Against eastern competitors, Great Lakes shipyards laid claim to the largest and most luxurious vessels to participate in any coastal passenger trade. Nowhere in the world was there a concentration of ships defining engineering advancement, customer satisfaction, and geographic opportunity as on the Great Lakes.

There exists a curious gap in the historic literature about this commercial niche. The body of material related to this topic is generally dealt with through various studies of transportation, immigration, labor relations, and so on. Herein a multifaceted story is presented in depth, covering nearly 150 years. However, it is not the intention of this volume to identify every vessel or rectify all arguments and omissions in the record. Instead, this narrative portrays the passenger ship industry on the Great Lakes through its growth, prosperity, and demise.

Boats have been part of my consciousness for as long as I've been aware. Of three memories prior to my third birthday, one involves a boat: my uncle's Chris-Craft runabout on Lake Charlevoix in northern Michigan. I would like to say that I remember the *South American* cruising past a family picnic on Belle Isle, near the neighborhood where I grew up on the east side of Detroit, but it's too hazy to claim as fact. However, the parade of ships that passed our picnics certainly impressed on me the fact that I lived in a seaport town.

My affinity for the water, which in my family began generations ago, is most easily traced to an Irish sailor and fisherman who moved his brood to Nova Scotia and was afterward lost on the Grand Banks. Two generations later I had a grandfather, Maurice Lagrou, who was a professional photographer. He grew up on the Detroit River and swam around Belle Isle on a bet. Later in life, he took Peshaesque photographs and very early moving pictures of vessel traffic on the St. Clair River. My other grandfather, Ferris Stone, was part owner of a small sailing schooner that competed in early Bayview Yacht Club races to Mackinac Island. My parents, Fred and Lenora Stone, brought this appreciation of water together, and their three children absorbed it in varying degrees. I seem to have been the most smitten.

When growing up, I was fortunate to live a mile or so from Lake St. Clair, the pass-through "pond" between lakes Huron and Erie. The city of St. Clair Shores claimed more registered recreational boats than anywhere on the continent. Sleepy, foggy summer nights meant steam whistle signals floating in off of the Detroit River. I was not very good at fishing, but my best friend Mike had older brothers who talked their dad into buying a sailboat, and we enjoyed that sloop to its fullest. My coming-of-age had a lot to do with sailing.

I considered joining one of the sea services but came no closer than a stint as disc jockey on the Bob-Lo boat *Columbia*, a daytime excursion ferry between Detroit and an island amusement park. Cool job. I got my Coast Guard papers.

I began to understand maritime history and the depth of the literature when I studied with Father Edward Dowling, an engineering professor at the University of Detroit and an avocational marine historian and artist. His personal collection of data and ephemera was vast, and I came to understand that there were similar collections in libraries, museums, and homes throughout the Midwest.

In putting together this acknowledgment, so many instructors, mentors, and partners come to mind. To mention a few does a disservice to the many, but inevitably there are the Miss Spoors and Mr. Baileys who encouraged writing and the Father Dowlings and Pat Labadies who loved the boats. Together with Denver Brunsman and Doug Fisher, I came to understand how a book was molded and learned to embrace the challenge when the opportunity presented itself.

The friends I have sailed with add flavor to every word that follows, remembering sloops named *Phoenix, MicJay, Aegir, Quicksilver, Aggressor, Patriot,* and, with most affection, *Sean Cára, Conundrum,* the Cal-25 *Christmas,* and her longer, more comfortable sister, *White Christmas.* The best way to know the lakes is to sail them, and I've been fortunate to see most of them from deck level. To all who made that possible and enjoyable, I am grateful.

Throughout this volume an attempt is made to recognize the people who contributed significantly to the historical record regarding passenger steamships or to the ability of historians to access those records. In many cases, these gentlemen and ladies also encouraged my pursuit of this topic, whether they knew it or not. Patricia Majher, editor of *Michigan History* magazine, and Dedria Cruden sparked this project. The staff of the University of Michigan Press has made this process a pleasure, notably Scott Ham and Kevin Rennells, who shepherded the manuscript through the gauntlet. Mary Peterson created a thorough index that future researchers will gratefully leverage. And once again my friend Doug Fisher coached the prose, returning it to within the bounds of accepted grammatical norms.

This chronicle leveraged decades of dedication by innumerable scholars. A few writers deserve note. Transportation historian George Hilton, formerly Professor Emeritus of Economics at the University of California, Los Angeles, wrote extensive on various aspects of Great Lakes steamship travel. His analysis of the Lake Michigan passenger industry remains the finest compendium related to that regional business. Likewise, the work of Francis Duncan on the Detroit & Cleveland Steam Navigation Company (D&C) and its associated firms, serialized in *Inland Seas* magazine, is the most complete analysis of that organization, based largely on original documents held in the Burton Historical Collection at the Detroit Public Library. James Elliott's *Red Stacks on the Horizon* offers a keen insight into the development and maturation of a single firm—Goodrich Transportation—during this period. Maurice Smith and the Maritime Museum of Great Lakes at Kingston, Ontario, are to be commended for published works about early British and Canadian passenger steam-shipping. A fine recent addition is *Great White Fleet* about the Canada Steamship Line passenger fleets by John

Henry. Also, a salute to the editors and contributors of topic-specific publications like *Inland Seas, Marine Historian, Telescope, Scanner, Anchor News* and many others.

A special nod is given to those who have compiled various electronic databases which proved invaluable. Walter Lewis, Brendan Baillod, Chuck Feltner, David Swayze, Gerry Metzler and many others, have transcribed tens of thousands of early manuscripts and newspapers into searchable tools whose value cannot be understated. This material is found at a number of websites, notably the *Maritime History of the Great Lakes*. Additionally, the Association for Great Lakes Maritime History has supported several projects that make primary source material universally available to researchers.

This book owes a great debt to the collection at the Dossin Great Lakes Museum in Detroit. From 1949 to 2006, three curators fostered its development and growth: Captain Joseph E. Johnston, Robert E. Lee, and John Polacsek. Countless men and women from around the lakes have donated time, skills, documents, memorabilia, and money to preserve a record of the passenger steamboat era as it was drawing to a close. As of this writing, the Detroit Historical Society (DHS) Maritime collection at the Dossin Great Lakes Museum (DGLM) is undergoing an accessibility upgrade by staff and volunteers who appreciate its importance and vibrancy.

Those mentioned here, and subsequently, are responsible for the success of this volume. Failures in the text are ultimately the responsibilty of the author. Every effort was made to present the available data in a cohesive, contextual, critical, and correct narrative. The ultimate goal is to entertain and intrigue the reader with a fabulous drama that has already been performed.

My family has been most supportive and forgiving, both Stones and Masts, and that is a wonderful thing to say. When families know their history, they foster stronger historical communities and continuity.

This book is adoringly dedicated to my lovely and loving wife, Linda Terrell Mast Stone, who has a quiet patience for my maritime passions that even I don't understand.

JLS

Contents

Introduction

Steam Navigation on the Great Lakes

O n an anxious afternoon in mid-autumn 1967, a sonorous, three-toned chime echoed mournfully off the skyscrapers of downtown Detroit. The throaty blast of a steam whistle had become rare in this gritty home of internal combustion capitalism. Along the river, a crowd gathered to bid farewell to the Great Lakes excursion steamship *South American*. On board were "more than 125 sentimentalists" headed for Montreal and the Expo '67 World Exhibition.[1]

Similar scenes of departure, in some manner or another, had been played out on this stretch of the Detroit River for a century and a half, less a year. On an August afternoon in 1818, the steamer *Walk-in-the-Water* arrived at Detroit from Buffalo on her inaugural voyage, signaling the beginning of the age of steamship travel on the upper lakes. Since then—and until this moment in 1967—the movement of people around the Great Lakes on boats had been a major industry and a defining cultural element of the region.

In the words of *Detroit Free Press* marine reporter Curtis Haseltine, "[I]t was a trip like the *South American* had never taken before." Throughout the five-day voyage, wherever the ship went, its guests were serenaded by passing boat traffic. Whistle salutes blossomed from the stacks of slender Great Lakes bulk freighters. Smaller tugboats and appreciative mahogany runabouts provided an escort along the route. Everyone knew that the lily-white "Sweetheart of the Lakes" was making its last run.

At a stop in Cleveland, the farewell scene was played out again. After passing through the tranquil waters and locks of the Welland Canal,

The *South American* boarding its final complement of passengers in Detroit. (Photograph by William Hoey, 1967, courtesy of the Detroit Historical Society Collection.)

the ship crossed Lake Ontario, traversed the upper St. Lawrence River, and pulled into its last freshwater berth in Montreal. Passengers reluctantly disembarked, and an era in Great Lakes history was concluded with appropriate ceremony.

A simple schedule for October 23, printed on company letterhead, declared that the decommissioning ceremony would begin at 1530 hours, or 3:30 p.m., with a muster of personnel. With everyone seated, Mr. E. J. Goebel, president of the Chicago, Duluth and Georgian Bay Transit Company—for decades known as the Georgian Bay Line—presented for delivery the formal documents completing the sale of the vessel. Clifton Weston of the Seafarers Union's Harry Lundeberg School of Seamanship accepted them. Located in Piney Point, Maryland, this academy for maritime cadets had been established that same year, and the *South American* was to serve as a student dormitory.[2]

The ship's last skipper, Captain Joseph A. Testyon, efficiently proceeded through a series of official protocols and then called on "Officer

Thomas Joyce to haul down the colors." He presented the ship's flag to Mr. Goebel, who in turn presented the flag and a key to Mr. Weston of the Lundeberg School.

At 1620 hours, or 4:20 p.m., Captain Testyon dismissed his crew. The era of passenger travel aboard fleets of elegant steamships on the Great Lakes was over. Sadly, the vessel's new saltwater assignment was never realized. The Lundeberg School was unable to convert the ship into a habitable craft that would pass Coast Guard certification. The *South American* survived in a steadily deteriorating state until 1992, when the cutting torch closed the book.

At this writing, there are still a number of boats carrying passengers across the magnificent lakes of North America. Most are ferries designed for short-haul excursions or utility players that also carry autos, trucks, and freight. Only the ferries SS *Badger* and RMS *Segwun* are powered by steam. A handful of the retired vessels survive under the care of loving and inevitably underfunded entities. Such valiant efforts attempt to preserve and relive one of the grandest eras in our binational experience.

The era of "steamboating" in the Great Lakes region has been gone for almost half a century. Those who study North America's history must not forget the incredible impact that passenger vessels and freshwater maritime culture had on the development of the region and, in turn, the continent. Steamboating was a way of life for both passengers and crews, involved hundreds of the sleekest and fastest ships in the country, and took guests to nearly every picturesque port around the lakes. For a period in the middle of the nineteenth century, the ships elicited the moniker "palace steamers." In fact, throughout their history, nearly all of the premier passenger vessels sailing the inland seas were palatial in the eyes of customers and competitors. Cabin class guests generally traveled in the elegance and style typically reserved for the very wealthy. Throughout the age, the steamship companies catered to passengers of every type, from immigrants to tourists. Everyone benefited from a comfortable voyage and standards of speed and luxury that only improved over a hundred years.

Steamboats across the country shared a similar glorious history and a similar fate. On the Mississippi River, the Hudson River, Long Island Sound, and all along the East, West, and Gulf coasts of North America, the public and historians alike lamented the passing of an industry that fostered and established a continent. Each region had its favorite boats and celebrated shipping lines. Each enjoyed a rich nautical history that shared technologies and business practices and went through similar aesthetic styles and trends. And each region infused passenger steamships into its history, its people, and their culture. The resulting nostalgia and affection seem universal, as aficionados and casual boat watchers can be found wherever a steamboat line used to run, anywhere in the world.

Predictably, factors such as geography, culture, commerce, and politics combined to give each area unique characteristics, and the Great Lakes region exemplifies that rule. The inland seas dictated how hulls were shaped and engines designed. Those living on the lands around them, all immigrants in one form or another, brought traditions of nautical management, construction, and decoration to the vessels. And the natural resources, available markets, capital, and seasonal nature of the trade determined what freight—including passengers—was viable and how profits were made.

Despite the beauty and romance associated with steamboats, in the final analysis, they were financial assets intended to generate returns for their investors. Throughout this era, creative captains and owners continuously adapted to changing business conditions, taking advantage of opportunities within and without the maritime community. But, no matter their inventiveness, a number of elements conspired to gradually, and then quickly, drive the beautiful floating palaces from freshwater.

In the following chapters, an examination will be presented that has never been offered in this comprehensive form. Surprising as that is, based on the rich trove of extant literature related to the Great Lakes, the following text will describe an industry that began to decline almost from its inception and can be easily separated into three distinct eras. The business enjoyed an era of absolute transportation monopoly in which competition between ships drove the industry to maintain high standards. There followed an era of consolidation in which the ships benefited from an increased population base but were faced with intense external competition, primarily from railroads. And, finally, as the rising standard of living of average North Americans allowed more leisure time, the steamboat enjoyed the final phase of its career as an excursion carrier and tourist attraction. This phase especially allowed the iconic arks to enter the fond memories of millions of passengers and to become ingrained in the social and economic legacy of this massive watershed.

Unique to the Great Lakes is the fact that it is possible to identify within minutes the beginning and end of the fleets. As it ended with the *South American* heading east on Lake Ontario, it began with the *Ontario* heading west on Lake Ontario. The popularity of steamboat travel over coach, buggy, or wagon grew quickly. The migrant wave moved rapidly westward to the "upper lakes"—those west and north of Niagara Falls in the great chain of lakes.

This volume is not intended as a complete and exhaustive exploration of the Great Lakes passenger steamship industry. It will not explore every nuance of the quadruple expansion steam engine, describe each ship in detail, or outline the history of each steamship line operating on the freshwater seas. Instead, it offers the reader a comprehensive overview of the businesses, leaders, and vessels, and the political, economic, and social factors, that allowed them to succeed or caused them to fail. With analysis, it is hoped that students of maritime history will perceive patterns and draw conclusions that facilitate further discussions about this topic.

An examination of steamboats on the Great Lakes necessarily requires background. Steam propulsion had a fascinating, century-long nascent period that, even then, brought the technology to the lakes in a fairly early form. European and North American experiments had not developed so significantly that Great Lakes pioneers were simply following prior efforts. With this in mind, an examination of the origin of steamboats and their pioneering role on the lakes will provide context.

This first era began on Lake Ontario and spread rapidly to neighboring shores, as did industry, population, and touring. Steamboats allowed the Old Northwest to grow and managed the task with elegance. Despite the high-profile catastrophes associated with early steamboat travel, the industry had a good safety record and leveraged passenger accommodations and service to improve the experience. Particularly in this first period, technology issues shared front page headlines with the grandeur and opulence of the Great Lakes palace steamers. Notably, both contemporary and modern literature on this era is narrowly focused on personalities, individual vessels, or notable events such as races or disasters. In the process of collating these accounts, original manuscripts, memoirs, and news accounts were revisited to draw in fresh details and perspectives.

The second era began with events that greatly affected the Great Lakes. To the south, the Civil War in the United States ripped the nation apart, slowing commercial development for a decade. Northern victory brought the vanquished back into the Union, but the experience created sectional animosities that lasted for generations. To the north, Canadian colonies were binding together in confederation. As the Dominion of Canada after 1867, the northland was an independent "kingdom" within the British Empire. These two experiments in democratic federalism gradually created the most comfortable and profitable international neighbors in the world.

The closing era saw the steamship business adapting to inexorable changes in travel habits. This included a blossoming continental fascination with automobile transportation, the growth of a trucking industry that carved large portions of profit from the steamship business, and the development of and dependence on a tourist trade that revered ships the way one loves a favorite old hotel. Literature for this period is the most prevalent and is available in numerous media. The spectrum of material includes abundant primary resources, as well as analysis that runs the gamut from scholarly publications to oral histories and personal memoirs. This era is likely the most familiar to the public by virtue of its extensive documentation.

With this in mind, the following narrative necessarily places more emphasis on the earliest development of the industry to put the familiar into a more complete context. This editorial focus also has been adopted to reflect the relative importance of each era: the beginning was the industry's birth and adolescence, and what came afterward was a healthy maturation followed by a graceful, inevitable decline. Extending the life metaphor, the final chapter is the golden age—the steamship's most fondly remembered period.

PART I

Steam Navigation from 1817 to 1860

CHAPTER 1

Harnessing Steam

Steam as a powerful force has been understood for centuries. Egyptian records indicate the use of steam, and the Greek inventor and mathematician Heron of Alexandria describes steam contraptions—not new in 280 BCE—in his *Spritalia seu Pneumatica*. He sketched and built the aeolipile, a small, steam-powered, rotating orb, and described an engine that used hot air to move heavy temple doors. Curiously, steam did not become a driving force in civilization for many centuries, first theoretically and then practically. The royal Spanish archives at Simancas preserve the story of Blasco de Garay, a Spanish naval officer, who attempted to move a ship using paddle-wheels. The 1543 entry infers that a "vessel of boiling water," somehow tied to the contrivance, was the motive force. Without illustration or description, we can only assume that Garay was the first person on record to imagine steam-driven boats as a feasible reality.[1]

Through the seventeenth century, advances in steam technology took place in Europe with varying degrees of success. Across the Atlantic, William Henry, a native of Lancaster, Pennsylvania, began experimenting with steam engines in American vessels. Henry was a gunsmith active during the American Revolution. His interest in atmospheric energy was sparked by a business trip to England in 1760. Having seen the inventions of James Watt and Thomas Newcomen, he returned to his machine shop with thoughts of putting engines of his own design into watercraft. Henry's first attempt, in 1763, suffered the same fate as earlier experiments: the paddlewheeled prototype was overwhelmed by the weight of the engine and sank immediately. Undeterred, Henry pressed on, and his business and inventions attracted critical, creative thinkers. Fatefully, his home on the Conestoga River was near the home of the aunt of Robert Fulton. Henry's preliminary experiments were witnessed by both Fulton and John Fitch, young protégés who eventually played important roles in the development of the steamboat.[2]

In the meantime, Virginian James Rumsey adapted a concept that had been suggested a century before. Instead of a bank of oars, Rumsey attempted to apply poles to drive a barge over the Potomac River's surface. George Washington was one of his investors. When this design proved unsatisfactory, Rumsey radically changed direction and began testing a theory preferred by the Frenchman David Bernoulli and mentioned offhandedly by Benjamin Franklin after he returned from his duties as American ambassador. It involved using steam to create "hydraulic power"—essentially jet propulsion—pumping water from bow to stern through a vessel to generate forward motion. This experiment successfully drove a boat at four miles per hour in 1786. Rumsey died seven years later, having received a patent from the State of Virginia. Such hydraulic propulsion essentially died for decades until it was revived for the quiet submarines of the Cold War era and for very fast pleasure boats of the "jet ski" variety.[3]

John Fitch was among the first Americans to be granted broad patent rights. These types of new business protections were being employed by European countries, particularly Great Britain, to control intellectual properties. Protected technologies included weapons manufacturing, textile machining, and the engineering that drove the mighty Newcomen and Watt steam engines. Americans could visit England and appreciate the technologies, but they paid dearly to export the machines across the ocean.

Practically, it was Newcomen's comprehension of the power of condensation, not vaporization, that allowed his engines to operate at low pressures and reduce the very real dangers of steam under pressure. Steam power requires harnessing pressure in a closed chamber. If the pressure becomes more than the chamber can handle, the chamber ruptures. Pressurized vapor meeting a thinner and cooler atmosphere outside the chamber expands at an awesome rate. A simple equation will suffice: a heated chamber, or boiler, breaching under only fifty pounds of pressure will become fifty thousand pounds of pressure in a split second. This expansion is evidenced as an explosion. Despite the existence of gunpowder, steam under pressure was the most potentially explosive force recognized at that time.

Steam did not come into prevalent use prior to the seventeenth century because the materials and skills needed to handle this pressure did not exist. Metalurgical technologies on an industrial scale were just beginning to be understood. Making a sword or a horseshoe took skill, but hammering iron sheets into boilers and forging rods into reliable shafts required precision and a command of chemistry that were still coalescing. Even under the most controlled conditions, eighteenth-century founding was a crude and imperfect science.

At the same time, components of early steam engines were undergoing enthusiastic experimentation, and Fitch's engineering patents were constantly challenged. From drive elements to boilers and heat retention, changes in the technology quickly threw patent protections into litigation. The demands of raising capital and subsidizing court battles began to be a drag on steamboat development. Despite this, Fitch put a boat into regular service between Burlington and Trenton, New Jersey, on the Delaware River in 1790. This craft also handled excursions to neighboring towns, logged a couple of thousand miles in its first year, and is recognized for placing the first advertisements for steamboat services. While not financially successful, Fitch also is credited with the first experiments in screw propulsion. He dabbled in this field after moving to Kentucky, reinforcing his earlier prophecy: "The time will come when steamboats WILL be used to navigate the waters of the Ohio and Mississippi Rivers."[4]

Fitch did not work alone. Many other visionary mechanics tinkered with propulsion mechanisms. Dayton cites Samuel Morey, Nathan Read, Oliver Evans, Elijah Ormsbee, John Stevens, and Nicholas Roosevelt as early notables. Morey's stern-wheeler made a trip from Hartford to New York in 1794 at six miles per hour. Passengers included Robert Livingston and Robert Fulton, gentlemen who came to dominate American steamboat development in the next era. Read created tube boiler designs that were state of the art for many years. Ormsbee is included for his successful "duck-footed paddle" craft, which made three miles an hour on Narragansett Bay. Robert L. Stevens produced a reliable engine that propelled a skiff from New York to Hoboken at eight miles an hour but did not represent a significant, marketable model.[5]

Robert Fulton maneuvered events so masterfully that he was anointed the "father of the steamboat." His success seems to be credited equally to his mechanical ability, political savvy, and magical timing. It had been a century since French physicist Denis Papin's first successful steam-powered boat. Apart from Finch, intelligent and enthusiastic experimentation had not produced a viable commercial vessel.

Fulton astutely grasped the technologies at work and in 1807 incorporated them into his first vessel, known to history as the *Clermont*. Traveling reliably over 130 miles on its first trip, the vessel created positive public relations at a time when the public was coming to understand the important potential of steam propulsion.

Fulton's story is well documented but should not be discounted. He began as an artist and designer who imagined submarines for the governments of France and Great Britain. He formed a partnership with Joel Barlow, an American merchant in Paris, and by 1803 they were partnered with the wealthy and powerful investor Chancellor Livingston. Their first boat, like so many before, broke under the weight of the engines. The second attempt successfully impressed guests and observers along the banks of the Seine. By 1806 the innovators were back in New York and were installing an imported Boulton & Watt engine in a Charles Brownne hull by August 1807. This first ship was not nimble; its hull was formed along the familiar lines of contemporary sailing vessels. With some redesign—a longer waterline, better cabins, and larger rudder—the *North River* steamboat was set on a regular run to Albany. Success led to success, and Fulton began planning larger boats.

At this point, insight and capital worked to Fulton's advantage. His partnership with Chancellor Livingston resulted in a number of boilerplate New York State patents that virtually shut out competition in the steamboat industry for several years, on both salt- and freshwater. In 1810 Fulton and Livingston joined Nicholas J. Roosevelt in a shipyard venture in Pittsburgh, Pennsylvania. The launch of their *New Orleans* signaled inaugural steamboat history on the western rivers in 1811. By the time steamships came to the vast freshwater seas of the northern Great Lakes, the Mississippi and its tributaries boasted a dozen steam-powered vessels.[6]

CHAPTER 2

Early Years on the Lakes

It was a crisp autumn afternoon in 1815 when Henry Teabout set out, in rather uncomfortable circumstances, to establish an important boatyard on the shore of Lake Ontario in the district of Upper Canada. The weather was not remarkable. It was October in the North Country, golden days ripe with a successful harvest, rich with the smell of moldering leaves, and dark in anticipation of winter snows. Exhilaration drove Teabout's steps as he visited a number of prospective sites for his yard. The task was historic and his chances of success well within his experience and expertise. He was about to build the first steam-powered ship on the wild western lakes of North America, and one of the first steamships in the world to venture out of protected rivers into open water.[1]

The technology was new. The land was new. The population was still thin, but the opportunity was tremendous. As he strode carefully up the gravelly beach of Finkle's Point, Teabout understood that several factors beyond his control could make or break this project and that several people were assuming—even conspiring toward—his failure. His companion on this walk was Henry Finkle, a business associate, an investor in the project, and one of the few friends he had in this endeavor. Owned by Henry's mother, the property they were viewing was near Earnestown, outside of Bath, Upper Canada. In deference to its appropriate location, its dependable resources in terms of timber and accessibility, and the obvious political implications, Teabout chose this spot as the place to build the steamship *Frontenac*.

The vessel project was directed and capitalized by a consortium of investors concerned about British control of Lake Ontario. It was 1815. A year earlier, war between the young republic of the United States and British Canada ravaged towns and villages throughout the frontier. The war had been especially vicious in this area, as well as the closely related towns near Niagara, Detroit, Mackinac, and Sault Sainte Marie. Militia actions around Lake Ontario resulted in massacres, rapes, and destruction of property that left bitter feelings on both sides for generations.

Anticipating the War of 1812, the international rivalry between America and Britain prompted the expansion of shipyards along the border. Tremendous effort was expended to outbuild the adversary and gain superiority on Lake Ontario. An American shipyard at Sackets Harbor rapidly manufactured several vessels for Captain Isaac Chauncey, commodore of the American fleet. Across the narrows leading to the St. Lawrence River, a government shipyard at Kingston churned out gunboats and frigates for Captain James Yeo to counter the American threat. In the end, the two fleets, afraid that even an hour-long battle would tip the balance for ultimate control of the Great Lakes, sparred but never closed to fighting distance. Instead, the showdown for superiority was left to Yeo's and Chauncey's subordinates—British Captain Robert Heriot Barclay and American Master Commandant Oliver Hazard Perry—and occurred on Lake Erie, above Niagara Falls. These falls had posed a strategic obstacle, both militarily and economically, ever since Europeans arrived with deep-draft vessels.[2]

On September 10, 1813, a fleet of warships built at Fort Amherstburg, Upper Canada was beaten in a short but bloody battle on Lake Erie by an American fleet built and launched at what is now Erie, Pennsylvania. Both crews were undermanned by half, with farmers and woodsmen serving cannon intended for garrison duty half a century earlier. Perry became an instant hero, and Barclay was exonerated for the defeat based on his sheer determination against overwhelming odds. This was the only open-water military fleet action on the Great Lakes during the Great Age of Sail, and it was conclusive. Despite being a hastily organized affair on both sides, it proved to be one turning point in the war, politically and in the court of public opinion. Treaties were signed in the last days of 1814, and within months business interests on both sides of the border were considering obvious economic opportunities.

The new steamship Teabout was to build at Finkle's Point was the crux of a Canadian effort to control steamship commerce on Lake Ontario. Curiously, during the war, Teabout had been an integral part of the American effort at the Sackets Harbor boatyard in New York. Teabout and his partners, James Chapman and William Smith, were American shipwrights. They had received superb training under famed New York shipbuilder Henry Eckford, who directed construction of nearly all the American vessels that defeated—or stalemated—the Canadians. Teabout, Chapman, and Smith had recently constructed the *Kingston* and the *Woolsey*, sailing vessels operating out of Sackets Harbor to Kingston, Ontario. That the Canadians had awarded a shipbuilding contract to Americans in this politically charged atmosphere was a curious turn of fortune.

The Canadian project was in direct response to efforts on the American side of the lake. With the war and bloody animosities fresh in the public's memory, both sides were anxious to gain control of future commerce on Lake Ontario. In the postwar era, the towns around the lake numbered residents from two to four thousand. Investors were gambling on a lasting peace and the influx of migrants to justify investing £17,000 in a steamboat.[3] By this time, John Molson had experimented with steamships on the St. Lawrence River. He had partnered with mechanical engineer John Jackson and shipbuilder John Bruce to build a steam-powered vessel to carry passengers between Montreal and Quebec. With an engine constructed locally by George Platt in Montreal, the *Accommodation* operated unimpressively after 1809. An English-built Boulton & Watt engine drove another Molson-owned boat, the *Swiftsure*, reliably after 1812, and Molson ran a moderately successful steamship venture for several years.

During the process of awarding the contract for the new Lake Ontario vessel, only two contractors were seriously considered: Americans Teabout and Chapman, and the Montreal builder John Bruce, whose successful ventures with Molson placed him in a fine position to get the job. With cross-border relations still volatile, there were public rumblings about prohibiting American steamships from trading at ports along the northern shore of Lake Ontario and in Canadian towns along the St. Lawrence River. Exclusion was emphatically evident in the owners' agreement, which stipulated that "No Alien shall hold a Share in the Boat either by Subscription purchase, or transfer."[4]

The twenty-three investors were mostly from Kingston, and many were related by either blood or other financial partnerships. There was backing from York (modern-day Toronto) and Queenstown, but the Kingston elites chose to keep their interests foremost and closely held. The fact that they were interviewing an American contracting firm was unpopular. On top of that, Bruce knew most of the investors through his work at the Kingston yards and was engaged in consultations with the syndicate well before Teabout and Chapman arrived for their interview.

However, the Americans had the backing of Finkle and his allies on the committee. Two merchants from Sackets Harbor named Hooker and Crane contacted Finkle and enthusiastically endorsed Teabout and Chapman. Coincidently, these merchants would be involved in the *Ontario* project in short order. Whether it was Finkle's intent to hire the best talent or keep two fine shipwrights out of Sackets Harbor is speculation, but when the votes were counted, Bruce lost to Teabout by a slim margin. The company defended its decision with a statement:

[E]very effort had been made to procure Canadian shipwrights, but that unfortunately . . . had proved unavailing. . . . [W]hile engaged in this fruitless search after a person among our fellow subjects competent to conduct an enterprise of such importance, two Americans, on whom the greatest reliance could be placed, presented themselves before the committee, and offered to contract for the immediate construction of this large vessel on moderate terms.[5]

In New York, the only American state fronting Lake Ontario, the race was on to place a steamboat into commission before the Canadian interests did. Heirs to the Fulton-Livingstone monopoly, which controlled steamboat rights in that state, were solicited in 1815. By January of the following year, arrangements had been made securing exclusive rights to use the Fulton technology on the US side of the lake by Charles Smyth, Joseph Yates, Thomas Duane, Eri Lusher, Abraham Santvrood, John DeGraff, and David Boyd.[6] The terms of the agreement stated that grantees were to pay one-half of the annual net profits in excess of a dividend of 12 percent on the investment. A bill was introduced into the New York legislature in February incorporating the "Ontario Steamboat Company," but it failed to reach a vote due to adjournment. Despite this minor setback, construction began in August 1816.

There has long been debate about which boat was the first steamboat on the Great Lakes. Arguably, the *Frontenac* won the race into the water, as it was launched on September 7, 1816, at Finkle's Point, three weeks after the keel of the *Ontario* was laid. A week later an article in the *Kingston Gazette* described the event.

On Saturday the 7th of September, the Steam Boat frontenac was launched at the village of Ernest Town. A numerous concourse of people assembled on the occasion. But in consequence of some accidental delay, and the appearance of an approaching shower, a part of the spectators withdrew before the launch actually took place. The boat moved slowly from her place, and descended with majestic sweep into her proper element. . . .

Her proportions strike the eye very agreeably; and good judges have pronounced this to be the best piece of naval architecture of the kind yet produced in America. . . . The machinery for this valuable boat was imported from England, and is said to be of an excellent structure. The frontenac is designed for both freight and passengers. It is expected she will be finished and ready for use in a few weeks. . . . Every friend to public improvement must wish it all the success, which is due to a spirit of useful enterprise.[7]

By contrast, a month later the *Buffalo Gazette* noted briefly, "A Steam Boat has been launched near Kingston, U. C., to ply upon the British side of Lake Ontario." Both newspapers failed to note that the vessel was launched without its machinery, which didn't arrive from England until late in the year. Following the launch, the *Frontenac* actually hoisted sails to traverse the lake from Finkle's Point, opposite Amherst Island, to the east and Kingston, where it completed its fitting out.[8] It would not travel under its own steam until May 23, 1817. The *Kingston Gazette* reported, "Yesterday afternoon, the Steam Boat left Mr. Kirby's Wharf for the dock at Point Frederick. We are sorry to hear that through some accident, the machinery of one of the wheels has been considerably damaged; notwithstanding which, however, she moved with majestic grandeur against a strong head wind."[9] This maiden voyage of "the Steam Boat" was a simple crossing of Kingston Bay. Unfortunately, nine days earlier, the American vessel *Ontario* claimed the honor of becoming the first steam-powered ship on the lakes.

Decades of confusion over "first in" claims were related to this. According to a number of eyewitnesses, construction of the American vessel *Ontario* began in early August 1816. The *Buffalo Gazette and Niagara Intelligencer* erroneously reported on August 6, "We learn with pleasure, that Charles Smyth, of Albany, and his associates, have *completed* a Steam Boat on Lake Ontario, of rising 200 burthen" (my emphasis).[10] Perhaps the writer meant "completed arrangements to build" or "commenced," which would render the report correct. Instead, other newspapers, notably the *Niles' Weekly Register*, picked up the story verbatim. Assuming that "completed" meant "launched," this misstatement led Americans—then and since—to brag that they could claim the first steamboat on the northern lakes. As it happens, they could. But that would not play out until the following year. In the meantime, the ship was under construction.

Details about the vessel's construction are scant. A report by the owners indicated that construction was stopped in December due to lack of funds. The ship was gradually completed, and the *Niles' Weekly Register* noted in March, "The steam boat *Ontario*, capable of carrying 2,000 barrels, is prepared for the lake, and will leave Sackets Harbor every Monday, and make a route from Ogdensburg to Niagara, stopping at several places to land or receive passengers. The fare for cabin passengers from Sackets Harbor to Ogdensburg is $5—from the same to Niagara, $10." Captain James Van Cleve, who sailed as clerk (and captain on the *Martha Ogden*, the next steamboat to be built at Sackets Harbor six years later), noted in his diary that the *Ontario* was enrolled on April 11, 1917. He also claimed that she sailed for the first time in April, perhaps as test runs.[11]

The *Sacket's Harbor Gazette* proclaimed that the *Ontario* made its first steam-powered voyage on Wednesday, May 14. In an article printed the following week, it noted, "The Steam Boat ontario on Wednesday last, left this port for the first time, in order to try the force of her machinery. A number of gentlemen, ambitious to be the first that ever navigated the waters of Lake Ontario in a Steam Boat, embarked on board. She started from the wharf accompanied by an excellent band of music, greeted by the huzzas from the people on the adjacent shores and the U. S. S. Brig JONES." Further insinuating the national interests at play, she was commanded by Captain Francis Mallaby of the US Navy.[12]

The vessel left Sackets Harbor and reached Oswego the same day, where it was met by crowds and jubilant cannon fire. After a gala celebration that ran late into the night, the *Ontario* left Oswego and reached the Genesee River (modern-day Rochester, New York) by evening. Soon after leaving the river for Niagara on the second morning, it encountered a stiff headwind from the northeast. On this course waves came in on the starboard side in what sailors call a beam sea, rolling the vessel acutely from side to side. This was a first in the history of steamboating.

Until two days prior, steamboats in North America and Europe had been operated only on rivers and protected bays. *Ontario* was the first vessel not propelled by sail or oar to travel on open water, well beyond the reach of shores and harbors. The quick pitch and roll of the boat played havoc with the paddlewheels suspended on either side of the hull. Secured in its bed only by its immense weight, the wheel shaft was eventually dislodged by the violent yawing of the boat. The revolving wheels instantly shattered their housings and damaged the paddles and wheels. Fortunately, the staunchly built craft remained sound, and the captain was able to hoist sails and return to Sackets Harbor. Damage kept the *Ontario* out of service for several weeks. Whether the *Frontenac*'s wheel issue and damage were similar or coincidental is not recorded.[13]

By July 1, following the *Ontario*'s repair, the American firm announced a weekly route running from Ogdensburg, on the St. Lawrence River, to Lewiston, just downstream from the falls at Niagara and Buffalo. Along the way, the *Ontario* would also call at Sackets Harbor, Oswego, Pultneyville, and the Genesee River. First-class passage for the full trip was $15, or $3 between ports. Steerage passengers, who traveled without taking a stateroom, paid half that. By the end of the year, the ship's managers had adjusted the schedule to a ten-day round trip.[14]

The design of these pioneering vessels was important. Differences between the two ships ultimately had an impact on their long-term success. There were similarities: both were built along the lines of existing hulls and in line with rapidly developing steamboat construction—broad and shallow to accommodate undredged harbors; both were quickly built of unseasoned timber and enjoyed rather brief careers; finally, both were strongly built, prepared to navigate open water and uncharted rivers. Illustrating their stoutness, both grounded on rocky shoals early in their lives with little more than cosmetic damage. The *Frontenac* went so hard aground on the only trip to Prescott that it took several days to affect its release. The only damage was a bit of keel rubbed away, but it never again attempted the river route to Prescott. As reported by the *Kingston Gazette*, when the *Ontario* was "driven on a ledge of flat rock near Oswego, . . . the damage done her is inconsiderable to what has been currently reported. It is expected she will be ready for further operations in a week, or fortnight at the least."[15]

In nearly every other respect, from design to management, the ships were markedly different. By comparison, the *Frontenac* was about 50 percent larger in length, width, and depth than the *Ontario*. Exponentially, this gave the Canadian hull about three times the measured tonnage of the American hull, yet its engines were not three times as large.

The steamer *Frontenac*. (Drawing by Captain James Van Cleve, c. 1817, courtesy of the Maritime History of the Great Lakes.)

The *Frontenac* had three masts to *Ontario*'s two, and its forty-foot paddlewheels were at least double the size. One passenger described the Kingston vessel as being slow to respond to its helm, yet the ship is on record as having the better speed of six to eight miles per hour. The *Ontario*, while it may have been handier, evidently seldom ran faster than five knots.[16] It wasn't long before Great Lakes sailors abandoned the traditional "knots" for "miles" per hour; the difference was minimal and miles was a bigger number.

The *Ontario* was modeled after a vessel already sailing on Long Island Sound near New York, the *Sea Horse*. Each vessel was 110 feet long and 24 feet abeam, drawing 8 feet, and weighing in at 237 tons. *Sea Horse*'s boilers are recorded at 17 by 3.5 feet, driving 20-inch cylinders, with a 3-foot stroke to a cross-head engine turning an 11-foot-4-inch paddlewheel with 21 horsepower. *Ontario*'s low pressure beam engine had a single 34-inch cylinder with a 4-foot stroke and was rigged as a fore-an-aft schooner.[17]

By August the *Ontario* had established a routine. Word of its reliability spread, and, according to the *Ontario Repository*,

The Steam Boat Ontario, Capt. Mallaby, touched here this morning from Niagara on her way to Sackets harbor, Ogdensburgh, &c. She was so much crowded with passengers that the captain was under the necessity of leaving a number of applicants at Niagara, for want of more extensive accommodations. Among those left was the Russian minister and entourage. One passenger lucky enough to be included noted, "It could scarcely have been anticipated by the most sanguine friends of the steam-boat establishment on this lake, that this route would be so soon have become so fashionable, although all particularly acquainted with the accommodations of the steam boat, the experience and politeness of Capt. Mallaby, as well as the beauty and novelty of the scenery on the passage, knew it could not be otherwise than pleasant.[18]

By all early reports, the ship was as fine as those sailing other waters. In a flattering report, the *Sacket's Harbor Gazette* promotionally touted, "The accommodations on board are excellent, as no pains or expense has been spared by her owners, in her construction or equipments. The facility with which the lake can now be navigated, will add new inducements to its commerce and that of the River St. Lawrence. Travelers whose curiosity may lead them to nature's grandest scene, the Falls of Niagara, will, we are convinced, hereafter [take] the route to Sackets Harbor, and then proceed in the Steam Boat."[19]

The *Rochester Telegraph* carried an advertisement for the *Ontario* in July 1818, noting that Eri Lusher, one the boat's investors, commanded that season. The nascent tourist trade to Niagara Falls continued to build and receive good reviews.

This fine boat continues to ply most successfully between Ogdensburg and Lewiston. It is well fitted up, . . . receives very liberal patronage and rides the lake with perfect ease and safety. . . . If an admirer of the works of industry and enterprise, what can more completely excite the admiration of the traveler, than to reflect, that but three or four years since a wilderness only could afford him shelter, where now populous villages greet his eyes and offer him welcome? And if a lover of the curiosities of nature, . . . [t]his route is now rapidly becoming the fashionable one for parties of pleasure to the falls of Niagara, and no part of our country abounds in grander and more variegated views.[20]

Not all was smooth sailing. In mid-August the *Ontario* was within a few miles of Niagara when it encountered a gale. Unable to power against the wind and waves, the ship was driven halfway back to Sackets Harbor but weathered the storm without damage. Occasionally upset by weather conditions, the regular westward route found the steamboat departing Ogdensburg every Saturday at 9:00 a.m. for Sackets Harbor, leaving there every Sunday at 3:00 p.m. for Hansford's Landing on the Genesee River. The next day, it would leave the dock at 3:00 p.m. and arrive at Niagara "with all possible expedition." The return trip, with all departures at 4:00 p.m., left Lewiston on Tuesday, the Genesee River on Wednesday, and Sackets Harbor on Thursday, arriving in Ogdensburg on Friday. Only departure times were stated on advertisements, suggesting that arrivals were highly uncertain. It is interesting to note that nearly every departure was in the late afternoon, so that much of the voyage took place at night. In the days before lighthouses and charts, this would have been risky, but it made it probable that the captain would have daylight with which to navigate the next harbor. In 1819 departure times and routes were refined a bit, with the boat leaving Prescott, Upper Canada (instead of Ogdensburg), and Sackets Harbor at 9:00 p.m. and Oswego and the Genesee River at 2:00 p.m. on respective days. All returning departure times were at 3:00 p.m.[21]

The Erie Canal reached Rochester to the west in 1822 and was opened eastward to Albany in 1823. "Clinton's Ditch" would change life on the Great Lakes in many ways. The *Ontario*, now skippered by Robert Hugunin, altered its schedule again, signaling a new era in lake navigation. "In order to facilitate the communication from the termination of the Canal," regular runs left the Genesee River every other day exclusively for Niagara. A weekly stop at Sackets Harbor was added in June. Ogdensburg and Prescott were dropped entirely until the following year as the canal neared Buffalo.

Once the direct connection to Lake Erie was made, the *Ontario*'s importance to westward migration would diminish, even as competition grew. By 1825 there were seven steamboats working the waters of Lake Ontario, including a smaller fleet mate, the *Martha Ogden*, Daniel Reed, master, in the American Steamboat Line, and the diminutive *Sophia*. Fares were being discounted—full fares dropped from $15 to $8— and the company declared that "freight, and families moving, will be carried at a reasonable rate." Following a saltwater tradition, passage that did not include a stateroom could be bought for about half price. Deck passengers lived with their luggage on the main deck exposed to the elements. For migrants traveling with all their possessions, this was often preferred, both for security and for thrift.

A report in the *St. Catharines Journal*—St. Catharines being a town located on the muddy construction route of the Welland Canal in Upper Canada—stated that the *Ontario* had been wrecked off Sodus Point in the early hours of July 23, 1826, "all on board supposed perished." Eleven months later the *Buffalo Emporium* reported, "We had a severe gale on Friday. . . . There is a report current that the stm. *Ontario*, has gone ashore at O[s]wego." If these groundings occurred, neither was fatal to the ship. The end came for the *Ontario* in 1832 at a breakers yard in Oswego. Newer, lighter, more comfortable vessels cruised at nearly double her speed and marked the new generation of passenger steamships on the Great Lakes.[22]

Although the *Frontenac* was a much different vessel, larger by far, the two crafts enjoyed similar careers. The *Frontenac* was designed based on the *Car of Commerce*, a steamship already operating along the St. Lawrence River. Soon after its maiden steam voyage, mechanical issues with its wheel were addressed. On May 31, 1817, the *Kingston Gazette* reported that the *Frontenac*, "having completed the necessary work at the Naval Yard, left this port yesterday morning for the purpose of taking in wood at the Bay of Quinte. A fresh breeze was blowing into the harbor, against which she proceeded swiftly and steadily to the admiration of a great number of spectators. We congratulate the managers and proprietors of this elegant boat, upon the prospect she affords of facilitating the navigation of Lake Ontario, by furnishing an expeditious and certain mode of conveyance to its various ports." On June 7, the same paper reported, "The Steam-Boat *Frontenac*, left this port on Thursday morning last, on her first trip for the head of the lake" at York and Niagara.[23]

Its competitor, *Ontario*, was 110 feet long and 237 tons. *Frontenac* was 152 feet at the keel, 170 feet overall, and rated about 700 tons. *Ontario*'s low pressure beam engine had a single 34-inch cylinder with a 4-foot stroke and was rigged as a fore-an-aft schooner. *Frontenac*'s engines were identical to those of the *Car of Commerce* and rated at 50 horsepower. Walter Lewis cites various sources for the *Frontenac*'s overall price. Teabout and Chapman received £7,000, and the Boulton & Watt engine cost investors upward of £5,000. A shareholder stated that the total bill was £14,500, and the company said it spent £16,000 for construction and outfitting on a petition to the Legislative Assembly.[24]

An 1819 advertisement in the *Kingston Chronicle* read, "The steamboat *Frontenac*, James McKenzie, master, will in future leave the different ports on the following days: Kingston, for York, on the 1st, 11th and 21st of each month; York, for Queenston, on the 3rd, 13th and 23rd days of each month; Niagara, for Kingston, on the 5th, 15th and 25th of each month." Towns along the route, including Earnestown, Newcastle, and Burlington, were also serviced. Passage from Kingston to York or Niagara was £2 in 1817, rising within two years to £3. The *Kingston Chronicle* ad went on to explain that children under three years of age would be charged "half price, above three and under ten years of age, two-thirds price. Passengers are allowed 60 pounds of baggage. Gentlemen's servants can not eat or sleep in the cabin. Deck passengers will pay 15 shillings, and may either bring their own provisions or be furnished by the steward. For each dog brought on board, 5 shillings."[25]

There is only one major incident recorded in the *Frontenac*'s record. On a Sunday morning in 1822, while returning to Kingston, it collided with the schooner *Lady Maitland*. About fifteen miles out, the two were crossing tacks at five or six miles an hour when "the stem of the frontenac struck the larboard bow of the schooner with such violence, that the latter immediately filled and sank to the waters edge." Fortunately no lives were lost, and the steamer was able to pump and tow the *Lady Maitland* into Kingston.[26]

Within a year from its launch, the *Frontenac* shared the lake with another Canadian steamer. The *Lady Charlotte* was built by Captain Henry Gildersleeve with funding from the more aggressive partners of the *Ontario* syndicate, including Henry Finkle. While the builder was Canadian, the engine was ordered from an American company. Within a few years, there were four faster and more reliable steamers running along the north shore. An ad in the *Kingston Chronicle* on December 10, 1824, listed the *Frontenac* for sale with everything aboard.

On January 14, 1825, the *Kingston Chronicle* reported, "On Monday last the Steam Boat *Frontenac*, was sold by auction at the Government Wharf, for the sum of 1,550 L (sterling). This vessel though eminently useful and convenient, as respected the accommodation of the public, did not, we understand, remunerate the proprietors. Indeed we believe she was quite a losing concern." The buyer was twenty-two-year-old John Hamilton, younger brother of one of the original investors, Alexander. John had recently come into an inheritance and used the *Frontenac* to start a noble career in the steamship industry, culminating in a position as general manager of the Canadian Inland Steam Navigation Company in the 1860s. He bought the boat for a mere £1,550, even though assessors had set the value of the engine and recoverable parts at £4,000. Most observers assumed that John's intent was to scrap the ship and reuse the engine. Instead, he brought the vessel up to snuff and sailed it against newer competition, for two years before bowing to the inevitable.[27]

In 1827 the *Kingston Chronicle* again advertised the *Frontenac* for sale at public auction. Drawing no serious bids, Hamilton set a crew to removing the useful parts. Curiously, one Sunday morning, Captain Mosier of the steamship *Niagara* was coming into harbor when he encountered the *Frontenac* loosed from its moorings and ablaze. Having been the captain of the *Lady Maitland* when it collided with the *Frontenac*, Mosier returned the favor and towed it back to port, extinguishing the fire on the way. A reward for information brought no results, but the most valuable equipment—the engine and boilers—was intact and eventually transferred to a new ship, the *Alciope*, owned by Hamilton's brother Robert. A few years later, the engines were again transferred to the *Adelaide*, the first British steamboat to ply the waters of Lake Erie. The burned hull of the storied *Frontenac* lies abandoned on a beach near Niagara.[28]

This closes the book on the Great Lakes' first two steam-powered vessels. By 1841 there were a number of steamships plying the waters of Lake Ontario and the upper St. Lawrence River. Because of the falls at Niagara, and despite efforts to build and expand locks along the Welland Canal, vessels on Lake Ontario serviced established routes on that lake, seldom venturing to the upper lakes. That traffic would be handled by a fleet that sprang up soon after the *Ontario* and *Frontenac* touched freshwater.

The first steamboat on the upper lakes was the *Walk-in-the-Water*. Named for a Wyandot chief and coming only a year after the launches on Lake Ontario, this new vessel enjoyed some of the historical celebrity and technological flaws experienced by its immediate predecessors. The *Walk-in-the-Water* was not unique in its design and boasted few innovations. Built on the frontier, this vessel was meant to be reliable and profitable. For three years it fulfilled expectations.

Unlike the situation on Lake Ontario, there was limited enthusiasm for building the first steamship on Lake Erie. Eastern American capital, interested in the land and mineral opportunities to the west, were promoting a canal to be built through the Mohawk Valley in New York State. There was certainly an incentive to have a steamboat available at the canal's terminus in Buffalo, running regularly to the only other large settlement on the upper lakes, Detroit. With stops at towns along the Ohio shore, the craft would remain busy enough to justify the investment.

Along the Canadian shore there was no such impetus. The northern shore of Lake Erie had no major commercial settlements, and it would be a few years before the government of Upper Canada could justify a steam-powered vessel to serve its small military and trading installations on the upper lakes. Thus, for its entire career, the pioneering *Walk-in-the-Water* had the lake to itself and was generally referred to simply as "The Steamboat."

During the winter of 1817–18, a group of New York investors, including seven men from Albany and four from the lower Hudson River valley, agreed to finance and build the *Walk-in-the-Water*. Two of them—Robert McQueen and Noah Brown, machinist and shipwright respectively—were to manage construction of the engine and hull. In the spring, the keel was laid along Scajaquada Creek, below Squaw Island, in the vicinity of the town of Black Rock near Buffalo.[29]

William Hodges, who grew up sailing during this era, beckons readers, "[I]n your mind's eye, then, go with me back to the year 1818, and imagine the situation and the appearance of Buffalo. . . . Then the blue waters of Niagara, unobstructed by the works of man, rolled and whirled in their hurried, turbulent, and precipitant way; washing in their haste the black, rocky shore, below the village, from which that locality derived the name of 'Black Rock.'" At this time, Black Rock was more commercially active than Buffalo, which had no harbor. David Wilkeson, captain of the schooner *Pilot* at eighteen years of age in 1818, remembered that "only small beginnings had been made by way of occupation and settlement" at either location. Between the neighboring communities, there was a handful of merchant warehouses and forwarding businesses and a proportionate number of homes and waterfront developments to accommodate about two thousand inhabitants.[30]

At Black Rock, *Walk-in-the-Water*'s hull was fabricated in a newly built shipyard in the wilderness, much like those in which the hulls of the *Frontenac* and *Ontario* had been built. An abundance of white oak, ash, maple, spruce, and white and red pine grew along the shores of Scajaquada Creek, supplying just about anything a shipwright might need except finished iron stock and cordage.[31] The 338-ton vessel had the profile of a schooner-rigged barge. Its graceful stem, with a small sprit, and the tapered bow belied a flat hull with shallow bilge and vertical sides that met at a tight chine. At 135 feet long and 32 feet wide, the craft drew only 8.25 feet of water. The deck was raised astern of the engine to give added headroom in the cabins below, and an elegant taffrail surrounded the afterdeck. Set amidships were two skylights open to the cabins below and a stout helm station from which the vessel was steered.

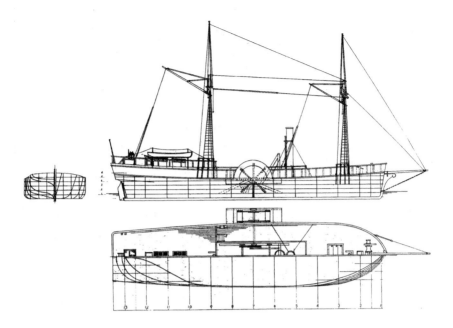

Plans of the *Walk-in-the-Water*. (Drawing by Great Lakes
Model Ship Building Guild. Courtesy of the Detroit Historical
Society Collection.)

There was a rectangular gap in the deck open to the bilge and hull
timbers and surrounded by a wooden balustrade. Within this recess
sat the low-pressure engine and boiler of the *Walk-in-the-Water*. Two
masts were stepped forward and aft of the recess. From the keel, a
guillotine-type structure rose above the deck. This frame sat above the
cylinder and piston, and rise and fall of the guillotine beam rocked cams
that turned two drive shafts. Above the boiler, the black tube of the
smokestack rose high above the deck. Set outboard on either side of
the engine were paddlewheels, covered above the deck by gracefully
arched wood-planked housings.[32]

Word of the vessel's construction had spread along the lake. At Detroit anticipation was high. On August 14, 1818, the *Detroit Gazette*
published a thankful note, stating that because of "a gentleman who
left Buffalo on the 6th inst. we have been favored with the *Niagara
Journal* of the 4th, which says—'We understand that the Lake Erie
Steam-Boat will be finished the present week, and that she will leave
here for Detroit, on her first trip, about the 15th inst.'" Upon hearing
this news, Detroit's educated leadership appointed a committee to pre-

pare for the steamboat's arrival. "The committee will be accompanied by such members, citizens, and gentlemen from the British side of the Strait, as choose to go down on the occasion." The committee let everyone in town know how important this was and renamed a street at Roby's Wharf Walk-in-the-Water Street. Additionally, Ben Woodworth replaced his moderate tavern with a three-story hotel and livery, conspicuously named Woodworth's Steam Boat Hotel. It was among the storied hostelries on the lakes for many years.[33]

Before its arrival, printed hyperbole suggested that the *Walk-in-the-Water* was "to be the finest Steam Boat in America, and in the world, excepting that recently launched at New-York." A week later the *Detroit Gazette* stated, poetically, that the Lake Erie boat had suffered sea trial tribulations similar to those experienced by its Lake Ontario predecessors.

> *Expectation.* having been "on tip-toe" for more than a week, "looking out" for the steam boat *Walk-in-the-Water*, has quietly sat down to rest herself, consoled in the reflection that in the late gale at Buffalo, the boat did not *walk on the land.*—We are informed that her detention is in consequence of some part of her machinery being out of repair.[34]

It would be another week or so before the *Walk-in-the-Water* took passengers aboard for what proved to be a celebratory event. Dignitaries of all stripes were aboard when the boat departed Buffalo, and more came aboard at every stop. The captain on this first trip was Job Fish, formerly an engineer for Fulton and Livingston on the North River and the skipper of the *Firefly*, which ran between Poughkeepsie and New York City. In what was to be a signature event for Buffalo and Detroit arrivals and departures, Captain Fish ordered a small cannon fired thirty minutes prior to departure, allowing passengers sufficient time to say their goodbyes. The gun also barked within a mile of the next destination, announcing the boat's arrival.[35]

Black Rock served as a good building site and provided reliable shelter from the often-angry waters of eastern Lake Erie. It was the obvious choice because Buffalo Creek had no harbor and often silted closed in storms. Unfortunately, a speedy current in the Niagara River at Black Rock was nearly more than the steamboat could handle. In order to reach the open lake at anything faster than a crawl, up to sixteen yokes of oxen were attached by a stout hawser to the steamboat, pulling it upstream as indelicately as any canal barge. Once past Bird

Island, the steamer proceeded to the river's head under its own power, pausing to board Buffalo passengers, who waited in small lighters. When all were aboard, "The Steamboat" turned its prow to the west and ground toward Detroit. On board were twenty-nine passengers and a considerable amount of freight.

In a story reprinted around the lakes, the *Kingston Gazette* reported:

Buffalo, Aug. 25th—The new Steam Boat, *Walk-In-The-Water*, lately finished at Black Rock, came up the rapids on Saturday, opposite to this village. On Sunday afternoon she left here for Detroit, touching at the intervening ports, on an experimental voyage, under the superintendence of Mr. McQueen, the engineer who constructed her machinery. Her motion through the water, from this place as correctly as could be judged from the shore, was at the rate of 7 miles an hour; and from every appearance, we doubt not that she will be found to fully answer the valuable purposes, for which she was designed.[36]

Once clear of Buffalo about 1:30 on a sultry summer Sunday afternoon, the *Walk-in-the-Water* steamed steadily across the lake's flat surface. Passengers listened while the ship's officers explained the steamboat's mechanics and potential. When the monotonous regularity of the marvelous machinery no longer captivated them, guests turned to the passing shoreline and watched as the hills and cliffs of the Niagara escarpment gradually leveled into a horizontal scribe of low prairie, irregular groves, and marsh. Along the northwestern reaches of the State of New York, the southeastern shore of Lake Erie provided the navigator with a steady horizon. Standing a few miles offshore to avoid sandbars, the *Walk-in-the-Water* made a brief stop at the small settlement of Dunkirk about five hours later. At a distance of twenty miles, the boat averaged four miles an hour, possibly into a slight headwind.[37]

As small groups of passengers wandered the deck, they would have remarked on ship characteristics that were familiar to them from other voyages. Wooden decks on a wooden hull were surrounded by wooden rails and yards. Two masts, likely made of spruce, were supported by hempen shrouds carrying sheets, guys, halyards, and lines of the same material. Unlike other voyages, the sails remained tightly brailed to the mast, as the ship drove along at five or six miles an hour. Also unlike other vessels, the central part of the main deck was an open balcony looking down on the magical gyrations of the engine and the lofty parts making up the vertical beam mechanicals. Despite the elegant paddle covers, windblown spray often encouraged the less adventurous guests to remain belowdecks. Modest lounges were provided for both men and women, with bright skylights open to the deck above. Guests could also avail themselves of private or semiprivate cabins, which the *Detroit Gazette* described as "fitted up in a neat, convenient and elegant style; and the manner in which she is found does honor to the proprietors and to her commander. A passage between this place and Buffalo is now, not merely tolerable, but truly pleasant."[38]

Sailing toward the late sunset, *Walk-in the-Water* kept the thin, tree-lined horizon to port. As the night wore on, Captain Fish checked the engines down, running at reduced speed to avoid passing the next fueling harbor at Erie, forty-five miles farther west. At first light, the steamboat approached Erie, a growing village of six hundred settlers. Situated within a fishhook-shaped archipelago known as Presque Isle, Erie enjoys one of the few natural harbors on the Great Lakes. Most lake ports are found in rivers or straits adjacent to the big lakes. Along this coast, geology, wind, and waves combined to craft a graceful break-wall that closed the harbor to prevailing winds and allowed lightly drafted boats to find shelter. Only a few years earlier, the brig warships *Niagara* and *Lawrence* had been unable to pass the bar with their nine-foot depth. The *Walk-in-the-Water* required nearly as much water to clear the sandbanks, but records show that it was able to enter the harbor in September.

Cautiously, Captain Fish took the ship into the sheltered bay and took on several cords of wood. A cord is a standard rough measure of split logs stacked four feet high, eight feet long, and four feet deep. Standard prices were $1.25 to $1.75 per cord, depending on the quality and seasoning of the wood. In this case, the fuel "consisted wholly of bass, pine, and hemlock wood. All split fine and well-seasoned. Hard wood would not answer: as that which would make a more lively and intense fire than was needed." Early steam plants consumed a great amount of firewood. *Walk-in-the-Water*'s boilers required more than one hundred cords per trip. At the start of each voyage, the crew piled wood on the deck, paddle box sponsons, and in nearly every nook and cranny. Despite this, frequent refueling stops were needed, and a substantial business developed in curing and delivering firewood to the steamship docks along the lakes. An advertisement running in a number of papers in 1819 foreshadowed a lucrative trade developing: "Notice—Sealed proposals will be received by Harry Thompson for supplying 600 cords of basswood for the steamboat Walk-in-the-Water, the wood to be delivered on the river bank adjoining the steamboat wharf. Payment will be made one-fourth on the delivery of the wood, the remainder on the first day of May next." Fortunately, in the Old Northwest, lumber was still plentiful.[39]

The boat spent a short time aground as it worked its way out of the bay at Erie, but by evening it was again steaming west along the forested shoreline. Nearly one hundred miles later, *Walk-in-the-Water* arrived at the small village of Cleveland, on the Cuyahoga River, sometime after daylight on Tuesday. Snugged to the dock by noon, crew and passengers helped to refuel. This visit had been anticipated for months, and, according to one report, "All Cleaveland swarmed on board to examine the new craft, and many of the leading citizens took passage in it for Detroit, for which place it soon set forth."[40] Six hundred townsfolk were likely joined by many of the six thousand farmers and settlers in Cuyahoga County.

On Wednesday the steamer ceremoniously left the Cuyahoga River and cruised fifty uneventful miles to Sandusky Bay. There barrier islands and a convenient peninsula provide a refuge from the prevailing westerly winds. After hosting visitors from the bay's old trading village, *Walk-in-the-Water* spent the night at anchor in the shelter of its marshes and low dunes. Thursday morning it sailed to neighboring Venice for wood, departing by midafternoon for the mouth of the Detroit River. Along that route Captain Fish navigated among the Lake Erie Islands. This uncharted archipelago of three moderate islands and numerous islets and reefs forms an incomplete barrier between most of the lake and its western end. Fish's previous experience sailing around these islands proved valuable, and his ship reached an anchorage within in the Detroit River by evening.

At sundown Captain Fish's large pocket watch read about 8:15. Being a respected skipper with saltwater experience, Fish probably also carried an accurate chronograph synchronized to Greenwich Mean Time. Set on gimbals in a hardwood box, *Walk-in-the-Water*'s chronograph was a valuable tool for navigation. On saltwater and out of sight of land, an accurate timepiece was required for navigation based on the sun and stars. On the Great Lakes, with the coastline as a guide, pilots were less dependent on clocks and primitive charts. Relying mostly on experience and dead reckoning, a compass, speed log, and the elapsed time allowed most skippers to bring their ships into harbor safely.

Ship's clocks were rare instruments on the frontier, where exact time was rather immaterial to most people. Farmers and trappers relied on the sun to dictate their activities. Church congregants were beckoned with bells when appropriate. A new class of industrial worker lived life to the tempo of factory whistles. Wealthier folks had watches and stationary clocks, but they required constant attention and were only as reliable as the clock from which they were set. With the growth of towns, steeple clocks on churches and courthouses created a shared local time. Gradually the need to accommodate a steamboat or railroad timetable necessitated a modicum of universality. It would be a century before time zones were defined in North America. During this period, not only did steamships bring news, supplies, visitors, and new residents to every visited port, but they were also the keepers of time.

At first light the next morning, Mr. McQueen, the engineer, fired up the boilers. When steam pressure was sufficient to crank the ship's engine, the crew hoisted the anchor, and the *Walk-in-the-Water* headed north. Coming into the main stream of the Detroit River east of Celeron Island, the steamboat was saluted by soldiers at Fort Malden of Amherstburg, the British fort opposite Bois Blanc Island. A newspaper reported that Native Americans "lined the banks above Malden, and expressed their astonishment by repeated shouts of 'Tai-yoh, nichee!' They had heard that this new craft didn't need oars or sails, but was pulled along by a giant sturgeon. Could there be any other explanation? Indeed, most of the people living in this region had never seen a steam engine, so they can be forgiven their naiveté."[41]

Powering against a two-knot current, *Walk-in-the-Water*'s paddle-wheels drove the ship steadily past farms and the small riverside hamlets of Maguagon, Brownstown, Petite Côte, Spring Wells, and Sandwich, where the mighty strait turned to the east. Passengers and crew appreciated passing the numerous small dwellings standing at regular intervals along the low banks on either side. In contrast to the long stretch of virgin forest that they had experienced between their last ports of call, these farmhouses gave the sense of arriving in a civilized neighborhood. Indeed, many of these farms were already over a century old. Most reflected the character of the ribbon farms that were carved from the woods during the French period, each claiming a narrow portion of riverfront—perhaps two or three hundred feet wide— and extending inland for two or three miles. This plan had the advantage of giving each family access to the river, as well as farmland and timber needed for survival. It also allowed the homes to be stretched along the river in close proximity to one another, enhancing safety and preventing complete isolation for these groundbreaking pioneers.

The town that the ship was approaching was preeminent on the upper lakes. About two thousand residents lived in and around a stockaded village that stretched for nearly half a mile along the river and triangulated to the north around Fort Shelby, a quarter mile inland. Despite being over a century old, Detroit had burned completely thirteen years before. Streets had been reestablished along the old lines but on a more modern template: wider, with improved drainage and room for planked sidewalks. Every structure was new and reflected a mixture of old French and New England architecture familiar to the inhabitants. Besides homes, there were merchant shops, bakers, blacksmiths, a church, modest hotels, and taverns—all the things that represented civilization in the Old Northwest.

By late morning on August 27, *Walk-in-the-Water*'s cannon rang out, announcing its arrival at Detroit. The *Detroit Gazette* reported that the "Steam-Boat Arrived!—Yesterday, between the hours of 10 and 11 am the elegant steam boat walk-in-the-water, Capt. Fish, arrived. As she passed the public wharf and the dock owned by Mr. J. S. Roby, she was cheered by hundreds of inhabitants, who had collected to witness this (in these waters) truly novel and grand spectacle." Steering easily to Wing's Wharf at the foot of Bates Street, the ship hosted many onlookers, who came aboard to marvel at the entire machine. Later in the afternoon, Captain Fish took a capacity crowd of invited guests for an excursion eastward into Lake St. Clair. While not recorded, it is likely that upon its return to the town, captain and crew were the guests of honor at a celebration appropriately held at the Steam Boat Hotel, the largest venue for such gatherings in town.[42]

The era of steamship passenger trade had commenced without incident. Within a day, the *Walk-in-the-Water* departed Detroit for Buffalo, mirroring the voyage westward. It was a routine that was repeated weekly throughout the navigation season. On its second trip, Captain Fish hosted thirty-one passengers. Among the party was the Earl of Selkirk, along with his wife and two children; Colonel Dixon, the British Indian agent for the Northwest; US Army engineer Colonel Jonathan Anderson, along with his wife and sister-in-law; Colonel Leavenworth, with his wife and daughter; Colonel James Watson; and Major Abraham Edwards. This list was related by Mrs. Thomas Palmer, a newlywed on her way to new adventures on the frontier. Coincidently, Mrs. Palmer and her husband also were aboard the vessel for its final voyage.

The first season proved generally successful for the boat and its owners. The *Niagara Patriot* reported that on Sunday morning, September 27,

> while passing the bar in entering the harbor at Erie, Pennsylvania, [the *Walk-in-the-Water*] was approached by a boat from one

of our public vessels, with the intention of boarding the steam boat. The men in the boat were cautioned against attempting to come aboard, but not withstanding the boat came up forward of the water wheel and was instantly drawn under it; the steam boat was stopped in order to save the lives of those in the boat and while this was being effected, she drifted on the bar, remaining there about 2 days before she got into the harbor. We learn the only injury she sustained was the breaking of one of her rudder irons.[43]

The *Walk-in-the-Water* proved a reliable emissary of westward expansion for the next few seasons. During its first winter, McQueen and his crew overhauled its machinery: "Some defects were remedied, and the improvements and those of lessening the diameter of the Water Wheel, which by the same power is enabled to make a greater number of revolutions in a given time, have had the effect to increase her speed nearly two miles an hour."[44] It was expected, though not reported, that the added velocity would be sufficient to propel the vessel up the Niagara River and avoid the embarrassing oxen-tow.

In 1819 the *Walk-in-the-Water*'s season began in the first days of April when enough ice had left the lake to make navigation possible. It departed Buffalo for Detroit with 156 passengers and much cargo. The summer schedule suggested that the craft would complete a round trip from Black Rock to Detroit once a week. More important, the owners announced a northern trip to the Straits of Mackinac in June. In promoting this excursion, publicity set the tone for steamboat vacations for many years to come: "The trip to Mackinaw [*sic*] . . . will undoubtedly attract a very considerable number of passengers, whose curiosity will be amply gratified by the splendid scenery of these inland seas. The Island of Mackinaw and the surrounding country in particular, is said to exhibit one of the most picturesque views in the world." Drawing on literary hyperbole, one New York paper suggested, "The swift steamboat *Walk-in-the-Water* is intended to make a voyage, early in the summer, from Buffalo, on Lake Erie, to Michilimackinac on Lake Huron, for the conveyance of company. The trip has so near a resemblance to the famous Argonautic expedition, in the heroic ages of Greece, that expectation is quite alive on the subject. Many of our most distinguished citizens are said to have already engaged their passage for this splendid adventure."[45]

Excitement about this trip grew, and when the *Walk-in-the-Water* departed Buffalo on June 15, it carried "a full freight of goods belonging to the American Fur Company." Upon leaving Detroit the following Wednesday, the ship proceeded north across Lake St. Clair and up the St. Clair River to Lake Huron. Once past Fort Gratiot, the site of present-day Port Huron, its paddles pulled it along the west coast, reaching Mackinac Island two days later. The *Detroit Gazette* described the passage as having taken fifty-two hours, "about 16 of which she lay at anchor for the purpose of getting wood, &c," for a total relative travel time of thirty-six hours. Over the 270-mile course, this translates into an average speed of about 7.5 miles per hour.[46]

Once in the Mackinac Straits region, the sixty passengers were in one of the westernmost outposts on the American frontier. It was a highly strategic location where two peninsulas lay within a few miles of each other, dividing the freshwater sea into lakes Huron and Michigan. The French built a small fort on the northern mainland as early as 1683, later moving to the southern side of the strait in 1715. After the British government inherited the lakes, it established a new fort on Mackinac Island. Under American rule, the citadel set high on a cliff remained an active garrison until 1895. Reflecting this, the steamboat's passengers included "Gen. Brown and suit[e], Cols. Smith and Jones, several navy and army officers, and many respectable citizens from different parts of the United States." Throughout this period, Mackinac Island suffered declining influence in the rich American fur trade. The arrival of the *Walk-in-the-Water* marked the beginning of a tourist trade that eventually supplanted furs, and later fishing and lumbering in the local economy and made the island one of the premier vacation spots in the country. Because of the importance of steamships to this burgeoning business, this text will visit Mackinac Island again in the narrative to follow.[47]

Paddling back toward Detroit, "The Steamboat" fought headwinds, and the engineer complained of fuel that was "very bad." As a result, the return trip "occupied 46 hours in sailing." Nonetheless, the ship arrived at Detroit seven days after its departure, a full day less than anticipated, and by reports, "the passage is represented to have been very interesting and agreeable." The vessel refueled, left for Black Rock on June 24, and fell back into a nominal routine. Having left Buffalo on June 28, the ship encountered a gale the following day that drove it from Erie all the way back to Black Rock. Nature was not so kind to several other vessels blown ashore by that storm.[48]

Throughout the summer, a number of changes took place. One correspondent noted that Job Fish had given up the fickle lakes for a job on the East Coast. Captain John Davis, master of the schooner *Michi-*

gan, took over the *Walk-in-the-Water*. Davis was reputed to be a better seaman than Fish, though one description suggested that he "amused himself by exciting his fears and magnifying the dangers of lake navigation." Perhaps not surprisingly, within a few months Captain Jedediah Rodgers (sometimes spelled Rogers) took command. It should be noted that the position of captain on a lake vessel was not yet a professional mariner's position but often reflected the participation of the builder or owner or was simply a perceived level of maritime or managerial competence. On uncharted waters in the Old Northwest, sailors were rare. Captains were often successful if they were "very polite, gentlemanly men, unexceptionable in their deportment, and [of a] disposition to please and make comfortable and pleasant the passage of all travelers while guests aboard their boat." An engineer made the paddles go, and a mate ran the ship.[49]

For the remainder of the first season, the advertised schedule generally described an eight-day round trip to Detroit and back. The fare for a through-trip in one direction was $18, with consideration made for shorter segments of the voyage. Over the winter, the owners of the *Walk-in-the-Water* must have realized that their investment was not reaching its potential. Customer pressure indicated that the fare was steep, so in 1820 the firm made a number of efforts to improve the public relations image of the steamboat. On April 1, the Lake Erie Steam-Boat Company was incorporated at Buffalo, projecting for the vessel and its owners an element of professional permanence. Additionally, it addressed competition from commercial sailing vessels. While there was only one steamboat, there were more than sixty commercial sailing vessels working the same market. Sailing ships spent little on propulsion, profiting in proportion to their cargo. Passenger fares on sailing ships were low and negotiable. Aboard the *Walk-in-the-Water*, in an attempt to fill one hundred cabin berths, the fare was reduced to $15, and there remained public pressure to lower it further.[50]

After two years, the novelty was gone. Price, paddle spray, black wood smoke rife with live embers, and the constant vibration of the engine became consumer considerations that engaging captains and general reliability could not entirely overcome. The ship's stout and stodgy hull and largely experimental technology operated with little incident, and the company actively promoted endorsements and improvements. An article announcing the opening of the season describes the *Walk-in-the-Water* as having been "altered in a manner to render her very strong, and we were told by the engineer that she sails much better than she did last summer." The article also reflects on pricing pressure: the following line hinted, "It is to be regretted the proprietors continue the price for passage and freight that was demanded last season; but if they study their true interest, a reduction may be anticipated." Within a month, Captain Rodgers would announce a fee reduction for first-class cabins from $15 to $13.[51]

The 1820 season opened later than the previous year due to ice at the eastern end of Lake Erie. Navigation at Cleveland opened in early April, but it wasn't until May 6 that the *Walk-in-the-Water* was able to open a channel out of Buffalo bound for Detroit. Aboard was Henry Rowe Schoolcraft, one of several notable passengers that the boat would carry this year. Schoolcraft, a geologist, mineralogist, and ethnologist, was one of a growing number of intellectuals and capitalists who were taking an interest in the newly opened lands to the north and west. Eventually he would become an Indian agent at Sault Sainte Marie and promote the mineral riches of the lands around Lake Superior. This year the scientist was arriving in Detroit as part of an exploratory party led by territorial governor Lewis Cass, which would leave for the north country later in the season.

This inaugural voyage of the new decade also brought officers and "120 handsome recruits" of the Third Infantry, and newspapers noted that "some addition was made to our permanent population." On Wednesday, June 14, the *Walk-in-the-Water* departed Detroit for its second trip to the north. Again it carried goods and personnel for the American Fur Company at Mackinac Island. The passenger list included the Reverend Dr. Jedediah Morse and son, General Alexander Macomb, Colonel John E. Wool, and Dr. William Beaumont. Morse was one of the nation's preeminent geographers and author of numerous texts that had earned him the name "Father of American Geography." His son Samuel was an aspiring painter whose experiments with electricity later in life would lead to development of the telegraph. General Macomb was a native Detroiter, scion of a wealthy landowning family. His exploits during the War of 1812 made him a national hero. A year after his experience on the *Walk-in-the-Water*, he would be named chief of the army's Corps of Topographical Engineers and later would be promoted to commanding general of the US Army. Colonel Wool, a Macomb protégé, was inspector general of the army, touring military posts to determine the fighting effectiveness and preparedness of the troops. Dr. Beaumont was en route to Mackinac to become the post surgeon at the fort. There he would have occasion to save a man shot in the abdomen. When the fellow's wound healed in an abscessed state, Beaumont was able to study the workings of the human stomach, securing his place in medical history.[52]

Lewis Cass, governor of Michigan Territory, was leading this phalanx of notables. Cass, whose exploits at Detroit during the War of 1812 earned him the federal position, spent much of his gubernatorial tenure politicking on the East Coast. His connections, as well as the nation's growing curiosity of the continent, allowed him to draw luminaries into this energetic and adventurous search for the source of the Mississippi River. After the steamboat unloaded provisions, equipment, and personnel at Mackinac Island, it wooded up and sailed west through the Straits of Mackinac toward Green Bay and the old settlement of Red Banks. One of the earliest trading posts in the north country, the French called it La Baie Verte, and later the English established Fort Edward Augustus at the terminus of the Fox River. This important byway led to the Mississippi Valley through a series of lakes and ancient portages to the Wisconsin River and its terminus at Prairie du Chien. The Cass party erroneously identified Cass Lake as the source of the great river. More importantly, it gave Cass an introduction to both the local Native Americans and the landscape, which would prove beneficial when he returned to demand treaty concessions in 1825.

Following this historic sojourn to the north, the *Walk-in-the-Water* returned to its regular route along Lake Erie's southern shore. The reviews were mixed. On August 1, the *Detroit Gazette* published one commendation, noting that the correspondent had "never had a more pleasant passage, so far as respects the goodness of the boat, the excellence of the accommodations, fare, attendance, &c."[53] Along with its regular duties, "The Steamboat" made another trip to Mackinac in mid-September. At the end of the season, a similar promotional piece ran in the Detroit paper, signed by ten gentlemen, that was clearly designed to bolster a negative impression of the boat and its management. In this unusual situation—a boat, only three seasons old, with an unblemished safety record and only minor published public antipathy—it can only be imagined that there was a grassroots reaction to the vessel's monopoly. Perhaps the availability of reliable transportation had created a perceived reliance, and the lack of other options fostered resentment. Nonetheless, the Lake Erie Steam-Boat Company aggressively addressed the situation in print.

The undersigned, passengers in the Lake Erie Steam-Boat *Walk-in-the-water*, aware that impressions unfavorable to the said boat have heretofore existed, unhesitatingly state that, in their opinion, the fullest confidence may be placed in her safety. During her last trip she experienced such violent winds as sufficiently tested the strength of her construction, and the great power of her machinery. Of Capt. Miller, his officers and crew, and of the accommodations of the boat, the undersigned cannot but speak in terms of commendation and praise.[54]

As in the previous year, the 1821 season started late. In Detroit John R. Williams, agent of the Lake Erie Steam-Boat Company, reported to the *Gazette* that, according to a letter he had received, Captain Rodgers hoped to have the ship out of Black Rock by the end of April. Williams predicted that it would arrive at Detroit by May 10. The weather stayed cold for weeks, and the *Walk-in-the-Water* wasn't able to clear Buffalo until late on the morning of the thirteenth, arriving in Detroit two days later. The boat, dodging ice flows across Lake Erie, carried three members of the US Boundary Commission and several families.[55]

Captain Rodgers scheduled a trip to Mackinac and Green Bay to leave Buffalo on July 9. In the meantime, he and his crew participated in a Fourth of July celebration in Detroit, which was reported in the *Gazette*: "The Anniversary of our National Independence, in the celebration of which, every American heart and hand should join, was also distinguished by a numerous and brilliant assemblage of the ladies of Detroit and its vicinity, accompanied by several of our citizens and the gentlemen of the army at this post, who embarked on board the Steam Boat *Walk-in-the-water*, at eleven o'clock. . . . The day was extremely fine, and the quarter deck of the boat, which, by the politeness of Capt. Rogers had been prepared for the purpose, was occupied by cotillion parties. The Declaration of Independence was read, and after partaking of an excellent dinner, a set of appropriate toasts were drunk. The boat, after passing Malden and making a short trip in Lake Erie, returned to her wharf at sunset." After returning east in regular succession, the northern trip was "unavoidably suspended" and did not commence for nearly three weeks.[56]

On July 27, the delayed cruise to the north and west finally left Black Rock. When the steamboat departed Detroit four days later, it had on board "upwards of 200 passengers, and a full cargo of Merchandize for the ports on the Upper Lakes." A large number of the passengers were officers, soldiers, "and public property destined for the posts on the Upper Lakes." By August 12, the ship returned to Detroit and, within a few more days, arrived in Buffalo after a voyage of about 1,800 miles.

For the remainder of the season, it maintained the standard route from Buffalo to Dunkirk, Presque Isle, Cuyahoga, Sandusky, and Detroit, at least until its last scheduled trip in October.[57]

At four in the afternoon on the last day of October, the *Walk-in-the-Water* departed Black Rock with a full cargo and a good number of passengers, including a few who left vivid descriptions of the events that followed. Captain Rodgers took the vessel into Lake Erie in a light rain but did not anticipate anything adverse. All was well until about eight in the evening. According to one report, "[S]he was struck by a severe squall, which continued to blow through the night with extreme severity." The shallow lake quickly became "rough to a terrifying degree, and every wave seemed to threaten destruction to the boat and passengers." With wind and waves in its face, the steamship ceased to make progress. To proceed west was impossible, but attempting to make the river and Black Rock was inherently risky. Captain Rodgers ordered three anchors dropped, one with a chain and two on rope cables. For a long while, the ship and its passengers and crew were at the mercy of the seas. The hull began to leak as the timbers twisted, creating a cacophony of creaks and groans to compete with the gale outside. The engines were used in a vain attempt to pump the bilge. Without significant assistance from the paddlewheels, the anchors began to drag across the bottom.[58]

Belowdecks, it is hard to imagine passengers coping through the long, loud night. One witness noted, "The passengers were numerous and many of them were ladies, whose fears and cries were truly heartrending." A Mrs. Welton, traveling with her missionary husband, Rev. Welton, and their family, recounts, "Tired out with anxious watching, I had taken my berth with my children, keeping my own and their clothes on. . . . I will not attempt to describe the anxious, prayerful, tearful upturned faces that were grouped together in the cabin of the 'Walk in the Water' on that terrible, cold morning as we looked into each other's faces for probably the last time." Not all passengers evinced the fear around them. As the other guests made their way on deck, prepared for the worst, a Mr. Thurston declared his utmost faith in Captain Rogers. "He promised to land me in Cleveland, and I know he will do it." With that he wrapped himself in his cloak and lay down on a settee for a nap.[59]

As dawn crept from the east, Rodgers realized that he was close to the beach, a few hundred yards from the Buffalo Lighthouse, then three years old. Observers afterward wondered why the captain had not been able to see the light through the night, as he lay anchored a few miles away. They were later assured that light was lit the whole

Wreck of the Walk-in-the-Water. Following the 1821 shipwreck, Mrs. Thomas Palmer hired a Buffalo painter to recreate the scene. Two oil-on-board images were created, one from the beach, and one from the main deck. (Painting by John Lee Douglas Mathies, c. 1822, courtesy of the Detroit Historical Society Collection.)

time and its obscurity bespoke the severity of the storm. Critics pointed to the poor optics and visibility of the government's mandated lamp and lens systems.

With no options, the captain ordered the anchor chain released and the cables cut with axes. Within a half hour, the hull hit the beach broadside. Mrs. Thomas Palmer, traveling with her husband and sister-in-law, declared that the first touch was a grazing pass, "the next swell let her down with a crash of crockery and of glass, [and] the third left her farther up the shore, fixed immovably in the sand. The swells made a clean breach over her. Some of the ladies were in their night clothes, and all were repeatedly drenched."[60]

Successive waves lifted the keel and pounded it into the sand, gradually driving it nearly clear of the lake. As daylight slowly grew, engineer Calhoun succeeded in getting ashore in a small boat with a long hawser. The line was attached to a stout tree, and gradually all the passengers and crew members were brought ashore, suffering from varying degrees of exposure and shock, but safe. Mrs. Palmer and Calhoun ran to the lighthouse. Having survived the terrible night aboard the steamer, the young lady recalled, "[I]t seems to me that I almost flew along the beach, my exhilaration was so great." The lighthouse keeper, aware of the steamer's plight, had a large fire burning in "his huge fireplace, by which we remained until carriages came down for us from Buffalo." The people of the town were amazed that the vessel had survived and made every accommodation necessary for the stricken passengers, who were taken to the Landen House, the principle hotel in the town. When the *Walk-in-the-Water* was stranded, it had a full and valuable cargo aboard, resulting in a loss to her owners of $10,000 or $12,000.[61]

Word of the incident was greeted with concern around the lakes. A businessman in Detroit opined, "This accident may be considered as one of the greatest misfortunes which have ever befallen Michigan, for in addition to its having deprived us of all certain and speedy communication with the civilized world, I am fearful it will greatly check the progress of emigration and improvement." Perhaps exemplifying the effect implicit in the loss of the steamboat, it took four days for word of the shipwreck to reach Cleveland and eight days to reach Detroit. Additionally, the story of the vessel's survivors is telling. Most of them eschewed another voyage on Lake Erie and took a wagon route through Upper Canada to Detroit, a two-week trek. The brave Mrs. Welton and her family opted to leave in the schooner *Michigan* on November 5, with the intent of finishing the voyage they had started. Unfortunately, the vessel was blown around the lake by a series of late season storms and did not arrive in Detroit until the first of December. A trip from Black Rock that should have taken four days kept the Weltons at sea for more than a month.

Survivors of this first steamship wreck commemorated the event with a published memorial, a piece that was rerun in the *Marine Review* more than six decades later: "In this scene of distress and danger, the undersigned passengers in the boat, felt that an expression of the warmest gratitude is due Captain J. Rodgers for the prudence, coolness and intelligence with which he discharged his duty, his whole conduct evinced that he was capable and worthy of his command. He betrayed none but the character of one who at the same time feels his responsibility and has courage to discharge his duty. He was if we may so speak almost simultaneously on deck to direct and assist in the management of the boat, and in the cabins to encourage the hopes and soothe the fears of the distressed passengers. The calmness of his countenance and pleasantness of his conversation relieved in a great degree the feelings of those who seemed to despair of seeing the light of another day." It was signed by Reverend Alanson W. Welton and seventeen other men and women. The *Walk-in-the-Water* lived on through its engine, which was quickly recovered and afterward placed in another hull.[62]

Before moving forward in this narrative, it is proper to take a final glance at these three pioneering vessels: *Frontenac*, *Ontario*, and *Walk-in-the-Water*. In a great number of ways, these ships not only laid the groundwork for early steam navigation but also established recognizable patterns in the coming era of growth for the passenger ship industry. Ownership was often held by capital syndicates that included the master and engineer as stockholders. Despite their monopoly status, managers of the steamboats were constantly concerned with improving their public image and catering to frontier travelers of all types, particularly the wealthy tourist and regular business passengers. Captains depended as much upon their skills as hosts and politicians as they did their navigational know-how.

The fate of these steamships foreshadowed much that was to come. The *Frontenac* suffered a collision and was later abandoned to inadequate management, succumbing to fire and premature retirement. *Ontario* enjoyed moderate success before being surpassed by newer technology, ending its days in the breaker's yard. *Walk-in-the-Water* carried immigrants and lords, generals and ladies, and arguably was the first entity to promote and enable tourism on the Great Lakes. Her demise upon a stormy beach bolstered a campaign to improve lighthouse efficiency and lifesaving capability. And in the case of all three boats, their valuable engines long outlived the original hulls. The same shallow harbors and uncharted hazards that they faced would threaten their successors for decades.

CHAPTER 3

Opening the Frontier

The loss of the *Walk-in-the-Water* was not tragic as shipwrecks are concerned. While frightened, the passengers were not hurt, and investors were able to recover much of their physical capital. The event did not plunge the region back into the Dark Ages, but the people of the Northwest were returned to a more primitive time as the fastest communication link had been removed. The loss of the *Walk-in-the-Water* was also a real moral and physical setback. There was a sense of loss expressed in towns along Lake Erie, as well as enthusiastic anticipation for the next steamboat to be built.

At the time, long distance travel was not taken lightly. As a rule, the people who were settled in North America by 1820 seldom ventured more than twenty miles from home during their lifetimes. Travel remained complicated by limited public transportation options and expense, inconsistent dining and living conditions, uneven regulation and safety, and the lack of a standard form of currency and consistent regional time zones. Standardization of currency was gradually imposed to simplify and encourage interregional commerce, but it was several decades in coming.

Admittedly, there were long-distance migrations of people and groups. Families left New England farms for mill towns or newly opened western reserves. Entire church congregations trekked toward the dream of vast forests of the west. These moves were dramatic, once-in-a-lifetime events and were rarely repeated. Once resettled, most emigrants concentrated their efforts on their new homes and seldom ventured far. An emerging and increasingly mobile professional class of government agents, politicians, merchants, evangelists, soldiers, and land speculators traveled greater distances on a regular basis.

When traveling to the continental interior, there were a few vehicular options. The East Coast offered a number of land and sea routes by which one could travel on foot, horseback, or coach or engage a berth on a coastal schooner, merchant packet ship, or—the emerging option—a packet steamboat. The term *packet* in a maritime sense indicates a craft operating on a particular route at predictable intervals. As travelers ventured westward, the availability of regular carriers diminished. Waterborne routes were limited. A few steamboats challenged rivers in the interior, with modest accommodations for passengers. Small sailing craft carried passengers, and scows threaded into countless tributaries, but these were essentially cargo carriers and not designed for the polite or impatient traveler. Prior to canals, excursionists took advantage of a variety of water routes, but at some point they ended up on a highway or, more likely, a byway.

The quickest and most efficient way to traverse nearly any terrain was on horseback, but this option was not available to all. Beyond the costs of owning or leasing a horse, it required physical stamina to cover long distances, and luggage options were limited. At the other end of the spectrum, foot travel was slow but ultimately affordable. Sprinkled in thousands of letters and diaries are comments by tired hikers who attest that they preferred walking to the jarring and intimate nature of early public transit in an open road coach.

In 1820 American stage travel was heading toward its heyday, and travelers encountered accommodations of every type. The busiest coach routes between Washington and Boston featured impressive coaches of the English style carrying eighteen to twenty people. Those who tipped the driver or booking agent obtained more comfortable seating positions, and, on the better lines, coaches were driven well and on time between first-class taverns and hotels. On the lesser routes, the age and design of coaches and available stopping points varied greatly. Until the arrival of the famed Concord coach in 1827, vehicle styles were an amalgam of two centuries of development. Some resembled fancy carriages; others were closer to modified farm wagons. Unlike the Concord vehicle, many earlier coaches were designed so that all passengers faced forward or inward, with entrances at the front or rear. When necessary, two additional riders could be perched next to the coachman on the front of the rig. Luggage and overflow passengers might be carried on top of the cabin or on a platform attached to the rear, with additional seating above.

The Concord coach, produced by an innovative company in New Hampshire, used leather straps to suspend the cabin. Between the vehicle's suspension and balance, frequent customers, such as Mark Twain, described the ride as a cradle on wheels. This design gradually took over long distance markets in the West, but several years passed before the technology was widely employed. Most riders suffered the imperfect jolt of heavier coaches, which often featured gracefully curved exteriors, belying the stiff, unforgiving frames beneath. In June 1811, Lydia Bacon was following her husband, a lieutenant in the US Army, from Philadelphia to Pittsburgh. Riding with a couple of other military wives in a coach, she noted "weather serene, the roads good, all nature appeared in its richest dress." It is significant that over these "good" roads, "Bounce would go my poor head against the top of the Stage, till my brains were ready to fly."[1]

For the land-bound traveler, the vastly different landscapes of the Great Lakes region presented an endless combination of road surfaces, and first-generation roads were defined by geography. Wagons might travel easily through the vast forests of the southern lakes. A mature oak tree offered such dense shade that almost nothing grew beneath it, and extensive oak stands provided miles of good traveling to a pathfinder. Unfortunately, the oak stands across the lower region predominated in areas interspersed with rivers and swamps. Rivers provided fine avenues for canoes and rafts when available, but they were obstacles when traveling by road. Shallow fords or bridges were required to cross them. Swamps, except when frozen, were nearly impassable, and areas like the Great Black Swamp of northern Ohio created pestilent roadblocks necessitating circuitous detours. Interspersed among the rocks and sandy soils were a spectrum of clays that allowed reliable riding when dry. Wet or flooded clay roads would swallow carriage wheels to the axle.

In the north woods, coach service was limited by the lack of viable routes. The road from Detroit to Toledo and Buffalo, long a swampy Indian trail, had been developed in places during the War of 1812. Even so, it remained impassable except when frozen or parched. Parts of it were corduroyed, with logs laid laterally along the path. This system improved the chances of getting beyond a rough patch of road but unfavorably influenced the rider's comfort level. The cost incurred when building corduroy roads was often addressed by tolls. The road through Ohio's Great Black Swamp and portions of the Sauk Trail from Detroit to Chicago offered the same obstacles. Regular coach service was subject to the weather; it developed regionally after 1822 but was not reliable until the 1840s. Chicago and Milwaukee had similar experiences. York began coach service to Fort Erie near Niagara Falls in 1787 but didn't have through-service to Kingston until about 1817, the year the *Frontenac* began sailing Lake Ontario.

The private carriages of wealthy travelers featured glass windows, but public stagecoaches usually had little more than simple canvas curtains. Wooden benches were padded and leather-covered, but the straw, sawdust, or horsehair used as filler was nearly as hard as the wood. During the winter, a modicum of heat might be provided by small, metal ash containers, refreshed with hot coals at every stage stop. Summer presented the opposite problem, and stifling interior warmth was only ameliorated when the coach was moving quickly. Generally, the horses were not pushed hard, and the average speed of a stagecoach was four miles per hour. Outside seats were at a premium, and summer travelers frequently chose to walk rather than endure the cabin's closeness.

Confinement—shoulder-to-shoulder for many hours—created a social dynamic unique to its time. Imagine the interaction among four to nine people sitting in a seven-by-ten-foot space, with knees interspersed and only modest ventilation. Social mores of this period regarding physical contact between the sexes were strict and likely affected human dynamics in the cab. In the age before a clear understanding of hygiene, traveling by coach was best enjoyed during the days of sunny late spring, when the lush fragrance of blossoming trees and new crops invaded the cabin through unshuttered windows. By comparison, the broad decks and weatherproof cabins of a steamboat offered civilized spaces and privacy, coupled with a faster and generally smoother ride to the towns that were popping up around the lakes.

When traveling by private or public coach, stops at coffeehouses, taverns, and inns offered respite, diversion, and repast. The frontier period saw development of businesses that served a rapidly growing, increasingly mobile population. Hostelers catered to wealthy travelers and local farmers, and accommodations ranged from rough-sawn sheds to solid, multistoried hotels. In describing such establishments, the historian Alice Morse Earle noted, "They were the centres of so much of [a village's] life and affairs, the resort at once of judge and jury, of the clergy and laity, of the politician and merchant; where the selectmen came to talk over affairs of the town, and higher officials to discuss the higher interest of the province." Traveling patrons of these rustic inns were also relied on to dispense news.[2]

Increased transient trade, particularly in the major towns of the Great Lakes and Mississippi regions, prompted tavern owners to adapt. Attention was paid to public rooms such as ladies' lounges to allow women to seclude themselves from the barroom, which often doubled as the dining room. In a trend that ran through the first two decades of the century, taverns began describing themselves as *houses* or *hotels* and catered to different types of clienteles. Visitors to Buffalo or Detroit in 1830 might stay at an upscale, multistoried residence, modern and bustling, or an older modified homestead. Many old log taverns bore the name *hotel*, but whether called a hotel, tavern, or inn, the quality of service was reflective of traffic, competition, and the landlord's temperament.

When traveling by coach or ship, people often stayed with relatives or acquaintances, particularly on extended visits to a town or region. In between, overnight stops on land involved hotels. Rates were dictated by each guest's choice of accommodation. Private rooms were expensive. Clients, from judges to peddlers, generally shared rooms that had two or more beds, and beds that had two or more occupants. Sharing beds with strangers was common practice, particularly on busy routes.

Most American taverns on popular routes served good food. An English traveler to Buffalo in 1807, prior to the steamboat age, described Gregory's Inn as equal to many London hotels, observing, "At the better sort of American taverns, very excellent dinners are provided, consisting of almost everything in season. The hour is from two to three o'clock, and there are three meals in the day. . . . English breakfasts and teas, generally speaking, are meager repasts compared with those of America, and as far as I observed the people live with respect to eating in a much more luxurious manner than we do."[3]

Whether settling a wager or a hotel bill, money was traded in various forms. Gold coins, hard currency dating to seventeenth-century France and sixteenth-century Spain and Portugal, were hoarded as savings. State-issued specie was valued against the British pound sterling, and currency values varied widely, with New England dollars generally trading at more than twice the value of Carolina dollars.[4] For the average American on the frontier, barter remained the common means of exchange throughout the century. Within communities like Buffalo, Cleveland, Detroit, Milwaukee, and Chicago, local banks served as accounting and capital investment firms, recording transferred funds and making loans, often without the physical exchange of cash. Many merchants operated almost entirely by means of commodity-based transactions.

As the number of transients and speculators in the western and northern regions grew, paying for services such as a hotel bed, food, and vessel or stage passage required cash—cash in the form of specie issued by hundreds of banks, which carried varying and dubious values. Only the most notable travelers were allowed to use letters of credit from their eastern or European financial institutions.[5]

Adding to the adventure of westward travel were challenges hardly contemplated two centuries earlier or later. Clothing, sanitation, medicine, and communication were complicated while one was on tour. By the late 1840s, some Americans had become accustomed to bathing once a week, but it didn't become common practice until the latter half of the century. Shirts, blouses, and underclothes were washed when possible, but outer garments—typically made of wool or cotton and invariable hand stitched—were washed irregularly.

Sanitation options were chamber pots and outhouses. It was here that ships had an initial advantage over taverns and hotels. As the size and sophistication of cabins and accommodations grew, facilities took advantage of hull characteristics. Some vessels featured rooms on the main deck wings forward of the paddlewheels. Appropriate seating allowed waste to be deposited directly into the paddle wash. Constant agitation and spray in this area assured a good "flushing." Another arrangement belowdecks placed private chambers at the stern of ships over flared fantails. Again, seats were placed to allow direct access to the lake below. In either case, sanitation aboard ship, without the use of chamber pots or outhouses, proved more sanitary, convenient, and comfortable than practices ashore.

Communication improved as transportation innovations extended the nation's reach and the timely reporting of information. In the early years of the century, the time required to send news from Atlantic ports to the frontier was measured in weeks. By 1820 the transfer time via regular post was cut to about ten days, with stage companies and steamers handling daily mail deliveries to major frontier towns. Telegraphy was generally introduced to the Great Lakes region in 1848, with regional lines spreading between large towns and connecting to the East—albeit without great initial reliability—by the end of that year. During this period, information about the riches of the Northwest was as alluring in the East and Europe as news of the world was on the frontier.[6]

Commercial tourism in the Northwest began soon after political tensions eased in 1815. People venturing into the Old Northwest and Upper Canada were encouraged by improvements in transportation. Initial capital improvements favored navigation. Eastern harbors were the first to have lighthouses and engineering improvements. Canals captured the commercial and scientific imagination of the new century and became magnets for speculative capital. When the Erie Canal opened to Buffalo in 1825, it increased the flood of aggressive adventurers and permanent new settlers that began after 1815. A growing transportation and hospitality trade struggled to keep up with the influx.

When letters, newspaper articles, and travel guides with positive reviews were disseminated, interest in pleasure travel soared. Touring satisfied a curiosity about this recently opened part of the primitive world, drawing people from eastern states and Europe. Notably, both men and women reliably included the freshwater seas in their North American itineraries. Niagara Falls was the continent's first natural wonder destination and was visited on a grand scale by people on tour. As peace and prosperity settled in, wealthy and curious folks ventured westward, accompanying migrating settlers on wagons, canalboats, and steamships.

Published accounts of the Great Lakes region had been available for centuries. The first European chronicler was Father Louis Hennepin, a Recollect missionary who recorded his 1679 travels through the lakes with René-Robert Cavelier, Sieur de La Salle. His description of the verdure and majesty of the freshwater seas was repeated in subsequent narratives written by all types of frontier inhabitants, including soldiers, merchants, wives, civil servants, and itinerant preachers. Alexis de Tocqueville became the first high-profile chronicler of life in a tourist's America, including his travels through the primeval forests of the north country in 1831. This young Frenchman wrote extensively on the democratic and egalitarian nature of citizens surrounded by "nature vigorous and savage." His detailed commentary *Democracy in America* was not the first account of the region but it gained wide circulation. Letters, diaries, and memoirs by hundreds of venturers added volumes to the travelogues of the era.

Perhaps the most widely circulated analytical report was by Edward Tiffin, surveyor general of the United States from 1812 to 1839. Tiffin's damning review of Michigan territory was contradicted soon afterward by the published reports of respected travelers William Darby and Henry Rowe Schoolcraft.[7] In early 1819, Darby published *A Tour from the City of New York to Detroit*. He was already known for his popular writings about Louisiana and the *Emigrant's Guide to the Western and Southwestern States and Territories*. With a respected voice, he gave the Great Lakes an overdue public relations boost. His measured and neutral voice described the region's demography, government, and business and economic potential. His conclusion—"All parts well situated for agriculture and commerce . . . a fine picture of agricultural and commercial prosperity. . . . The face of nature in her richest garb"—was that its welcoming harbors awaited settlement and commerce.[8]

In 1822, Henry Rowe Schoolcraft had been appointed US Indian agent at Mackinac Island. A scholarly man, trained in geography, geology, linguistics, and ethnology, he became an astute observer of the native population with which he interacted. His detailed notes, papers, and diary entries remain an invaluable asset to researchers. More important, his writings about the north country based on knowledge gleaned while traveling with Michigan territorial governor Lewis Cass in 1820, were respected by investors and pioneers in the east. While traveling from New York, he noted the "wonderful degree of celerity, comfort, and ease, afforded by the line of internal steam boat navigation," which took him to Albany in only two days. Arriving at Buffalo, he was delayed by ice on Lake Erie and thence visited the falls at Niagara.[9]

Upon returning to Black Rock, Schoolcraft was able to depart aboard the steamboat *Walk-in-the-Water* on May 6 and arrived at Detroit late on May 8, averaging five miles an hour. He describes the boat as "uniting in its construction a great degree of strength, convenience, and elegance, and [it] is propelled by a powerful and well cast engine on the Fultonian plan, and one of the best pieces of workmanship of the original foundry," McQueens in New York. "Accommodations of the boat were all that could be wished, and nothing occurred to interrupt the delight, which a passage at this season, affords."[10]

Notable is the fact that Schoolcraft studied a number of accounts of the West, including those of Louis-Armand de Lom d'Arce de Lahontan, Baron de Lahontan; Pierre François Xavier de Charlevoix, S.J., Alexander Henry, Jonathan Carver, Alexander Mackenzie, and William Darby, and cites them frequently. "From the terms of high admiration of which all continue to speak of the riches of the soil, and the natural beauty of the country, and is central and advantageous position for business," he wrote, "we are led to suppose that it presents uncommon incitements to enterprising farmers and mechanics." After suffering fourteen days of headwinds as it proceeded up Lake Huron, the party arrived at Mackinac. His narrative reveals that, by 1820, Mackinac Island tourist attractions like Giant's Arch and Skull Rock were already on a visitor's must-see list.[11]

The growth and importance of the Erie Canal were mentioned earlier and deserve additional discussion and detail. The final section, from Black Rock to Buffalo, was opened with much ceremony on October 26, 1825, and despite derisive remarks about the folly of such a project, the $7 million canal was the engineering marvel of its day. Uniformly 4 feet deep for 363 miles, its 40-foot width allowed canalboats at the end of a towrope to pass in either direction carrying 30 tons of freight each. Aqueducts traversed ravines and rivers, and 83 locks lifted boats 568 feet between the Hudson River and Lake Erie. A trip from New York City to the Great Lakes could be accomplished in relative comfort in less than ten days, slightly fewer than by coach and eminently more comfortable and affordable. In 1812, the 300-mile, six-day coach trip from Philadelphia to Pittsburgh cost $27, including tolls and baggage fees. Fifteen years later, the 363-mile trip along the Erie Canal by packet boat took nine days and cost about $14.

Freight rates fell from $100 per ton by wagon to $10 per ton by canalboat. Within nine years, the State of New York had recouped its investment and was planning to expand the original canal and an extensive system of feeder canals. Cargo tonnage and passengers were counted annually in the millions. Like steamboats, canal packets and line boats were an important type of passenger freighter. A typical early passenger packet was 50 or 60 feet long and a dozen or more feet wide. A single, long cabin housed a lady's salon, a kitchen, and a main salon, which could accommodate up to fifty people comfortably and often handled more. Fares on passenger-only packets averaged four cents per mile throughout this period, bunk and food included.

The success of the Erie Canal spawned a number of similar projects designed to connect the hinterland with the lakes or the lakes with the rivers leading to the Ohio and Mississippi rivers. These included the Ohio and Erie Canal, the Miami and Erie Canal, the Illinois and Michigan Canal, and two efforts to breach Michigan's Lower Peninsula from Lake Erie or Lake St. Clair to points on Lake Michigan. Of the dozens of proposals, some enjoyed modest and brief success. All eventually succumbed to railroad competition.

The Erie Canal rapidly monopolized the eastward flow of goods, something the British government recognized with some alarm and addressed. Americans realized a system that met their immediate needs, but it was shallow—physically. Reactive efforts in Upper and Lower Canada strove to draw deepwater traffic through Montreal and Quebec. Canal and lock systems were envisioned connecting Lake Erie eastward to saltwater. Construction first took place on the Rideau Canal, drawing traffic along the north shore of the St. Lawrence River near Montreal, and a second effort drew shipping along the north side of the upper river to Prescott. The Rideau and LaChine canals were completed in 1832, effectively connecting the Great Lakes to the North Atlantic. The third great feat traversed the Niagara peninsula and connected Lake Erie and Lake Ontario. Planning and construction of the Welland Canal began in 1824; five years later it produced an interlake route between Port Dalhousie and Chippewa, eastward then to the Niagara River, and south against the current to Lake Erie. The route from Lake Ontario directly south to Port Colbourne was completed in 1833 and became hugely profitable. Plans to expand it were developed immediately.

Canadians were also the first to tame the Sault Sainte Marie rapids between lakes Superior and Huron with a short canal and lock that the Americans destroyed during the War of 1812. After that, it wasn't until 1855 that Americans would reopen this natural choke point between the vast mineral riches around Superior's shore and the lower lakes.[12]

As news of the region's wealth circulated into investment communities to the east, the Great Lakes basin came alive. The difficulty and annoyance of overland travel, refinements in maritime shipbuilding technologies related to steam propulsion, and development of Canadian and American canal systems launched local companies into an era of design and professional development directly related to moving people—many people—around the region.

CHAPTER 4

Birth of an Industry

Even before the engine, boiler, and other machinery were removed from the broken hull of the *Walk-in-the-Water*—physically dragged from the beach where the hulk had been driven into the sand, overland through a slash carved in the woods—competition between Black Rock and Buffalo for the terminus of the Erie Canal had become contentious. It was obvious that the town that won the honor as primary western port for canal barges and lake boats would enjoy a tremendous economic boom. At various times, the *Walk-in-the-Water* had refused to stop for passengers waiting in yawl boats off of Buffalo Creek as the steamboat pulled out of the river. While stopping was a common and profitable courtesy during these early years, the vessel occasionally passed by with a hearty hail from the taffrail: "Gentlemen, . . . the port from which we sail is Black Rock."[1]

Despite this enthusiasm and hometown pride, Black Rock's geographic placement made it less than desirable for the canal trade. Located a mile or so down the Niagara River, all vessels leaving that port for Lake Erie had to be towed against a hefty current that reached fifteen miles per hour in midstream. Along the banks, the current was more placid, but boats on a canal leading to Buffalo would experience no current at all.

Buffalo Creek opened directly onto the lake, and would seem to be the most likely place to put a harbor. Unfortunately, as the people of Black Rock frequently pointed out, prevailing westerly winds and the resultant waves and ice conspired to keep the creek closed. Understanding the importance of a harbor, Buffalo's city fathers commenced harbor improvements in May 1820. According to a report two years later, the work was "composed of square timber, connected by tiers twenty feet in width; it is raised seven feet above the water, and is filled with stones." A pier built of parallel piles filled with brush and stones was planked out into the lake 55 rods, or about 900 feet. The following summer the pier was extended another 300 feet, culminating in a large "block of 181 feet, where there is about 12 feet water. Here, during the most severe gales last fall, vessels remained with perfect safety." So it was possible for a visiting vessel to dock in deep water. But what about getting a vessel built on the creek out to deep water?[2]

Within days of the *Walk-in-the-Water*'s wreck, rumors were rife suggesting that up to three new boats might be built. Just prior to Christmas, less than two months after the event, the *Buffalo Journal* stated that "the proprietors of the steam boat WALK-IN-THE-WATER are about to commence the building of another boat, of smaller dimensions, and that she is intended to be ready for the lake by the first of May next." Competition for the new ship's loyalties intensified, and both Black Rock and Buffalo committed to providing wood for the vessel at reduced cost. Black Rock investors sweetened the pot enough to get the nod, but they made a strategic error in holding the contract-signing ceremony at the area's finest tavern, the Mansion House—in Buffalo. An agent for the Buffalo concerns buttonholed Noah Brown, the steamboat company's representative and builder, before he signed the papers and assured him that when his vessel was done, Buffalo Creek would accommodate it. Buffalo backed this promise by offering a guarantee: if the ship couldn't pass the bar, the city would pay the Lake Erie Steam-Boat Company $150 every day it was detained. Brown accepted these terms, and Buffalo became a shipbuilding town.[3]

The piers and cribs of the breakwater were complete. Now the shifting slurry of sand, marl, and organic matter had to be removed. This was an incredible task with the primitive tools of the day, but nearly everyone in the village got involved, putting in long hours with shovels, scrapers, and oxen or preparing food for the hundreds of workers at the waterfront. However, "many were the obstacles that the Harbor Company were continually encountering. A heavy bank of ice, resting on the bottom of the lake and rising several feet above its surface, had been formed during the winter, extending from the west end of the pier to the shore. This ice-bank arrested the current of the creek, forming an eddy alongside the pier, into which the sand and gravel removed by the flood were deposited, filling up the channel, for the distance of over 300 feet, and leaving a little more than three feet of water where, before the freshet, there was an average of four and a half feet. This obstruction of the harbor produced not only discouragement, but consternation. . . . [A]t length piles were driven down, and scrapers, formed of oak planks, were set to work, and by the 15th. of April, much more than half the work was accomplished, and every doubt as to the practicability of completing it removed."[4]

Noah Brown returned from New York to direct construction of his second freshwater steamboat, this time on the north shore of Buffalo Creek slightly upstream from the big lake. By February, one resident reported, "The new Steam-Boat Walk-in-the-water [*sic*], is building on Buffalo Creek, and not at Black Rock. It is a fine model, and will be much stronger than the old one. The ladies' cabin will be on the quarter-deck, which will render it airy and pleasant, and make it more roomy than the former boat. The workmen have begun to plank her, and it is confidently expected she will be ready to launch as soon as the ice shall be out of the creek in the spring."[5]

A couple of points are worth noting. First, despite the success of the *Walk-in-the-Water*, no other syndicate, American or Canadian, jumped at the chance to put a competitive boat on the upper lakes. The Lake Erie Steam-Boat Company had almost new furniture, an available engine, and the associated machinery, representing more than half the initial investment required for a new boat. It was a relatively simple and inexpensive matter for that firm to pick up where its first vessel had left off. Prior to the completion of the canal, though, the frontier population had not grown enough to support a second or third steamboat. Second, just as the *Ontario* was smaller than the *Frontenac*, so the new Lake Erie vessel would be shorter and narrower than the *Walk-in-the-Water*. Despite the shallow harbors that had been a nuisance for the first boat, the second was designed to be two feet deeper, resulting in a slight increase in tonnage. Theoretically, this vessel was more stable in heavy weather, but also its access was limited to deep or improved harbors.

On April 23, 1822, the secretary of Lake Erie Steam-Boat Company, J. I. Ostrander, issued a notice from Albany announcing the new season. With Jedediah Rodgers as master, "Will sail from Buffalo for Detroit on or about the 2d Tuesday in May next, and thereafter during the season, will leave Buffalo or Black Rock for Detroit on Tuesday of every week, at 9 o'clock, A.M. & Detroit for Buffalo every Friday, at 8 o'clock, P.M. and will stop to land and receive passengers at Erie, Grand River, Cleveland and Sandusky, unless prevented by stress of weather. The Boat will make a trip to Michilimackinac, and leave Buffalo for that purpose, between the first and twentieth days of June next." Emphasis was placed on the strength and seaworthiness of the ship, but "With respect to provisions, stores and attendance, it is only necessary to say, that the new Boat will not disgrace her name": *Superior*.[6]

In the same public relations announcement, without explanation, the steamboat company gave notice "that all goods, wares and merchandize, furniture, plate, jewels and specie, which may be shipped or transported on board the Steam Boat *Superior*, shall be at the risk of the respective owners or shippers thereof." Evidently, three years' experience on the *Walk-in-the-Water* evinced problems with luggage, baggage, and other cargo subjected to the vagaries of lake travel, which necessitated such a disclaimer. Customer satisfaction issues related to mishandled or damaged possessions would be a headache to pursers, porters, and dockhands for decades to come.[7]

Launch day was April 13, a Saturday. Hundreds of Buffalo's two thousand residents and folks from Black Rock, Tonawanda, and the rest of the region came to the creek to see *Superior*'s hull touch the lake. According to G. W. Jones, a young shipbuilder, a number of men climbed aboard, and when word was given, "then commenced the rattling of the sledges of the ship carpenters who lay under the boat, knocking out the blocks. Soon she started. All watched with breathless anxiety as the boat was sliding down the ways." Her successful splash was greeted with a "shout that made the welkin ring." The only casualty was one of the lads onboard, who broke a leg when *Superior* lurched into the water. Once afloat, the ship's cannon cracked thirteen rounds in salute, and the injured fellow was attended to. Once secured, her final fitting out took place.[8]

Then the moment of truth. Could *Superior* make it to deep water? The channel had been scraped well, but there was a bar that frustrated progress. Everyone in town understood the penalty for failure, and there was a last-minute communal effort to clear the channel to the necessary ten-foot depth. Captain Miller, the pilot, acquainted himself with the shallows, and with the whole village watching, he took the new steamboat toward blue water. Slipping over the bar, *Superior* hesitated in the sand. One report details a kedging maneuver being used to pull it clear with the anchor, but another account suggests that it passed the bar without incident. In either case, as the boat passed the breakwall, it was clear to most observers that more work needed to be done. While Captain Rodgers put the familiar machinery through its paces out on Lake Erie, the scraping continued. After a few hours the vessel returned, cleared the bar, and docked. The citizens of Buffalo breathed a little easier, but only for a moment.[9]

The new steamboat departed on its first foray to the west, stopping at the ports of Erie, Grand River, Cleveland, and Sandusky. It arrived at Detroit for the first time on Saturday, May 25, with "a full freight of merchandize and ninety-four passengers, sixty-eight of whom were citizens of or emigrants to Michigan." Upon its return to the east, the craft docked at Black Rock after the first few runs. Its schedule was much like that of its predecessor, and it completed a round trip between Black Rock or Buffalo and Detroit in seven to nine days, venturing to the northern frontier on occasion. The first northerly voyage departed Buffalo on June 11 in late afternoon. *Superior* arrived in Detroit on Friday and left for the Straits of Mackinac the following morning with "a full cargo of merchandise destined for the Indian trade." The *Detroit Gazette* delightedly reported that more than half of the one hundred passengers that arrived in town had come to settle in the area, having "since left this place to examine the U.S. lands in the interior." Another modest wave of land speculators and farmers arrived each week on the steamboat.[10]

The ship returned from Mackinac, making all the usual stops on the way to Buffalo. It immediately reprovisioned for another venture, this time not only to Mackinac but to the northernmost village on the St. Marys River, Sault Sainte Marie. This trading town was among the oldest settlements on the lakes, a prime meeting place for fishing and trading, and the gateway to Lake Superior. Native Americans used the Sault as a base for centuries prior, and Europeans became a permanent part of the population before 1668. Americans built a small garrison at Fort Brady, which mirrored a small British installation across the river. Between them flowed the rapids that separate Lake Superior from the rest of the maritime world. Navigable in a canoe, this impediment kept the deep-draft trading vessels sequestered above or below the dancing waters of the Sault, unless, of course, they were hauled overland on log rollers through the center of town. It was thirty years after the opening of the Erie Canal at Buffalo before Michigan businessmen and legislators would muster the funds, without federal support, to build an industrial lock system that opened the gates of commerce to Lake Superior.

In July 1822, *Superior* arrived in the northern straits with more than two hundred troops of the Second Regimental Infantry, from Sackets Harbor, "in good health and spirits." Having disembarked a number of them at Mackinac, the ship sailed east to the entrance of the St. Marys River. Guests watched mile after mile of lush green pine horizon highlighting a rocky shore to the north, while the vessel coasted for the elusive entrance. Once through Detour Passage, Captain Rodgers, without the aid of charts or surveys, navigated the complex series of twists and turns, false passages, and marly banks that still commands the respect of today's pilots. Despite his skillful maneuvering, Rodgers was not able to reach the town. Soundings revealed less than seven feet of water at a bar at the north end of Lake George near the head of the river, keeping him six miles from his goal. Anticipating this problem, the captain had secured three "northwest boats"—thirty-five-foot canoes capable of carrying four tons—from fur traders at Mackinac and towed them behind *Superior*. When they reached Lake George, the anchor was set and Colonel Hugh Brady went off with two light companies of soldiers at about nine in the morning. Captain Rodgers also lowered the ship's small auxiliary yawl and began shuttling passengers ashore himself. The unloading of troops, passengers, luggage, and supplies continued for two days.[11]

One of the passengers taken ashore in the yawl boat was Henry Schoolcraft, who was returning to the Sault where he was now the US Indian agent. He and his wife, Jane Johnston, lived in a sturdy frame home on the southern bluff of the river. On this particular trip up Lake Huron, he commented, "The *Superior*, being the second steamer built on the lakes, had proved herself a staunch boat." Unfortunately, it was too deeply drafted to reach the docks of the Sault until 1827 under the command of Capt. W. J. Pease. It must have been a rare moment of high water, for it was another eight years before the steamer *James Monroe*, under Captain Harry Whitaker, reached the village.[12]

During the latter half of the season, *Superior* experienced two unfortunate incidents. The *Detroit Gazette* reported in August that a young man, traveling from Cleveland with his parents and brother, had been lost overboard. The item was brief, with few details other than his name—Thomas Thomas, Esq.—and the fact that his family was coming to Detroit from Windsor, Vermont. A month later *Superior*'s engine, having performed admirably all season, was overcome on a rough passage from Detroit to Cleveland, with serious results: "[A] heavy sea struck the water-wheels with such force as to overcome the power of the steam, and produce a reaction which carried away one of the crank wheels of the engine though formed of cast iron, and of immense weight. . . . The boat rode out the gale at anchor, after which the passengers were landed at Grand River." Rodgers was able to sail the ship back to Buffalo, where the *Cleveland Weekly Herald* announced, "This is the second accident of this kind the present season, and it is found by observation to be owing to the improper location of the engine. It is placed too high on the boat which gives such length to the arms of the water-wheels as to render the engine incapable of controlling them in a rough sea. The boat is now laid up for the season, and is to be thoroughly repaired the ensuing winter, under the immediate supervision of the engineer, Mr. Calhoun."[13]

The Detroit newspaper noted the incident a few days later, but it is easy to suppose that word had rippled through town by the time the paper hit the street. The passage of freight and personnel was again in the hands of schooner men and stagecoach drivers. It was September. Detroit would not see the steamboat again until April.[14]

The boat operated without major incident for the next several years, but by 1827 it was outmoded and offered for sale "with her Engine, Furniture, Tackle, &." The advertisement, published by the Lake Erie Steam Boat Company of Albany, outlined its features. "This boat was built in 1822, of the best materials; is uncommonly staunch and well found, chain cables, butt bolted and salted; is about 340 tons measurement, and her accommodations are inferior to no boat in the state. Her engine is in good order and furniture complete, and may be put in operation in the spring at small expense. Conditions of sale will be liberal, and made known on the day of sale." To sweeten the deal, the company also made available "1200 Cords Seasoned Hemlock wood, cut and split for steam-boat use; and a quantity of Stores, such as Wine, Brandy, &c. belonging to said boat." The tactic was evidently successful, and the boat was sold. One report suggests that portions of *Superior*'s power plant ended up in the *Waterloo*, and later at a sawmill in Michigan's Saginaw Valley. *Superior*'s hull was rerigged, and one source described it as a full ship's rig. Such an arrangement, with an array of square sails that required skilled personnel to handle, grew rare on the lakes. Regardless, the boat continued to be commercially viable, said to be capable of carrying one hundred thousand feet of pine lumber. In 1838 the *Buffalo Commercial Advertiser* boasted, "She draws ten feet water, with her present load. Our harbor floats her handsomely, and has some to spare."[15]

When *Superior* was launched in 1822, Buffalo was a silty backwater on a leeward shore. The town's finances were soon bolstered by the canal traffic, particularly in the transshipping business—that of transferring freight from one conveyance to another. Cargos transferred from a canalboat to a schooner or steamboat—luggage or freight—required strong backs and generated harbor fees for lighters, dredgers, chandlers, and eventually tugs. Facilities were refined to cater to two trades: passengers, particularly westward bound; and grain heading east. By 1838 the town was rapidly becoming one of the nation's leading ports. Demand for vessels fostered a shipbuilding industry, with steamships vastly outnumbered by sailing vessels. Smaller schooners, while slower, could carry nearly as much freight as a large steamer, without fuel costs. A steam engine, boilers, and cords of wood consumed nearly all the prime cargo space in a paddlewheeler's hold. Yet a fast steamer's cabins could be profitable, and the baggage light.

Steamship owners gradually nurtured a healthy relationship with the other new steam-powered phenomenon: railroads. Rail transportation initially lagged behind steamships in comfort, speed, safety, and reliability. For a time Great Lakes steamers maintained a distinct advantage over railroads. They were more reliable and far more comfortable than any railroad car or roadbed of the time. Most western towns were located along waterways, and many travelers preferred steamships simply because there was room to stroll. Both modes were physically constrained in their geographic scope—ships by the lakes and associated waterways, railroads by the extent of their tracks. In the nascent years, the balance between industries was relatively even. Eventually, the rail lines grew like vines, forcing steamships to become more efficient at servicing a static shoreline "track." The early rush to partner with the growing railroad business resulted in a scheme to provide an entire travel experience—for tourist or immigrant—that was startlingly fast, visually intriguing, and, even in the humble conditions of steerage, relatively clean and comfortable. It was an advantage that sustained Great Lakes steamships for another century.

To only the most jaded traveler was a steamboat voyage not a captivating experience.

Upon arrival at the wharf or pier, persons about to board were drawn into the bustle before departure. At the major terminal ports of Buffalo, Detroit, and later Cleveland, Chicago, and Milwaukee, the ship would be tied to the wharf taking on all types of merchandise, produce, crates, and animals. As luggage was passed to porter carts, ticket holders would embrace the excitement, wishing relatives and friends farewell while soliciting prayers for a safe voyage.

The broad side of the vessel was intimidating as one neared the gangway ramp. Looking up, there were two tall, lean smokestacks, quietly but insistently churning out a gathering black flume. Depending on wind direction and the quality of the wood or coal in the firebox, small flecks of ash or sparks could be falling—but this was common in any city. Passing the side of the ship, passengers took in its massive length, and felt its power even as the paddlewheels sat still in their ornately

City of Detroit Michigan. (Lithograph from a painting by William J. Bennett, 1837, courtesy of the Detroit Historical Society Collection.)

scrolled boxes. In contrast to nearly every structure ashore, steamships were a symphony of angles and curves, rich in cambers and lines designed to please both the human admirer and the much less forgiving fluid forces in which the hull worked and lived. This type of travel was new and popular, in no small part because of the aesthetic nature of the boats. Not only did steamships represent a cutting-edge technology—they were beautiful.

Arriving at the entrance, travelers generally boarded the vessel over a broad, wood-planked bridge, the gangway, which led to the main deck forward of the paddles. A clerk collected tickets or fares and directed porters to see to the luggage. Those with cabin assignments were directed to their quarters. Deck passengers were shown to large salons or deck spaces around the boat. In the matter of an hour or two, hundreds of people moved into a floating village, and the village sounded its steam whistle, engaged its engine, and departed.

The experience would have a slightly different script in the whistle-stop communities where the ships touched briefly. Wagons of freight and anxious passengers congregated on deck or dock in anticipation of the steamer's arrival. When the vessel arrived and was secured by lines to the shore, there was an energetic effort to transfer the appropriate people and freight, on or off, and depart for the next port. One docking technique used in river ports involved lashing the vessel to the dock while the paddlewheels remained slowly churning ahead, countering the current. This easily forced the appropriate part of the ship to the wharf, facilitating the crossing of people and freight, and allowed the skipper to be on his way without working up much forward momentum.

Fares varied a little between boats. The larger, newer, and faster vessels could generate enough traffic to justify slightly higher prices, but increased competition and efficiency served to drive them down. In 1820, without competition, *Walk-in-the-Water* was able to charge $18 for the trip between Buffalo and Detroit, but in the interest of good public relations it later lowered the fare to $13. Twenty years later the standard cabin fare was about $8 and deck passage only $3. Fares for shorter trips were nominally higher per mile, with a Buffalo-Cleveland passage costing $6. This was half the 1820 price. Of course, rates on prestigious liners, those generally adopting the "Queen of the Lakes" sobriquet for publicity purposes, would be markedly higher, that is, until a faster or more popular boat came along. The *Illinois*, largest in the fleet in 1839, charged twice what a two-year-old vessel could, and more than triple for steerage.[16]

The men and women employed aboard a Great Lakes steamer were as varied as the passengers they served. Officers and engineers were professional men with varying degrees of charm and grace. Service personnel fulfilled the full range of duties that the staff of a large hotel would address. Deckhands and firemen performed the tough, repetitive tasks necessary to keep the vessel safe and on time. These varied classes lived together in close proximity, along with hundreds of passengers, working shifts around the clock. Their lives were dictated by a code of maritime law and tradition that was many centuries old but was adapting to new crew positions such as fireman and barkeeper.

The shipboard hierarchy was strictly top down, with attention to duty and obedience etched in legal stone. There was only one person aboard a ship who took no orders. The captain had to be obeyed, and his opinion was accountable to no one else on board. At the heart of this absolute authority was responsibility for the vessel, as well as everything and everyone on it. It was a position that required years of service and eventually licensing to qualify for, and often a pecuniary investment, too. Great Lakes captains of the earliest era were often career mariners who had served aboard navy or merchant vessels in saltwater. As the regional maritime community developed, this position shifted to men who had grown up on freshwater schooners. Paramount to a successful career was an understanding and intimate knowledge of local waters, particularly in the age before nautical charts and aids to navigation. A captain was usually qualified—though perhaps not certified—as a pilot in the waters he sailed. This was not the case on saltwater, where vessels picked up local pilots when they reached a designated port.

A typical steamboat captain in 1839 commanded a crew of thirty, more or less, depending on the passenger load and whether a musical ensemble had been engaged. Figures related here to describe a "typical crew" were taken from the Lake Erie steamboat *Erie*, a fast and stable hull that was 176 feet long. In the upper lakes trade, there were only four boats larger than *Erie* that year. It was in its second season—sound, broken in, but still fresh and lovely. Travelers knew the reputation of each boat, and *Erie* was popular. Captain Thomas J. Titus generally took it into five or six harbors between Buffalo and Detroit—at his discretion based on weather and capacity—and reversed the process heading east. The vessel was capable of accommodating 150 cabin passengers and perhaps 400 deck passengers. It covered the 320 miles in a day and a half, averaging about 14 miles per hour. Great Lakes steamboat men and promoters did not deal in knots per hour; miles per hour was a slightly larger number and so perceived faster. Besides, knots meant little to migrant farmers. That season the vessel's managers scheduled the ship to leave Buffalo every six days.[17]

Captain Titus of the *Erie* received a yearly salary of $1,000. He had a small stateroom and office below the main deck, close on the outboard side of the engines. Nearby was the dining room and water closet he shared with the engineers and mates. Most of his days were spent attending to the needs of his ship, crew, passengers, and cargo. Attending to passengers could be either a delightful or a demanding part of a captain's job, and his personality dictated how he embraced this task. Captain Titus operated a tight ship and was a serious, conservative man who spoke his mind. However, he also had a sense of humor and was known to be gracious and attentive to his guests.

The skipper had five people to help manage the steamboat's operation. The person immediately subordinate to the captain was the chief engineer. This man was responsible for all mechanical aspects of the vessel, primarily the engine works. Some in the engineering profession, especially early on, insisted that they were on an even plane with the captain. Indeed, captains generally gave engineers wide latitude to do their jobs, as long as everything worked. Likewise, engineers left navigation, cargo, and passengers to the captain. With the advent of steam navigation, the two departments established their territories, and that arrangement remains little changed today. Aboard *Erie* the chief engineer and his assistant received annual salaries of $600 and $400 respectively.

In addition to the engineers, the captain relied on first and second mates and a clerk. The first mate was the captain's immediate surrogate and was charged with the care and navigation of the ship from an operational and maintenance standpoint. The second mate likely handled tasks like loading, unloading, and fueling, as well as keeping the deckhands busy. Both men stood alternating watches and managed navigational activities on the bridge while underway. The first mate was paid $70 per month and the second mate just $30.

The clerk also reported to the captain and was tasked with all the business activities of the ship. Accounts were closely kept and involved everything from fuel and machinery to paint and food. At every stop along the route, the clerk had to monitor disembarking and boarding passengers and make sure that the appropriate baggage and freight were taken on or off the boat. After every trip, the books had to balance. Clerks were paid $50 per month. Also in the housekeeping realm were the steward and cook, paid $30 and $35. The steward's staff included three waiters ($18 or $12), two porters ($15 and $5), and a chambermaid ($20). The kitchen staff included two assistant cooks ($20 and $15). Eight deckhands and two deck boys ($20 and $8) handled docking, rigging, anchors, freight, and the like under the eyes of the mates. Six firemen fed the boilers in the hold around the clock ($20). In addition, *Erie* carried a barber and a barkeeper who worked without salary, presumably for tips.

The crew lived aboard during the season. Room and board were considered part of their compensation. Persons in similar crew positions shared quarters. The firemen would have been in a bunk room near the boilers. The deckhands traditionally lived in close quarters near the bow. Porters and waitstaff were also likely housed forward. Cooks had a small room near the kitchen. The lakes traditionally opened for navigation in mid-April and closed in mid-November—seven months—but crews were usually hired for a full nine months. This allowed captains to maintain a stable work force from year to year, as well as allowing time to prepare the boat in the spring and close it properly in the fall. For the normal deckhand, a year's salary placed him in a basic wage range. More senior crewmen were solidly middle class, which allowed their families ashore a comfortable life. Captains were usually considered among the local elite, both socially and economically.[18]

When *Superior* was launched in 1822, it had Lake Erie to itself for two seasons. Within five years, nine American steamers were operating on Lake Ontario and Lake Erie. By 1836 there were forty-five steamboats cruising the upper lakes, and three years later that number was sixty-one. In stark contrast, Upper Canada had launched only two small steamers, the *Adelaide* and the *Lady Colbourne*; the latter burned during the Patriot War of 1837, a brief attempt by disaffected residents of Lower and Upper Canada to overthrow their government. The average boat was about 150 feet long, weighed 449 tons, carried a 160-horsepower engine, and cost roughly $50,000 in 1839 dollars. The largest boat was more than 200 feet long and cost $120,000. Most lake boats employed low-pressure steam engines, unlike their counterparts on the western rivers, which favored high-pressure systems.[19]

Competition became stiff, as the profitable routes were limited. Larger, more beautiful boats were launched every year. Small vessels operated between neighboring ports, making connections with larger vessels at major settlements. Astute entrepreneurs refined their business strategies and began to carve niches created by the new steamboat business. Some became talented navigators or engineers, revered as much for their technical skills as their pioneering spirit and bravery. Others were successful shipwrights or chandlers, founders or victualizers. Another group thrived as maritime business managers, owners, investors, and bankers. Gradually, they came together to form associations and trade groups to strengthen their industries. Several of the early leaders stand out, in part because they were involved in the Great Lakes steamboat trade from its infancy and helped launch many ships. Each man personifies both his industry and personal vision.

Henry Gildersleeve arrived in the upper lakes region as a young man. Born into an old American Puritan family, he was a third-generation shipbuilder. The family thrived on Long Island, and Henry learned the trade before moving west by 1814. He assisted with the construction of the USS *New Orleans*, a full ship of the line laid down at Sackets Harbor during the War of 1812 but never launched. Henry quickly came to understand the opportunities available in the upper lakes region. Embracing British roots, he moved to Kingston, Upper Canada, in the summer of 1816 and then to nearby Ernestown to assist in the construction of the steamboat *Frontenac*.[20]

After running aground during its inaugural run to Prescott, the *Frontenac* was taken off the St. Lawrence River in lieu of a regular run from Kingston to York and Niagara. Gildersleeve recognized the need for a smaller vessel to handle the trade that waited in Prescott, farthest east on navigable water toward Montreal. He convinced investors in the *Frontenac* to join in construction of the *Queen Charlotte*, generally referred to simply as *Charlotte*. Launched at Finkle's Point with engines from the Ward Brothers in Montreal, the vessel developed a route between Prescott and the Carrying Place at the far western end of the Bay of Quinte. Stopping at every small settlement along the shore that could afford even the crudest dock or crib, the *Charlotte* quickly made itself a welcome asset along Lake Ontario's northeastern coast. It remained profitable for twenty years, repaying its investors many times over.[21]

Gildersleeve kept close tabs on this business, shipping out as a purser in 1819 and qualifying for his captain's papers two years later. His time at Finkle's Point brought him close to that family, and in 1824 he married Sarah Finkle, young Henry Finkle's sister. Gildersleeve proceeded to bolster his shipping concerns, launching the *Sir James Kempt* at Finkle's Point in 1829. He took command of the new vessel, running it in tandem with the *Charlotte*. Four years later the *Commodore Barrie* was launched and began carrying the Royal Mail between Prescott and Niagara.[22]

The opening of the Rideau Canal in 1832 boosted the fortunes of Kingston as a transshipment point and prompted Gildersleeve to keep expanding his shipping interests. Partners at the time included influential men of Upper Canada and Montreal. Of particular note is his association with John Hamilton, the ambitious youngest son of a maritime family. When Henry launched a vessel in 1839 that bore his surname, the Honorable Mr. Hamilton managed it. The *Gildersleeve* initially ran between Kingston and Bowmanville, about halfway to York, but when the St. Lawrence canals were enlarged, it took up the Montreal trade from 1843 to 1850. During the winter of 1841, engines from the *Sir James Kempt* were installed in the new *Prince of Wales*. Under Captain Bonter, the vessel was capable of twelve miles an hour and was the flier of the lake.[23]

Henry Gildersleeve was one of the earliest entrepreneurs to embrace railroad growth and imagine a partnership between steamers and railroads. This was contrary to the adversarial perspective adopted by most other steamboat owners, including his friend Hamilton. Gildersleeve saw the possibility of direct trade with New York as a way to expand trade and facilitate immigration to Upper Canada. Perhaps his Yankee upbringing removed for him a stigma in Canadian trade that other men considered paramount; for the good of the British Empire, trade with Americans was not encouraged. Gildersleeve worked hard to encourage cross-border trade and the expansion of railroads.[24]

Gildersleeve died in 1851 at the age of seventy-five. His recently launched *New Era* was joined after his death by the *Bay of Quinte*, with management of the company's three vessels falling to his son Overton. Trained as a lawyer, the young Gildersleeve inherited the firm just as the wedding between railroads and steamships matured into a golden age on the lakes. A year after the founder's death, a daily train between New York City and Cape Vincent, on the St. Lawrence River, became a reality, and the Gildersleeve fleet was there to meet it. Scions of the family expanded the business, until 1913, when the family's Lake Ontario & Bay of Quinte Steamboat Company was one of ten companies merged into the Canada Steamship Line.[25]

James Van Cleve was an enthusiastic mariner, a vessel owner, and—fortunately for future generations, an artist. As an innovator, he is notably remembered as the first freshwater entrepreneur to recognize the potential of propellers rather than paddlewheels. He helped secure from innovator John Ericsson patent rights for his propeller design on the lakes.

Van Cleve's career began in 1825, when he served as a clerk aboard the *Ontario*, the historic vessel recounted earlier. Within five years he took command of the *Martha Ogden* and eventually owned and commanded several ships. A colorful man, he has been attributed with being in the midst of a number of historic events, some actual, some apocryphal. One of the latter type, related by historian Richard Palmer, was a prank that the captain and another passenger played on Joseph Smith, the prophet of the nascent Latter Day Saints. The passenger was Charles Stuart Dickson, who purported to be the son of Britain's King George IV, to whom he bore a certain resemblance. All three were heading east, Smith from his home near the Genesee River in western New York with a stock of his new *Book of Mormon*. The year was likely 1830, as the Smith family had moved to Ohio by early the following year. Captain Van Cleve conspired with the "royal" to convince Smith that peddling his "Mormon Bibles" in Kingston would be a violation of local statutes and would likely lead to incarceration. Evidently the prophet was convinced and returned to Rochester.[26]

Van Cleve was later master of the steamer *United States*, which played a well-documented part in the Patriot War. A few Americans publicly endeavored to aid this rebellion, and on November 11, 1838, several hundred men boarded the *United States* at Sackets Harbor under the direction of General Von Schultz. The captain insisted afterward that the owners of the vessel had ordered him to leave for Ogdensburg over the objections of the ship's officers. That destination lay directly across the St. Lawrence River from Prescott, the vital Canadian transfer port.[27]

Soon after entering the river, the steamer took two schooners in tow, one to each side, again at the bidding of the owners. Once secured alongside, it was clear that the schooners were also full of patriots. When the vessel arrived in Morristown nearly all the passengers departed and marched to Ogdensburg. The *United States* reached Ogdensburg early the next morning, after which it was forcibly boarded and directed downstream to drop a number of men. While steaming back upriver, the vessel was fired on by British cannon, killing a wheelsman. Thereafter, the patriots deserted the vessel, leaving Van Cleve to do some fast talking to avoid losing his boat.

As mentioned earlier, Van Cleve was one of the earliest visual chroniclers of Great Lakes ships. His watercolors are often the only graphic record we have of the earliest vessels and the rapid development of their successors. Toward the end of his life, Van Cleve's family moved to the Canadian town of Sandwich, across the river from Detroit, where the captain continued his artistic endeavors.

Above the Niagara River, at the east end of Lake Erie, another energetic entrepreneur set up shop. Benjamin Bidwell came to the lakes and helped build the American naval fleet on Lake Ontario during the War of 1812. He later became a journeyman ship's carpenter and joiner apprenticed to Asa Stanard, master builder of the steamer *Walk-in-the-Water*. Bidwell also was employed on Buffalo Creek building the steamer *Superior*. Stanard and Bidwell became partners, and following Stanard's death the firm became known as Bidwell & Davidson, then Bidwell & Carrick. Benjamin Bidwell joined the talented Jacob W. Banta by 1843 to form Bidwell & Banta, the most prolific builder of large "palace steamers" prior to the American Civil War. Banta had trained as a ship's carpenter under master builder Henry Eckford of Eckford & Westervelt in New York, birthplace of many fast packets and clipper ships. Banta was recognized for the grace and speed of his vessels. Bidwell's brother Vincent was also an integral part of this firm. Banta is reported to have moved to Chicago about 1860, and the Buffalo firm passed to a number of owners before being incorporated into the American Ship Building Company in 1899.[28]

Samuel Ward was involved in eastern lake navigation from an early date, but he came to the steamboat industry later than his contemporaries and pushed farther west. Born into a Baptist preacher's family in the farm country of Vermont, Sam and his brother Eber headed west as the new century opened and found themselves on the shores of Lake Erie during the War of 1812. They ran a small coastal craft, stealthily transporting food and matériel for the American army until that boat was burned by the British. Following the war, Sam built the *Salem Packet*, a small schooner that traversed the lakes from Buffalo to Green Bay. There were many tiny hamlets not served by steamboats where Captain Ward's floating general store was a welcome visitor. His arrival at small frontier settlements along the Lake Huron and Lake Michigan coasts—mere dots of civilization set amid hundreds of miles of ancient forest—was cause for celebration.

Ward eventually settled his family at "Yankee's Point" on the St. Clair River. There he built a number of boats, and when the town was renamed—for the fourth time—it became Marine City. Sam helped earn this title by taking a rather bluff little canal-type boat from the upper lakes through the Welland and Erie canals to New York, the first cargo vessel to make this trip and return fully loaded. The voyage cleared $6,000 in profit, but was not repeated. Ward used the money to steadily increase his fleet of schooners.

The Ward Line began with an investment in Detroit merchant Oliver Newberry's steamship *Michigan*. As railroads began to influence travel, Ward built the *Huron* in 1839 on Lake Michigan, designed to pick up the new mail route that was running on the Michigan Central Rail Road from Detroit to New Buffalo, Michigan, and then by ship to Chicago. This boat was small even by Lake Erie standards and likely experienced some exciting rides crossing southern Lake Michigan. The route was profitable enough to prompt construction of the *Champion*, a moderately sized vessel more suited to those waters. Ward's prompt reaction to this new route was savvy enough to catch the attention of the new managers of the Michigan Central Rail Road. The relationships he made within regional business circles proved far more important than the profits he reaped from the forty-mile ferry traffic.

About this time, his nephew, Eber Brock Ward, joined the business. Samuel's brother Eber had been employed for a time as a lighthouse keeper on Bois Blanc Island in northern Lake Huron. The family came to Marine City in 1822 and returned east a few years later. Young Eber Brock stayed behind, quickly earning his way aboard one of his uncle's ships. Learning the maritime business from the bottom up, Eber B.

started as a deckhand on a schooner and eventually became clerk and captain. Others have drawn him, verbally and visually, as a man "habitually brusque" of "average stature, cold blue eyes, weathered face, and . . . an iron jaw."[29] Sam saw the perfect partner and heir. The business thrived, and the Ward family enterprises spread in many directions. At the core of the Wards' fortunes were maritime concerns. Their shipyards built boats, which carried their lumber and their iron ore that fed their mills and smelters and were serviced by their interest in the Pere Marquette Railroad and related manufacturing facilities. While not the first to develop a broadly integrated business model, Ward was the first in the Great Lakes region to exploit it to this degree.

Steamboats were gems in the Ward empire. In response to a Canadian line taking passengers along the northern route of Lake Erie directly from Buffalo to Detroit, the Wards built the *Atlantic* and *May Flower* to handle Michigan Central Rail Road traffic. These were big boats at 1,100 and 1,300 tons, and they quickly established themselves as favorites between the two railheads. The company had one of the largest fleets on the lakes entering the boom years, and its political influence drove construction of the Soo Locks at Sault Sainte Marie and steered state and federal investment toward dredging the St. Clair Flats. Samuel died in February 1854, having seen the early days of the Great Lakes shipping industry ripen. His nephew would see it through to the next level.[30]

To the west of Buffalo on the American side of Lake Erie, another strong-willed investor developed a growing fleet. Charles Manning Reed was a native of Erie, Pennsylvania, born to a father who owned sailing vessels. Much like Overton Gildersleeve, Charles was educated as a lawyer and represented a second wave of vessel owners. Unlike Bidwell and Gildersleeve, Reed was not actively involved in building or operating vessels, instead creating opportunities as an owner and manager. He was involved in banking, railroads, and politics and served as a colonel in the Pennsylvania militia, retiring as a brigadier general. His fortune came from maritime endeavors. Over the course of his career, he was sole or part owner of at least twenty-five crafts, including a number of steamboats.[31]

One of his first investments was in the *Peacock*, the ship bearing the unfortunate distinction of being the first Lake Erie steamship to suffer a catastrophic boiler explosion. It occurred in 1830 while the ship was moored at a wharf in Buffalo, and the concussion was powerful enough to kill more than fourteen people. Reed acquired it the following year, and with a rebuilt superstructure the ship sailed for several more seasons. The first steamer he commissioned to be built was the *Pennsylvania*, launched in July 1832. The largest vessel on the Great Lakes at the time, it gave the firm nine years of service. At various times, Reed's organization owned the *New York*, *Thomas Jefferson*, *Louisiana*, and the popular and successful *James Madison*. At almost 180 feet long, the *James Madison* was part of a new breed of lake boat. Launched in 1838, the ship was fast and comfortable and ran regularly between Buffalo and Erie. The *Erie Gazette* noted that on May 25, 1837, "General Reed's steamboat *James Madison* came into this port from Buffalo with upward of one thousand passengers and a heavy cargo of freight. The *Madison* cleared $20,000 on this single trip." Not all voyages were so lucrative, but amid stiff competition Reed ran a tight business.[32]

The next boat in "Reed's Fleet" was the ill-fated *Erie*. Heavily involved in migrant transportation, this ship was the scene of a conflagration that killed more than one hundred Swiss immigrants. The company at one time or another had an interest in the *Buffalo*, *Rochester*, *Missouri*, *St. Louis*, *Sultana*, *Baltic*, *Michigan*, and *Ohio*. Ultimately, Reed was associated with a number of the magnificent palace steamers that marked the golden age of lake transportation prior to the American Civil War, including the *Empire State*, *Globe*, *Queen City*, and *Keystone State*.[33]

Throughout the history of Great Lakes steamships, there are names that stand out: Goodrich, Playfair, McMillan, Ashley, Dustin, Graham, Morton, and many others. Gildersleeve, Bidwell, Van Cleve, Ward, and Reed were among the pioneers in an industry they helped guide from infancy to a vital part of the continent's economic development.

Of course, steam navigation would not have survived if the business model was flawed. Competition was stiff, both from fellow steamship operators and from railroads. Illustrating the increasingly interwoven nature of transportation, the *American Railroad Journal* in 1841 published a detailed financial explanation of how the steamship business operated and the viability of the industry at that time. The original text was written by a man who was employed by a number of publications to analyze businesses around the nation and in Europe. The day-to-day details of the steamship business that L. Klein relates stand in contrast to more common narratives written by wealthy tourists and migrant travelers. He wrote, "The means of internal communication in the United States are furnished principally by railroads, canals, and steam navigation; all three are of nearly equal importance . . . but while railroads and canals have always received due attention, on the part of the engineer . . . the progress of steam navigation . . . appears to be regarded with much less interest, and even with indifference." Advocates for steamboat companies likely welcomed Klein's comments. Trade groups representing the owners and investors were raising the tenor of their pleas in Washington, DC, repeatedly soliciting funding for navigational aids and maritime infrastructure. Klein succinctly made clear the opportunity for success in the steamer trade.[34]

Briefly described earlier, the steamboat *Erie* operated on a regular course between Buffalo and Detroit, performing the 720-mile round trip every six days. Assuming an eight-month season, there were forty round trips. Dividing the annual costs of crew, fuel, laundry, food, and even depreciation on investment, Klein pegged the cost per trip at more than $800, or about $1.11 per mile—on a par with the railroads. Freight rates varied based on direction. Cargo westbound up the lakes out of Buffalo cost on average $0.38 per hundredweight or about 2¼ cents per ton per mile. Cargo heading east from Chicago to Buffalo averaged slightly more than 1.5 cents per ton per mile.[35]

It is interesting to note that produce going east included tobacco and deer hides. Products shipped west were commonly finished lumber and salt, commodities being shipped to a region that would soon supply much of the nation's wood and salt. Klein pointed out that the rate steamships charged for freight was lower than that charged by canals or rail, and so the industry should not fear competition if it can command sufficient traffic, and the routes remain direct. These assumptions were increasingly less certain, but in the meantime a ship like the *Erie* could expect to earn its investors an annual net income of $12,000, or 15 percent of the cost of the boat. If natural disasters or accidents were avoided, these coastal vessels were a sound investment.

Klein extended the analysis to the largest boats of the time, using the *Illinois* as an example. Recently launched, the ship was the queen of the Buffalo-Chicago run. It commanded $20 for a cabin and half of that for deck passage on a voyage of a thousand miles. Cargo prices were twice what the *Erie* charged for one-third the distance—a bargain. Yet the vessel was so efficient, and in such demand, that it averaged $5,000 in gross receipts for the round trip—two-thirds from passengers and a third from cargo. Expenses, according to Klein, were $3,523, leaving profit of $1,477 per trip. With thirteen trips likely in a season, the company took in $19,200, or 16 percent of initial investment. The opportunity was clear, and North American investors increased their building activity to the point where there were too many boats, particularly following the economic downturn of 1837, and profitability

Ticket and timetable from the steamship *Illinois*, 1843.
(Courtesy of the Detroit Historical Society Collection.)

dropped. Rate wars drove a couple of competitors out of business, while the others looked for a solution.

In 1839 owners of the thirty largest boats formed an association to establish regular routes between Buffalo, Detroit, and Chicago and to regulate the vessels on those routes. The intention was to spread the work and share downtime, as well as set prices for passengers and freight at a rate that ensured a profit. Under a board of directors, the association established twice-daily runs between Buffalo and Detroit, with ships continuing on to Chicago on alternate days. Profits were pooled; 15 percent was allocated to a general fund, and the rest was divided based on each owner's shares in the organization. Owners were responsible for their own operating expenses and were required to maintain their vessels in a manner appropriate to the association, clean and mechanically fit. This agreement was similar to one drawn up by the canalboat owners on the Erie Canal in 1838 and successfully kept the steamboat companies healthy—at the expense of the traveling public.

Before moving to the exciting era of the 1840s and 1850s, a moment more should be spent in the 1820s and 1830s. A number of events affected the region and nation during these decades, events in which steamboats played a pivotal role. Of course, the opening of the Erie, Welland, and St. Lawrence canals, already discussed, had a tremendous impact on the region, as migrants flocked to new territories.

In 1832 a Native American chief, Black Hawk, became a lightning rod for the fear and enmity of a huge wave of settlers arriving in the Great Lakes territories. Americans recalled the powerful legends of Pontiac, Blue Jacket, Round Head, and Tecumseh and feared that Black Hawk had the same ability to incite a broad spectrum of Indians to wage war against the white settlers. The true horrors and exaggerated narratives of the War of 1812 prompted a military reaction from the US government that has been labeled Black Hawk's War. Troops were rushed to northwestern Illinois, an action that had unfortunate consequences for thousands of people living well outside its sphere.

Recalling that this was the draconian era of Indian removal under President Andrew Jackson, perhaps the rapid military reaction is not surprising. Lewis Cass, former governor of Michigan Territory, became Jackson's secretary of war in 1831 and successfully imposed treaties on various native clans that forced them to cede rights to vast tracts of northern woods and prairies. Black Hawk was a Sauk, and treaties involving the Sauk and Fox lands dated to 1804. Sauk and Fox peoples had loose relations with local Kickapoos, Winnebagoes, and Potawatomis. By 1830, they had complied with government directives and moved west across the Mississippi River.

When Black Hawk led about a thousand men, women, and children back east across the Mississippi, he came at the invitation of the Winnebago prophet White Cloud, who maintained a settlement on the Rock River in Illinois. The chief was sixty-five years old and not inclined to go to war. Anti-native sentiment in Illinois was high, with eastern settlers often crossing the Mississippi to shoot the Indians' livestock and burn crops. Federal agents were not supplying the natives with the food stores that had been promised, and Governor John Reynolds had inflamed the populace with talk of invasion and extermination. On top of that, many on both sides thought that British forces at St. Joseph Island and Malden would support the Indians—a throwback to the War of 1812. Militia and regular army troops rushed in. Faced with overwhelming military odds, Black Hawk decided to withdraw to the Mississippi. That move was marked by rearguard skirmishes, which resulted in the killing, by both sides, of innocent farmers and native stragglers. A final showdown took place on the banks of the big river. Within a few weeks, Black Hawk's group had dwindled to a shadow, yet federal troops and angry militias poured into the territory.

At the onset, the militias came from the immediate region, and federal units were shuttled by steamboat from St. Louis—one of the earliest instances of steamboats moving soldiers to a battlefield. In June, just as the "war" was winding down, General Winfield Scott embarked almost a thousand troops at Buffalo for Chicago. They boarded four vessels: the *Henry Clay, William Penn, Sheldon Thompson,* and *Superior.*

One report claims that the *Henry Clay* carried immigrants exposed to Asiatic cholera, a virulent strain recently arrived in North America at Montreal from Europe via Russia and India. At Niagara the ship loaded New England troops that were generally healthy. This bacteria does not spread from person to person but is transmitted through contaminated water sources or food. Infection results in rapid and fatal dehydration. Improper treatment of related sewage and infected surfaces encourages the contagion. Perhaps most unfortunate, there is a time lag between exposure and the appearance of symptoms.[36]

The *Henry Clay* and *Sheldon Thompson* left Buffalo with troops, as the other ships remained to load supplies and ordnance. The *Clay* arrived at Detroit first, and within a day two soldiers succumbed to cholera. A general panic ensued. The ship was made to leave the dock, and it anchored upstream of the town, near Belle Isle. Medical knowledge suggested that the disease passed through the air as a vapor, and the Belle Isle anchorage was downwind of Detroit. Unfortunately, we now know that the cholera pathogen is waterborne, making Belle Isle the worst possible location. The rivers, lakes and canals provided both "fresh" water and sewage disposal, fueling an outbreak.

By the time the *Thompson* arrived, refueled, and departed for Lake Huron, conditions on the *Clay* had deteriorated. As the vessels passed, General Scott, his staff, and a contingent of fifty troops went aboard the *Thompson.* The troops and much baggage were later offloaded at Fort Gratiot at the head of the St Clair River. Captain Augustus Walker, skipper of the *Sheldon Thompson,* recalled, "The next day the *Clay* arrived in the St. Clair River. The disease had become so violent and alarming on board of her that nothing like discipline could be observed. Everything in the way of subordination ceased. As soon as she came to the dock, each man sprang on shore, hoping to escape from a scene so terrifying and appalling; some fled to the fields, some to the woods, while others lay down in the streets and under the cover of the river banks, where most of them died, unwept and alone."[37]

Walker's ship remained healthy for a few days but dropped five sick soldiers and sailors at Mackinac. Two survived. Between the Manitou

Islands and the settlement of Chicago, twelve men were committed to the deep. Scott and his retinue left the boat immediately, and over the next four days fifty-four members of the party died. It might be perceived as fortunate that Chicago was a small gathering of rough buildings and about fifty residents, not including the soldiers. This was to a pandemic what a firebreak is to a forest fire. So primitive was the post at Chicago that to get enough wood to return to Mackinac the captain purchased an abandoned log house and the rail fence surrounding the farm and had soldiers cut and split it for the steam engine's firebox. The pestilence seemed to have stopped at the southern end of the lake, ironically not affecting the military conflict that drew it there.[38]

Retracing the path of the plague, it seems that Mackinac, and by extension Beaver Island and Sault Sainte Marie, remained relatively untouched. Detroit fared badly. Fear spread quickly after 2 citizens were afflicted on July 6, two days after the *Henry Clay* arrived. Many people tried to escape the town but found hotels and taverns unwelcoming. Pontiac residents, twenty miles north of the city, turned outsiders away with guns, and Rochester citizens, to the east, tore up their bridge. Mail stopped being distributed. Migrants were told to leave. Despite a spate of homeopathic remedies and prayers, 96 people died, including Father Gabriel Richard, a Roman Catholic pastor and a leading political citizen. The point of origin—Buffalo—buried 120 people in two months.[39]

The "visitation" was repeated in 1834. By August, Buffalo residents felt under siege. This round was less lethal, but the constant funeral bells and despair prompted one diarist to lament, "Oh the melancholy days! Oh Buffalo, Buffalo, thou little Babylon of helots and harlots and infinite stinks!" It was unsettling to greet someone in the morning and find out in the evening that they were dead: "People are dying all around me. I may not have long to stay in the place. Death or my better destiny may remove me."[40]

This same pandemic spread through other lake ports, claiming significant portions of the populace. At the time, and for years afterward, it was generally assumed that a rapid spread of the disease was related to the rapid transportation afforded by steamboats. In a decade, travel time from the Atlantic coast to the middle of the continent was reduced from months to days, and the influx of immigrants had been tremendous. The lightning strike of cholera seemed to blossom in large port cities like Buffalo and Detroit, so it was easy to suspect the steamboat as the prime carrier of the disease. This theory has since been disproved, but it was a consideration when choosing steamboat travel in the early years of the technology.[41]

In a similar spirit, steamships enabled the rapid spread of rumor and conspiracy, and became victims of the same. During the early 1800s, a portion of the Canadian populace began a governmental reform movement. Over time power in Upper Canada became concentrated in the hands of a few noble families. Political and financial resources allowed members of this "Family Compact" to enrich themselves and their friends. The "Patriots," a loyal opposition mentioned earlier in this chapter, were frustrated when their diplomatic and political efforts were stymied. By 1836 the threat of revolt was being actively stoked with rhetoric akin to that of Americans Thomas Paine and Patrick Henry sixty years before. Canadian reform efforts were encouraged by a significant number of Americans, who for years had entertained the idea of a northern neighbor free of Great Britain.

As with many civil actions, eruptions occurred with little planning. In Lower Canada, a general uprising broke out in October 1837 and was quelled by the army within a few days. In Upper Canada, with political efforts exhausted, William Mackenzie crossed the border to Navy Island in the Niagara River and set up a Patriot headquarters. His organization grew as word of his intent became common knowledge. In the spirit of neutrality, American officials attempted to discourage his efforts. Then one evening three boats from the British garrison at Chippewa crossed to Navy Island and cut Mackenzie's small steamboat *Caroline* from its moorings, sending it over the great falls in flames. In the whole action, there was one casualty, but word spread that the ship had taken its entire crew over Niagara Falls.

It was a dramatic time that evoked memories of the War of 1812. Canadian Captain Andrew Drew and his crew became heroes upon their return from the raid, and Colonel Allan McNab, their commander, was knighted. Americans, most of whom knew nothing of the Patriots, immediately saw destruction of the *Caroline* as an affront to their sovereignty. President Martin Van Buren declared to Congress that an armed British force had come ashore on American soil, destroying property and taking American lives. The secretary of state protested to the British minister in Washington, and militias were placed on alert along the northern border. At the end of May 1838, a group of Americans boarded the Canadian steamer *Sir Robert Peel* at a wooding stop on the upper St. Lawrence River. After chasing the passengers and crew ashore, this band towed the hull offshore and set it afire. The British minister countered, and these two steamboat incidents became rallying points for an escalating conflict. Over the next several months, inept planning on the part of the Patriots and concerted efforts on the part of royal and federal troops and militias caused the movement to gradually die of frustration.[42]

In two decades, the Great Lakes steamboat fleet had grown from a few pioneer vessels to several dozen comfortable and reliable ships. Operators developed new business models, quickly adapting to a clientele which had a variety of needs. They profited from the influx of people to the frontier, but in turn made the rapid expansion of the region possible. This situation allowed steamboats to play key roles in significant historical events. For the most part this activity was limited to the four southern lakes. To this point, Lake Superior's part in early maritime history involved canoe-based commerce. Thousands of tons of provisions and furs traversed the big lake every year in birch bark-sheathed hulls. A few small schooners were launched by Oliver Newberry and other fur interests. By 1837 there were eight small sailing vessels, the large schooner *Napoleon*, one propeller—the *Independence*—and one schooner-converted-to-steamer, the *Julia Palmer*. The latter two registered 280 tons, according to the *Detroit Free Press*. Growth of the steamboat business on the northernmost lake came slowly during the next era, and blossomed with the maturation of mining and lumber harvesting after 1870.[43]

CHAPTER 5

Regional Development

For roughly twenty years, the Great Lakes steamboat passenger industry climbed to a commercial and stylistic peak. There would be other peaks, and for decades afterward the business expanded to encompass vessels of all sizes and builds. Between 1837 and 1857, there was a highly focused period of maritime development that saw commercial profits reinvested in the region and attracted significant additional outside capital. A public relations war forced shipping interests to build bigger, faster, grander, and more economical ships. Pride sparked a technological leap in many respects that was not matched for another half century. Most established economic relationships would change by the end of this period, moving the industry from its pioneering stage to practical maturity and making a profit by seeding the region with future customers. The dramatic adolescent phase described in this chapter was both glorious and fiery.

The number of vessels grew dramatically, as did their size. In 1839 there were twenty-five "principal" steam packets on the upper lakes. The *Illinois* was the only ship longer than 200 feet, and was one of only two—the *Great Western* being the other—registered at more than 700 tons, nearly 20 percent larger than the next vessels afloat. Two decades later, in 1857, at least twenty-eight boats topped 200 feet. Five boats were longer than 300 feet, and one weighed in at 2,000 tons. Incredible lengths demanded changes in construction techniques, and competition for passenger fares required more luxurious accommodations. New technologies such as propellers and improved drive systems redefined accepted practices, while changes in maritime safety policy, commercial politics, and demographic shifts constantly changed the nature of Great Lakes shipping industry.[1]

Throughout the world the steam engine was transforming transportation. Railroads spread a web across Europe, and novelty was being replaced with pride in their efficiency and technology. In America steam locomotives were breaking away from the East Coast and plunging westward. One of the first railroads in the country ran from Albany to Schenectady, following the Erie Canal by only six years. Connection by rail directly from Albany to Buffalo in 1847 greatly increased traffic to the Michigan Central Rail Road, Michigan Southern Railway, and other lines joining the Atlantic to the Great Lakes. Advertisements in the following years featured three of the largest steam vessels in the world, an exciting itinerary, and guest lists read like a midcentury Who's Who.

During a transitional period that lasted until after 1875, railroads and steamships shared the nation's transportation burden. Palace steamers were the most luxurious and often the most direct travel option. Following a trip from New York to Albany by packet steamer, the journey from Albany to Buffalo offered a choice of slow canalboats or fast trains traveling along nearly identical routes—a choice usually determined by budget. Early on, the trip from Buffalo to Detroit to Chicago was a remarkable steamer ride around Michigan's Lower Peninsula. In 1849 a train route from Detroit to Lake Michigan was completed, requiring only a short steamer trip to reach Chicago. That year saw one hundred thousand people make the passage. A rail extension to Chicago was completed three years later by both the Lake Shore & Michigan Southern and Michigan Central railroads, meeting fresh tracks already laid to the west.[2]

By comparison, other rail capitals such as St. Louis and Memphis began sending tracks westward at about this same time, but Memphis was not reliably connected to the Atlantic until the late 1850s, and then only by an irregular route. St. Louis did not have regular East Coast connections until after the American Civil War. On the Great Lakes, there was a successful effort to bypass the established Mississippi connection at Chicago via Toledo. The Toledo, Wabash and Western Rail Road met lines traversing Indiana and Illinois that would connect the lake port of Toledo with Mississippi River ports just above St. Louis in 1859.[3]

While early railroad lines made gradual thrusts into the hinterlands, steam-powered ships proved their mettle on the open ocean. In 1818 the American sailing packet *Savannah* was built in New

York with an auxiliary steam plant from New Jersey installed as an afterthought. Its hold was filled with an engine, boiler, coal, and firewood, leaving no room for cargo or passengers. The paddlewheels, collapsible and generally stored on deck, were used for only eighty-five hours of the crossing—about 13 percent. However, the vessel is recognized as the first steam-powered ship to cross the Atlantic, having traveled from Savannah, Georgia, to Liverpool, England, in twenty-seven and a half days. While early historians award this honor to a Liverpool-built vessel, the *Conde de Palmalla*, which crossed to Brazil and back to Spain soon afterward, the claim has not been supported by subsequent sources.[4]

The *Rising Star*, a full-rigged ship with steam propulsion, has long boasted the first east-to-west steam passage, in 1821–22 (the *Savannah* having returned across the Atlantic entirely by sail). Unlike conventional side-wheelers, the *Rising Star*'s copper boilers and twin cylinders drove two paddlewheels located within its hull instead of outboard. H. Philip Spratt describes the small, 13.5-foot wheels "enclosed in an airtight casing; this was open to the sea by apertures in the bottom of the vessel, between the centre keel and the two outer keels on either side." The paddle floats, or boards, extended below the hull's bottom by 39 inches. After some difficulties off of the Portuguese coast, the vessel reached Valparaiso, Chile. Its top speed was recorded at twelve knots, but there is no mention of how much time was spent steaming.[5]

In 1833 the *Royal William* became the first Canadian steamboat to cross the Atlantic. Schooner-rigged, it was built in Quebec and towed upriver to Montreal for engine installation. After a career spent along the coast, the staunchly constructed craft left Pictou, Nova Scotia, for Europe under power. Off of Newfoundland one of the two engines failed. Under the remaining Bennett & Henderson engine and auxiliary sails, it finished the crossing to England in twenty-five days. This was roughly comparable to elapsed times under sail, but it reinforced the promise of steam.[6]

In 1837 the London vessel *Sirius* became the first hull to traverse the North Atlantic from Cork, Ireland, to New York entirely under steam power. It was a small, hearty coaster with brigantine sailing capability. A regular route from London to Cork made the tough Irish Sea its testing ground. Fitted with Samuel Hall's surface condensers, the boilers could be continuously fed fresh water, an innovation that prevented costly corrosion and maintenance and proved absolutely essential for extended cruising. With forty passengers, thirty-five officers and crew, and moderate freight, the *Sirius* arrived in New York after eighteen days and ten hours, a mean speed of more than six miles per hour.[7] Vessels under sail often surpassed this pace, but they also might drift without wind for days. Assuming that the reliability of the steamers could be proven, powered voyages were greatly anticipated. The arrival of the *Sirius* caused much excitement in New York, and it departed ten days later to a seventeen-gun salute from the battery and cheers from thousands of spectators. Eighteen days later it was home. It repeated the feat the following year, retiring afterward to the rigors of the European coasting trade.

As an exclamation point upon the triumph of 1837, another British pioneering vessel, the *Great Western*, followed the *Sirius* into New York Harbor a few hours later. The *Sirius* weighed 703 tons. The *Great Western*, less than thirty feet longer, was nearly double the tonnage. Powerfully built, the *Great Western* was the first triumph of the builder Isambard Brunel, capable of carrying two hundred passengers under the care of sixty crewmen. The transit bested the *Sirius*'s time by three days and five hours. Both vessels were powered by low-pressure, lever engines. The *Great Western* traversed the North Atlantic sixty-five times, became a Royal Mail carrier to the West Indies, and finally reached the scrapyard in 1857. A third British steamer reached New York in 1837—a small boat coincidently called *Royal William*—and steamboats gained credibility in the public's perception with each arrival.[8]

On the inland seas, the *Great Britain* on Lake Ontario and *Great Western* on Lake Erie marked the first major step forward in passenger comfort with the installation of a spacious cabin that covered much of the upper deck. Prior to this, cabins and communal accommodations were below the main deck, which was reserved for fuel, cargo, and a bit of open space for promenading. In 1833 Oliver Newberry's *Michigan* featured a number of staterooms and a salon on the main deck, with a promenade above. When Newberry rebuilt the barge *Illinois* as a steamer in 1838, the concept went a step further with the addition of an upper deck, which was partially enclosed forward and offered a broad, sheltered promenade aft of the tall cross-head engine.

The *Great Britain* of 1834 may have been the first steamer to be dubbed Queen of the Lakes. An article in the *British Whig* proudly opined that "the *Great Britain* is undoubtedly the Queen of all the vessels which navigate the Western waters, and few persons can regard her without feeling mixed emotions of pleasure and astonishment; pleasure at the sight of her unrivalled size and beauty, and astonishment that a country so new and so poor as Upper Canada, should have had the laudable temerity to build so stupendous a steamboat."[9] The *Great*

The steamer *Great Britain*, c. 1834. (Courtesy of the Detroit Historical Society Collection.)

Western, launched at Huron, Ohio, in 1838, had a ladies' lounge on its main deck, as well as a number of staterooms. The upper, or hurricane, deck was enclosed from the pilot house aft, save for a narrow exterior walkway encircling the boat. Another ladies' salon was located near the stern, adjoining the dining room, and a long central cabin ran forward to a men's lounge, which served as the barroom. Sixty staterooms containing about three hundred berths opened off of the main salon. Including steerage passengers, the vessel accommodated more than 550 people. As the palace steamer era proceeded, this layout and guest complement remained the standard, with variations, for ships between 200 and 230 feet.[10]

Palace steamer is a romantic appellation adapted to the megaships of this era as a class. As early as April 1835, the Kingston *Chronicle & Gazette* described the *Great Britain* as "That Leviathan of the Lake, and Monarch of our Marine; that floating palace, the splendid result of . . . princely enterprise," and these boats remained "those magnificent floating palaces" through the American Civil War.[11] It was not until the 1880s, when the Great Lakes maritime industry recovered sufficiently to have large boats again under construction, that the epithet *palace* was revived to describe new builds. Even then it was only in complimentary comparison to their magnificent antebellum predecessors.

Within the current lexicon, most historians would agree that *palace steamer* refers to the largest, purpose-built, side-wheel or stern-wheel passenger vessels of post-Jacksonian America. More than twice as long as most other vessels—longer than a city block—the Great Lakes version stood out gloriously in any harbor, arches gracefully exuding strength and sharp prow the essence of speed. Nearly all were topped with two smokestacks set athwart the ship and employed a walking beam engine. Stylistically, wheelhouses morphed from utilitarian boxes set on the upper deck into elegant octagonal command stations, often topped with a sculpted eagle or finial and later with an upper pilot station.

The palace class as a whole will be explored further in the next chapter, but it is important to introduce these vessels for context. Of the inaugural prototypes, the *Illinois* sailed for only twelve years before it was considered redundant. By that time the ship had been involved in two collisions and had machinery damaged in two storms. Its engine and boilers were moved to a new vessel with the same name.

The *Great Western* was only a year old when it burned at Detroit. Rebuilt, the ship ran for fifteen more seasons before being dismantled. Its career on the Buffalo to Chicago run included three severe groundings, four collisions, and one disabling storm. Neither craft finished its career without a near-complete overhaul. However, both vessels ended their days in the breaker's yard. Many of their peers were not so lucky.[12]

Arguably, the first steamer in the palace category was the *Empire*. Launched in 1844, it rivaled any ship in the world at 253 feet and 1,140 tons, Old Measurement (OM).[13] Two low-pressure engines drove paddlewheels 30 feet in diameter. The power system is worth noting in three respects. First, the two engines were twin-chambered "compound engines" in which cooling steam from a primary cylinder was released into a secondary cylinder, applying a secondary thrust that smoothed the rotation. Second, the inclined engine—as opposed to vertical or horizontal—was designed to optimize space within the hull. Third, the *Empire* carried six locomotive boilers manufactured in Pittsburgh.[14]

By contrast, most steam vessels at the time employed a single, vertically configured engine driven by one cylinder infused with steam from one boiler. A few ships had two complete sets of single-cylinder engines and a single boiler, each driving a paddlewheel. The experiment aboard the *Empire*, which had a twin-cylinder inclined engine and multiple boilers, proved successful and insightful. Nonetheless, vertical engines would remain the norm on the lakes and horizontal the norm on the riverboats of the West. Boiler pressure in most lake vessels remained low, while high pressure was favored on western rivers. Both types had benefits and drawbacks, and both suffered catastrophic failures.

The *Empire* was a very sleek ship and must have presented a spectacular impression sitting alongside a dock. Wharf-side buildings, stacked chockablock on Buffalo streets, and small schooners and canalboats were dwarfed by its singular presence. Contemporary images show the pilothouse nearly on the bow, with a single gaff-rigged mast stepped just behind it. Most ships of this period sported two or three rigged masts to offer auxiliary propulsion for the ship and psychological reassurance to passengers. Typical of ships in this adolescent era, the *Empire* was crippled by a burst steam system pipe within the first five years and had the engine entirely replaced with a newer, more powerful plant. The engine was nearly as valuable as the investment in the rest of the vessel. The *Empire* endured at least one major collision or grounding every year until it was laid up in 1857, statistically adding to industry calls for federal intervention in navigational improvements. The Lakes were a tough place to be a mariner, and it took legislators in Washington many years to understand that.

Within several months of its launch, the *Empire* was joined on the upper lakes by the *Niagara*. Though slightly shorter at 230 feet, the new vessel was the first major launch by Bidwell & Banta of Buffalo, a company whose name became synonymous with the palace steamer era. Like a sporting event, the frequent ship launchings in Buffalo were announced in the papers and anticipated in taverns. On June 2 Buffalo's *Daily National Pilot* announced the 2:30 p.m. launch of Charles Reed's new flagship and three days later carried a positive report of what likely was an inauspicious wetting for this steamer.

> Yesterday afternoon, an immense concourse of people assembled to witness the launch of the NIAGARA. Everything seemed favorable, the ways well laid, and nothing appeared to hinder the boat from going off in fine style, At 4:00 she commenced moving and had got half her length into the water when she stuck fast having struck against a sunken piece of timber. She proved to be very strongly put together, as when she struck she bulged very much amidships; which in any ordinary built boat would have broken her in two. They expect to get her off without much difficulty.[15]

The *Niagara* was indeed sturdily built. According to marine archaeologist John Odin Jensen, a pair of arched keelsons ran along each side of the keel, comprised of oak beams sistered together with huge bolts. Such arches would become more prominent in later vessels. Beneath the engines, the greatest point of load, the keelsons were four feet thick and thirty inches wide. Five smaller keelsons added stiffness to the length of the ship. The framing of the hull was reinforced with thick strakes and liberal use of thick through bolts and nuts. To further accommodate the increased length, ceiling planks were attached to the frames. The *Niagara* was a stanch boat, a trend in steamship building that changed soon afterward.[16]

In the minds of sailors and landsmen alike, suspicion or superstition arises when a ship's launch does not go smoothly, particularly when the vessel gets hung up in the slip, as did *Niagara*. It is considered an unlucky sign. Yet the record shows that the *Niagara*'s career was typical—no more lucky or unlucky than those of its contemporaries. Running from Dunkirk, New York, to Detroit, and later in the more lucrative trade between Buffalo and Chicago, the ship grounded in successive years at Erie, hit a reef near the Straits of Mackinac, and went ashore at Charlotte, New York. Soon afterward the ship struck the schooner *Poland* as that vessel sat trapped in the mud on the St. Clair Flats.[17]

Mention of the St. Clair Flats occurs frequently in newspapers, logs, and letters of the period, generally in tones of frustration. Three of the five Great Lakes funnel into a bottleneck at the bottom of Lake Huron. This massive watershed generates 82 million gallons of water a minute as it enters the St. Clair River. For about fifteen miles, the flow is constrained in a channel seldom more than a mile wide before gradually branching in a southwest quadrant and forming the largest freshwater delta in the world. Initially, the northern branch of the river, which passes in a hook around Algonac, was favored by navigators. However, its confluence at Lake St. Clair is comprised of miles of shallow and shifting sands in Anchor Bay. The southern route was shorter, generally less hazardous and preferred—except for one spot. The hang-up, literally, was a stretch of the lower river: "the Flats."

It was at the far end of the delta, and depths varied from thirty feet to mere inches. Five feet of water over shifting sandbars in the main channel was common. It was often less. The shallows were identifiable by means of water plants or water color, but that changed with the seasons, and visual clues were not clear at night. Ships regularly stopped at nightfall waiting for first light and, despite crews' best efforts went aground in broad daylight. A thriving towboat business sprang up, dragging nonpowered vessels over the bar or pulling stranded steamers from the shallows. Most sailing ships engaged a towboat at the head or mouth of the St. Clair River, following a local pilot who lived on the river and understood its foibles. Despite this, groundings and collisions were common, and the lost revenues generated complaints that gradually filtered up the political ladder.

As the *Niagara* was one of the largest boats on the continent, it is not surprising that it languished at the Flats on its first foray toward Chicago. Returning to Detroit, it discharged cargo and took on a load of eastward-bound iron, hides, and flour. Within a month water levels rose, and the *Niagara* sailed confidently past Newport, St. Clair, and Fort Gratiot for the cruise to Mackinac, Milwaukee, and Chicago. Moving west, it carried cargo and dunnage that included all the fruits of the Great Lakes region: migrants and speculators, finished lumber, and salt; on the return trip, the products of the farm, forest, and mine heading to markets along the East Coast and overseas. This balance of items inbound and outbound generated freight and passenger revenues that served the steamship companies well. As new craft came down the ways, they were more purposeful in their design and technology.

When the *Niagara* finally reached Milwaukee, the *Sentinel* reported, "The arrival of this splendid steamer created quite a sensation," coming into town "on Monday afternoon . . . with all her colors set and music playing. Every body hurried down to the piers to look at her, and a very general verdict of approval and admiration was returned. The *Niagara* is, in truth, a noble boat; well modeled, capacious, convenient, swift and most strongly built. Her after Saloon, on the upper deck, is superbly fitted and furnished and the accommodations for steerage passenger on the main deck are unsurpassed."

Later in 1846, a grounding at Skillagalee, a reef in northeastern Lake Michigan, proved the strength of the noble boat. After dumping hundreds of barrels of flour and beef and cords of wood, it cleared the reef and headed for Mackinac. Grounding was a tough but accepted part of navigating the lakes. Ships approached known shallows slowly, with a crewman checking depths regularly by dunking a lead-weighted line. Without charts, even the best pilots found themselves aground occasionally on shifting sands. The *Niagara*'s captain, Tommy Richards, wrote to his wife, "Louisa join me in sending thanks to Him who alone is able to bring us safely though [*sic*] the perils by Sea & Land." During a storm, Richards had been forced to shut the engines down. The sails were deployed but were unsuited to more than support propulsion.

With a damaged rudder and both smokestacks blown down, the battered *Niagara* limped to Detroit for a refit.[18]

The late 1850s saw the growth of steamboat racing. At first record-setting passages were often instigated when owners were aboard. C. M. Reed prompted a speed test when aboard the *Niagara* in 1856. So impetuous was his zeal that the ship made only brief stops at appointed ports, leaving dawdlers on the dock. Later contests involved competing boats and were often impromptu affairs meant to generate good publicity. It did not escape the operators that these events enlivened the long passage for the passengers. Editorialists decried such dangerous games, but newspapers broadcast the challenges. The *Niagara* engaged the newly repowered *Empire* later that year, to the latter's benefit. In 1857 Captain Gil Appleby, owner of the new *Sultana* out of Cleveland, offered a wager of $5,000 for any comers on a run between Buffalo and Chicago. The *Detroit Free Press* reported that General Reed took up the challenge. But, despite growing anticipation, there is no evidence that the race actually took place. The *Niagara* was involved in a collision in the Detroit River on August 5.[19]

The *Niagara* remained on the Buffalo-Chicago route until 1851, when the New York and Erie Railroad reached its new terminus at Dunkirk, New York. Charles Reed chartered the *Niagara*, *Empire*, and *Keystone State* to the railroad companies for the season. The figure cited for the deal was $65,000, and it marks a trend in the palace steamer trade. Increasingly, the largest vessels were put on time-critical routes between railheads. The *Niagara* and its well-traveled fleet mates became the principal vessels running between Dunkirk and Detroit. By this time, the Michigan Central Rail Road was completed from Detroit to Chicago, so the Reed boats served as quick and comfortable ferryboat extensions of the railroads. This business paradigm was part of several successful syndicates into the next century.

Following the run-in with the *Poland* in the spring of 1849, the *Niagara* was involved in two collisions in 1851. It collided with the schooner *Traveler* on Lake Michigan in September and ten weeks later sank the *Lucy A. Blossom*, loaded with 10,000 bushels of corn, lying at anchor at the mouth of the Detroit River. Sometime afterward it grounded in Lake Erie, requiring repairs in dry dock, and within a few months it struck its near sister ship, *Cataract*, in the Niagara River. Damage to both boats amounted to $2,000.[20]

In 1855 the Northern Railroad was completed from Toronto to

Collingwood on Lake Huron's Georgian Bay. This route was destined to be important because it shortened travel to the northern lakes and became closely associated with the Great Western Railway and the Grand Trunk. Traveling between Collingwood and Milwaukee, the *Niagara's* captain, Fred S.Miller, described what was probably a typical voyage.

> The Clerk informed me, after leaving Collingwood, that he had on board 105 tons merchandize and passengers' baggage, 21 horses and several wagons, and about 75 cabin passengers. On arriving at Mackinac, we took on six more; does not know the number of steerage or deck passengers; the weather was fresh, northerly; arrived at Mackinac on Tuesday at 12 o'clock noon; left 20 minutes past 3 o'clock P.M., and arrived at Two Rivers about half past 10 o'clock A.M., on the 23rd inst., on arriving there stopped at Manitowoc about half past 11 A.M., and landed some passengers and things; one or two came aboard at this place; left Manitowoc and arrived at Sheboygan, and landed 15 horses, some wagons, and quite a number of passengers, and some merchandize; left Sheboygan about half past 2 o'clock, P.M.[21]

Reportedly, Captain Miller had been up all night as the *Niagara* passed around Waugoshance Point west of Mackinac, and through the Beaver Island archipelago. After leaving Sheboygan, the captain retired for a nap, and

> getting up, discovered that the boat was on fire, and suppose it was about the stove pipe, aft; I first met the 3rd. engineer and told him to get the hose on to the pumps. I then turned to go forward, and found the hall full of smoke; I went to the pilot house, gave the signal to the man to put up; the boat was headed towards the shore; the engine then stopped; was about five miles from shore, and four to five miles from Port Washington; I left the pilot house; the first mate then came forward; I ordered him to get the axes, and man the small boats and get them over; mate replied that the stern boat was over and capsized; we then went to work and broke the state-room doors off and threw them overboard; I then went aft to the larboard side and kicked the doors off and threw them over, together with wash stands, chairs, and everything I could get hold of; I remained aft as long as I could.[22]

In proper form, this narration avoids any description of panic gripping the passengers. By all reports, the captain and his crew managed the situation amid chaos. When passengers discovered the fire, their reaction, according to one, "beggars all description—consternation seized upon almost everyone and men, women and children rushed to and fro about the boat, shouting and crying." The crew's instructions were generally ignored. All but one boat was swamped by the rush of bodies and frightened ineptitude. Captain Miller later recounted that he had no more control over the passengers than a flock of wild pigeons. Several survivors described dozens of people jumping from the deck into the water and disappearing. Some people found bits of wood to float on. Despite September's late summer warmth, the water was likely about 50 degrees Fahrenheit, a temperature that allows good swimmers about an hour of consciousness. Unfortunately, swimming was not a common pastime in 1850, and few people knew how to stay afloat.

The conflagration was defined by all observers as happening very quickly. From first flames to a smoldering hulk probably took less than thirty minutes. The fireball attracted a number of rescue ships, including the steamers *Traveler* and *Illinois*, and three schooners, one the *Dan Marble*. Over the next several days, an estimate of the dead was compiled by printing the names of survivors or descriptions of the bodies recovered on the shore. Naturally, all passenger records had been destroyed with the ship, and the clerk, George Heley, perished. His son Harry, the second clerk, survived but was in serious condition for weeks. Deduction indicated that more than sixty people had perished, and losses ranged from two to three hundred thousand dollars, including cargo, the value of the ship, and the large amount of cash that many travelers carried. By the end of the month, a letter was published by Captain Miller, stating, "I am confident that the boat did not take fire from the machinery, nor from the boilers, as every portion of her firehold was fire-proof. My opinion is that the fire was caused by some combustible material . . . from the fact that it enveloped the boat in flames almost instantly."[23]

Miller also addressed a lingering rumor that arson was the cause. Through his narrative, which was reprinted in newspapers around the region, a mystery unfolded. Readers learned of ill feelings between a group of passengers leaving Collingwood for Green Bay and the *Niagara*'s managers. As the boats on the Green Bay line were generally less reliable and missed sailing times, tickets were sold for passage on the Milwaukee-bound boats only as far as Mackinac, where folks might find passage on a vessel from Buffalo or Detroit heading to Green Bay. This option aboard the *Niagara* cost $7.50, instead of the $10 fare to southern Wisconsin. Those who chose this plan frequently found themselves stranded at Mackinac. Passengers saw the company as opportunistic and felt that the "Chicago line" should provide some type of forwarding arrangement to accommodate them. Conversely, the steamship operators said they were assisting Collingwood traffic with a viable next step, for other westward-bound ships stopped regularly at Mackinac. Animosity developed. Captain Miller knew before the boat left the dock at Collingwood that among his passengers were "quite a number of those disaffected ones." Then the steward, Mr. Clark, found a letter in his room and took it to the captain. It read, "Look out!—Save yourself, the boat will be burned tonight; everything is in readiness, we have made ample preparations to take care ourselves. (signed) a. passenger." Miller consulted with his chief engineer and another skipper traveling as a guest. Security was bolstered to the point where the captain said he felt confident that the letter was a hoax. After the fire, he concluded that neither the ship nor its machinery was to blame. Readers were left to draw conclusions of their own.[24]

There were numerous conflagrant disasters, but dangers came in many forms. A report in the *Buffalo Courier* reported a horrific event aboard the *Passport* that left the ship intact.

We learn from the Toronto Globe of Saturday that a most frightful accident occurred on board the steamer PASSPORT, on Thursday evening, on her passage from Montreal to Kingston. It is represented by passengers that the engineer was absent, the assistant in his berth, and the boat left in charge of an incompetent person. When off Lancaster, 16 miles from Cornwall, about 9 o'clock in the evening, the boat struck the ground. The under deck was loaded with steerage passengers. The order to stop the engine and back out was promptly given, but the ignorance of the person in charge of the engine, led to a most sad catastrophe. Instead of backing, he opened a cock which let the hot steam in among the steerage passengers. A shriek instantly broke forth which was heard for several miles. The nature of the accident being for some time unknown, the steam continued to be discharged upon the poor creatures, adding to their insufferable agony. Four persons jumped overboard, two of whom were drowned. The nature of the accident being at length ascertained, the steam was at once shut off. Medical assistance was soon procured, when it was found that forty-four persons were severely scalded. The scene during the night is represented to have been horrible in the extreme; men, women and children, in dreadful agony, continued their shrieks throughout the night. When the boat reached Cornwall, nine persons had died. About twenty were left at that place and the remainder taken to Kingston, where four others have died, and many others were in a critical state. They were all immigrants. A number of passengers signed a card exculpating the Captain from all blame. If he was aware of the employment of an incompetent engineer, we do not see how he can escape censure.[25]

In the 1840s, several significant changes took place in the steamboat business. Boats got bigger, propellers were introduced, east-west cargoes reached a profitable balance, the politics of internal improvements became more heated, and confidence in the national economy excited interest in developing the West. As steamships offered the most economical form of transportation for both investor and passenger, demand drove expansion of architecture in the maritime world at an unprecedented rate.

About 1847 shipbuilders began to address the wooden steamer's primary structural problem: the integrity of long, wooden hulls. As the boats grew longer, they did not grow exponentially wider or deeper. Slender and shallow were necessary for negotiating the tight confines of early harbors. Slender was also considered structurally faster on open water, as evidenced by new construction. For instance, the *Great Western* of 1838 was 183 feet long and 34 feet wide, drawing 13 feet of water. Seven years later the *Empire* was 70 feet longer, 2 feet slimmer, and only a foot deeper. The efforts by shipwrights to manipulate wooden hulls to ever-greater lengths while retaining shallow drafts had reached the edge of the technological envelope.

Long, tubular hulls undulated fiercely in heavy weather. Front to rear they vibrated along the keel slowly, like a sound wave. Laterally, bulkheads were stressed like a sausage twisted in opposite directions at either end; the middle had little substance, relying on the outer skin to maintain the integrity of the whole. That combination was especially hard on a wooden hull already bearing heavy engines and boilers strung amidships. Similar to the *Niagara*, the inner timbers of other steamships had been girded with iron-strap, cross-hatched for several years. However, new approaches and apparatuses were required.

The internal and external arch trusses were evident in Great Lakes shipyards in 1847. Trusses had already been tested in bridge construction, and the remedy was immediately adopted for all large vessels on the ways and retrofitted into the larger ships in operation. Arches were a distinguishing feature of the palace steamers and were adopted by other wooden vessels afterward. The truss concept was most often employed in tandem, with two parallel arches running fore and aft, reinforcing keel rigidity along a line roughly 80 percent of the vessel's length at the farthest convenient point outboard.[26]

These experimental architectural arches came in three forms. One version sent laminated boards, clasp by long, two-inch-thick bolts, curving gracefully skyward through all decks, sistered to vertical braces falling from arch to bilge braces with the regularity of Grecian columns. Another created asymmetrical trussed arches that were less uniform yet easier to fabricate. In both cases, arches identified the vessels as first-rate packet ships. The third fix—simplest, lightest, and the longest lived—was the cable truss. Visually less prominent guy cables were strung diagonally upward from strategic deck locations to a stout central mast or pairs of masts, stepped along the keel. Three or four of these systems ran the length of the ship, creating a passive system that worked to support and stiffen the hull but was not an integral part of the structure. Many designs integrated combinations of the beam and cable concepts.

Although paddlewheel hulls were slim, they carried wide deck housings. Horizontal decks, with a slight camber, extended outboard from the slender hull to the outer edge of the large paddlewheels. This bulge nearly doubled the width of the ship at the centerline and gave it a teardrop shape when viewed from above. This configuration prevented damage to the paddles from collisions or alongside wharves. The large semicylindrical paddle boxes added further protection and reduced excessive spray on the passenger decks. Paddle boxes became dockside billboards, usually decorated with the name of the ship in large letters, as well as the company name, U.S. mail affiliate, or elaborate scrollwork. The teardrop profile of the decks and the need to protect the paddles demanded that these boats docked, when possible, with their bows to the wharf to allow for easy egress. This was also a favorable position in currents.

Wider beams allowed wider deck spaces. Early vessels took advantage of the overhangs to place their explosive boilers outboard, perhaps assuming that in the event of a disaster the hull would remain salvageable. Later steamers positioned their "water closets" on the overhang in front or behind the paddlewheels. Much of the commercial cargo that came aboard was stowed forward. Typically, a packet steamer heading west might load salt, lumber, fine furniture, clothing, oysters, and young livestock. Eastbound cargoes were mostly products of the frontier: furs, fish, potash, flour, and ingot iron. Steerage passengers were provided with partially enclosed spaces on the main deck, generally aft of the engines. Within a designated deck plot, families stowed their gear and set up temporary housekeeping. When they could afford it, women were housed in private cabins, leaving the men to stay on the main deck, surrounded by the valuable tools and furniture they had paid dearly to bring from the East Coast or Europe. The wealth of each family was represented by grindstones, saws, chisels, plows, wagon wheels, beds, chairs, books, and a few small toys. Many adults carried their life savings in gold sewn in their belts or the hems of skirts and coats.

When traveling for pleasure or business, a passenger engaged a cabin. Generally on the upper deck, these rooms had access to the upper promenade, a broad section of deck that allowed travelers to wander freely around the full circumference of the ship. Chairs and benches encouraged socializing alfresco. The cabins might also open onto the main public salon. Rooms were small but socially quite private for the era. Standard accommodations offered two mattresses on berths, one above the other. People were not expected to share beds as at taverns and hotels. Privacy was a luxury and a major draw for the steamboats, even into the railroad era. While cramped, the staterooms were twice as large as a stagecoach cabin at a fraction of the cost.

Passengers did not spend much time in their rooms when aboard these modern marvels. They meandered and mingled about the promenade and conversed in the dining room. In unpleasant weather guests lounged indoors where early Victorian upholstered chairs and divans were scattered liberally over well-padded carpets in the main cabin. This long, narrow room with arched ceiling and clerestory windows extended nearly bow to stern, lined with stateroom doors. At night candles or whale oil lamps provided warm illumination.

Common areas that were previously used for dining or dormitory sleeping evolved into specialized accommodations for ladies, and later for men. Ladies' salons were generally located aft, considered the most stable location on the boat. Comfortably appointed, the lounges provided a refuge from the elements and rougher passengers. Men's lounges were generally found near the bow, below the pilothouse.

Deep in the hull, a tough group of men tended the machinery. Engineers, oilers, and wood or coal passers kept the steam up and the physical plant in working order. Four decades from its inception, steam propulsion was better understood, but glaring issues remained regarding manufacturing standards, training, and regulation. During the early 1840s, engine size did not keep up with the growth in ships. Because of their value, engines were salvaged from wrecks and installed in larger vessels. When the *Boston* was wrecked near Milwaukee in 1846, the year-old engines on this 207-foot boat were salvaged and installed in the 251-foot Trenton, Michigan–built *Globe* in 1848. The only way to make a small engine push a longer ship fast is to lengthen and lighten the vessel. This became a trend in 1848.

When launched, the *Empire State* was about 13 inches shy of 300 feet. Built in the yard of John Griffin on the St. Clair River, the goal for master carpenter Captain A. Walker was to build the longest ship on the lakes. The project began in 1846, with an eye to constructing a vessel that was 20 percent longer and 36 percent heavier than anything afloat on the lakes. Proportionally comparable to the *Empire* of 1844, the *Empire State*'s beam grew by only 13 percent and its depth by just a few inches. All additional tonnage was extended forward and aft. This was a period of experimentation; long and slender designs seemed aesthetically perfect.

Engineers and shipwrights compensated for the weight of the arches and internal braces required to stiffen ever-longer hulls. Wooden braces, knees, planking, paneling, and hardware were optimized to realize the lightest, fastest vessel. The result was a very delicate ship. Additionally, arches and substantial upper decks elevated the center of balance on very narrow boats. Considering the rigors of the packet trade and the unpredictable nature of the Great Lakes, shipbuilders pushed the limits of practical frugality. Within eight years, six additional vessels were launched at more than 300 feet, representing more than a quarter of the new hulls. The 1850s brought the peak of the palace steamer era, a maturing of the Great Lakes maritime industry in terms of professionalism, and a genuine political concern for economic opportunities and improved navigational safety.

Disadvantages inherent in the nature of long, wooden, side-wheeled vessels were addressed as new materials and technologies became available. Long, thin boats were preferable as long as ships were limited by the dimensions of locks throughout the Great Lakes system. New applications of steel began to address some issues related

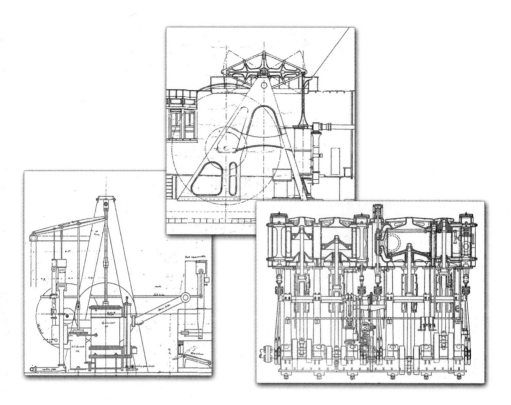

Illustrations of common steam engines: (*left*) vertical or cross-head engine from the *Frontenac*, 1817; (*center*) rocker beam engine from the *Darius Cole*, 1885; (*right*) quadruple expansion steam engine from the *South American*, 1914. (*Frontenac*, courtesy of the Maritime History of the Great Lakes; *Darius Cole* and *South American*, courtesy of the Detroit Historical Society Collection.)

to narrow hulls. Additionally, builders and owners evaluated emerging alternatives to traditional paddlewheels.

The possibility of building a boat out of iron had been beyond technical capabilities until 1784. Engineers and promoters had reasonably proven that iron construction was feasible, but primitive puddling techniques and trip-hammers turned out iron bars and rough plates not suitable for shipbuilding. The Englishman Henry Cort developed a practical rolling mill that produced large iron plates of a uniform gauge. British foundries first applied this finer sheeting to the construction of watertight boilers, and by 1787 they began experimenting with the construction of canalboats. The processes were similar: boilers were designed to keep vapor in and boats to keep water out. Successive experiments over the following decades resulted in larger hulls. Overlapping plates in a lapstraked style were through-riveted, stiffening wooden frames to an amazing degree. Sheathing for a number of vessels was rolled in Britain, deconstructed for shipment to the United States, and then placed over traditionally wood-framed hulls. The engines and mechanicals were increasingly of American manufacture.

The first American iron ship built completely of native material by local talent was the *United States* in 1838. This unusual vessel, of catamaran design, was fabricated at the West Point, New York, foundry to be employed farther upstate on Lake Pontchartrain. Within a year the second plate-sheathed, all-native ship was launched. Significantly, the *Valley Forge* splashed in Pittsburgh, an example of that town's influence as a western river port and growing iron center. Also notable, the ship's sheathing was attached to an all-iron frame with an all-iron deck. This experiment created a very light, strong craft capable of carrying four hundred tons in less than five feet of water—remarkable for the time. Unfortunately, the expensive iron sheathing did not deflect hull-rupturing snags as promoters had hoped. Remarkably, in the anthracite-coal- and iron-rich lands of the Ohio and upper Mississippi valleys, where the cost of producing and marketing a gross ton of iron had fallen almost 30 percent by 1842, to $25, such construction measures proved incongruously prohibitive. It wasn't until the 1870s that iron, and then steel, construction was seriously revisited on the rivers.[27]

Industrywide interest in commercial iron ship construction was underwhelming, particularly in North America. Boats had always been made of fiber and hide—wood, papyrus, bark, or reeds, often wedded with light skins and resins. In the British Isles and parts of Europe, shipbuilding wood had become scarce at a time when quality iron became inexpensive. Iron prices in America were such that even in the northern lakes region, wealthy in timber of all descriptions, it was cheaper to build an iron-sheathed ship than a wooden vessel. Yet wood remained the favored material. Throughout the maritime world, there were logical reservations about ships built of iron. Of primary concern, wood floated, while iron did not. Also, wood's flexibility allowed boats to work and undulate through waves instead of rigidly fighting them. That quality, long perceived to be an asset, proved a liability when constructing longer vessels. Builders stiffened existing hulls by installing iron strapping and created elaborate crosshatched grids to gird the frames of new vessels.

From a commercial manufacturing standpoint, the tools used to build a wooden ship were simple, proven, and inexpensive: blocks, tackles, saws, drills, chisels, and adzes. Most of the work could be performed by general laborers, and Great Lakes shipyards were established anywhere along shorelines where the timber was promising. The investment was small. Conversely, the equipment required to construct ships from iron was expensive, untested, and involved entirely new infrastructures and labor skills. The specialized machines were not initially available in the West, and various raw materials, from ore to cordage, involved additional shipping and processing costs. Great Lakes builders stuck with wood for several decades, with a couple of notable exceptions.

The Great Lakes was the scene of nascent developments in the use of iron hulls for naval vessels. In December 1843, the US Navy constructed and launched two such ships. The newly formed Lake Survey office of the US Army Corps of Engineers splashed the USLS *Abert*, a revolutionary research vessel. Almost 100 feet long and shallow-drafted, this unique craft was the first iron hull in the navy. Additionally, it had paddlewheels mounted horizontally instead of vertically, with paddles, or floats, extending laterally from the ship's side far enough to expose the paddle's face. Paddlewheels were protected from damage by a deck skirting similar to that on a side-wheeler. Intended as protection from cannon fire, the design was operable but slow and difficult to maintain. Within a few years, the *Abert* was refitted with traditional vertical paddles, and it served the navy well for forty-five years.[28]

The USS *Michigan* gets the nod as the first iron-hulled warship in the US Navy. It was launched before the *Abert* but not commissioned until several months later. Cutting-edge and fast, the *Michigan* was a project spearheaded by Secretary of the Navy Abel Upshur. He considered the undertaking a matter of national security but promoted it with equal vigor as a way to encourage and subsidize the nation's young iron industry. A contract for both the hull and engines was awarded, with limited bidding, to a reliable Pittsburgh company managed by Samuel Stackhouse and Joseph Tomlinson. This contract stirred controversy, but Upshur—a businessman, not a career mariner—drove it through the bureaucracy in order to modernize American naval capabilities. Design of the project fell to Samuel L. Hartt and Charles W. Copeland. It was Hartt's first attempt at iron construction. After studying other vessels, he created a generally traditional wooden frame and wooden forms that mirrored the final framing for hammering out the iron plates. Copeland developed a low-pressure, twin-cylinder, condensing

The steamer USS *Michigan*. (Painting by Charles Robert Patterson, c. 1927, courtesy of the Detroit Historical Society Collection.)

engine. This direct action, inclined system had a low center of gravity, an advantage in the *Michigan*'s shallow hull.

Plans and modeling were completed in four months, framing filled the summer, and plates were rolled in the autumn. During the winter of 1843, the hull was assembled, disassembled, and shipped to Erie. Over the summer and autumn, the ship was reconstructed and finally launched into the frigid December waters of Lake Erie. The USS *Michigan* was christened by no less than President John Tyler. It took nearly a year for the engines, boilers, final decking, and accommodations to be installed. By October 1844, following sea trials, the vessel began a career that lasted sixty-eight years. In a very short time, it elicited praise for its handling and speed. Under a normal head of steam, the ship easily cruised at fourteen knots when others averaged ten, making it one of the fastest ships in the world at the time and the swiftest in the US Navy for several years.

Constructing and outfitting the 167-foot USS *Michigan* under frontier conditions cost about $150,000. Comparably, the 175-foot wooden frigate USS *Cumberland,* built conventionally in the Boston Navy Yard in 1842, cost $320,000. The *Michigan* also weighed half as much as a similar wooden steamer, thereby consuming about half the fuel. Fully loaded, the keel drew only 7 feet 6 inches; the *Cumberland* needed 21 feet of water. The frigate carried a crew of four hundred, the steam cruiser less than a quarter of that. Its flat-bottomed hull—hardly possible in heavy wooden construction—proved more stable in a seaway, rendering the paddles more efficient and allowing the *Michigan*'s gunners to be consistently more accurate than those of any other American warship. Despite the economic and military advantages clearly demonstrated by Secretary Upshur's successful Great Lakes experiment, iron construction was not embraced by the naval establishment for many years. For commercial shipping interests on the lakes, where lumber was cheap, a substantial wooden hull could be commissioned for $8,000 to $10,000.[29]

In Canada West, prescient entrepreneurs built two iron-hulled passenger steamships. At the yard of Fowler & Hood, located adjacent to the Kingston Marine Railway, John Hamilton launched his *Passport* in November 1846. William McAusland (also spelled McCausland and McCauseland) oversaw the rolling of the plates in Glasgow, Scotland, and supervised construction of the 180-foot hull. At 346 tons (OM), it got good speed from an eighty-horsepower, horizontal engine, yet registered a depth of less than ten feet. Under the direction of Captain William Bowen, this hefty hull began a career that lasted until 1922.[30]

At the other end of Lake Ontario, on the lower Niagara River, a syndicate of investors led by Captain James Sutherland launched the *Magnet* in 1847. Its dimensions were similar to those of the *Passport* with plates generated through Liverpool merchants. This vessel was designed for trade between Hamilton, Toronto, and Montreal. Canals along the St. Lawrence had been enlarged during the 1840s, and both craft were built to the maximum allowable specification.

Both of these vessels were ostensibly not military ships, in an effort by the British government to comply with provisions of the Rush-Bagot Treaty, the agreement crafted after the War of 1812 specifically restricting armament on ships of the lakes. However, the hulls were built to naval standards and the Admiralty paid 40 percent of the building costs on the condition that the ships would be available immediately in the event of a crisis. Since the government had historically appropriated private vessels as necessary, this was rather transparent federal patronage. The arrangement created sufficient strategic tonnage, without the government maintaining the vessels or violating diplomatic protocols. By 1850, enthusiasm for further quasi-military iron vessels had waned, and builders returned to wooden construction for profitable production.[31]

The propeller, a more important technical advancement, was developed during this same period and had a profound effect on maritime interests. Based on the ancient screw principle, propellers installed at the stern of a hull addressed a number of issues that shipbuilders identified with side-wheelers.

From a military standpoint, it was assumed that the exposed paddlewheels would be vulnerable to artillery or close action, although this seldom proved to be the fatal event for steamers in battle. However, in an effort to counter the perceived flaw, engineers experimented with a single paddlewheel mounted between catamaran hulls. The horizontal wheel plan of the USLS *Abert*, mentioned earlier and designed by Lieutenant William Hunter, was another experiment in paddlewheel protection and also addressed a common consumer complaint: the surging ride.

Single-cylinder engines, the standard of the time, drove cams that required a push on the upstroke, a brief pause before an easy descent on the downstroke, and a hesitation before the push upward commenced again. Directed to the paddlewheels, this translated into a slight surging motion, the boat speeding and slowing as the engine rested or worked, perhaps every second or two. Some passengers found its gentle undulations reassuring and steady, just as later generations found the clickety-clack of railroad trains relaxing. To those less at home on the water, the surge was a source of discomfort. Hunter's horizontal design replaced the surge with cavitation, a less noticeable vibration. It also reduced the likelihood that the floats, or paddles, would come clear of the water as a ship rolled in large waves. While very stable on rivers and canals, a side-wheeler on open water canted from side to side in the troughs of a heavy sea. The paddlewheels alternately pulled clear of waves or were plunged to the hub. The yawing transferred the load of propulsion rather violently from one wheel to the other, occasionally resulting in critical equipment failures.

While addressing these issues, Hunter's design did not fix the two biggest problems. First, side-wheelers could not navigate the locks and canals between lakes Erie and Ontario. They were wider than the 22-foot maximum, and a commercial boat built to the stern-wheeler prototype designs would also be too wide. The second problem was that Hunter's design required that the middle of the boat be designated for engine spaces. This was an issue with any design involving paddlewheels: the engines, boilers, gearing, wheels, and fuel took up almost half the available deck space and absolutely had to be set in the middle of the boat. When the profitable trade was passengers and incidental cargo, this obstacle could be overcome. As commercial freight transfer became an increasingly important part of the steamship business, the spatial requirements of side-wheelers became an issue begging for a solution.

About the time that Lieutenant Hunter was selling his idea to Secretary Upshur, the lake-savvy captain James Van Cleve, former skipper of the *Ontario*, was getting an education in New York. At the behest of a fellow Lake Ontario skipper, Van Cleve went to the foundry of Hogg and Delamater to see the "spiral paddle-wheels" on display. Under a patent given to John Ericsson, Van Cleve bought rights to the new propeller for use on the Great Lakes. Much like Fulton, Ericsson was keen to disseminate his idea and defended his patents in court for many years afterward. Ericsson furthered many other successful maritime designs, including that of the *Monitor*, the first commissioned ironclad gunboat in the US Navy.

Van Cleve contracted with Sylvester Doolittle's Oswego yard to build a new type of steamship. At this time, schooners handled a growing commodities trade to the west and returned with the early fruits of the abundant plains. They were generally built to the lock dimensions of 110 feet long, 22 feet wide, and 8 feet over the sills and had no competition in freight trade with the upper lakes. They naturally suffered from uncertain schedules based on available wind. Buffalo steamships controlled the passenger trade to upper lake ports but could not travel to the lower lake. Van Cleve proposed to challenge both monopolies by exploiting their weaknesses: trumping wind-borne vessels by providing reliable timetables; and besting the steamer fares to Chicago by departing from Oswego on Lake Ontario, which would be less expensive than departing from Buffalo.[32]

Van Cleve's *Vandalia* was launched in November 1841. It had the lines of a modest sailing ship, sloop-rigged, 91 feet long, 20 feet wide, and 8 feet 3 inches deep, canal lock dimensions. Two 6-foot screw propellers were powered by a twin-cylinder, fifty-horsepower engine mounted horizontally. The propellers were a modified Ericsson design, which omitted the characteristic outer ring, likely the first side-by-side installation in an American ship. The result was a sound vessel that moved reliably at six to seven miles per hour and consumed only ten cords of wood per day—a quarter of the fuel needed for a traditional steamer—saving money and freeing deck space.

The engine was far smaller than the *Empire*'s six-hundred-horsepower plant and was mounted at the stern. This cleared most of the forward part of the hold for commerce. Engines and props, contracted through Dennis, Wood, and Russell of Auburn, New York, were built at the state prison for about $2,000, an important savings. Without the paddlewheels amidships, the *Vandalia* was able to negotiate locks with ease and could unload cargo at a wharf by means of a number of gangways along its vertical sides.

Lake sailors took to propellers quickly. According to James L. Barton, in a published letter to US congressman Robert McClelland, there were forty-eight steamboats on the upper lakes in 1840. Five years later there were fifty-two steamboats and eight propellers. Lake Ontario's seven steamboats competed with eight propellers. New construction in 1845 tells the tale. Upper lake yards launched seven steamboats and nine propellers. Yards on Lake Ontario built two new propellers and no paddlers. The following year the numbers were essentially the same, but tonnage increased. Twenty propellers ran with fifteen large steamers on the Chicago route.[33]

Palace steamers retained their reputation for fast, reliable, and comfortable travel. They also retained a significant competitive advantage over propellers, which ran at half the speed, at least for the time being. Gradually, the fast steamers were relegated to a decreasing niche of lake commerce. Powered bulk carriers had adopted propellers almost exclusively by 1870. Mixed freight vessels that operated on the open lakes soon came to favor propellers, as did towing vessels.[34]

The efficiencies of propellers forced rates down. Between 1839 and 1841, the cost for a room and meals—published as "cabin and found"—was generally $30 to "any place on the lakes," meaning from Buffalo to anywhere beyond Detroit. In 1845 fares fell by 40 percent: a $20 found ticket—just meals—to Milwaukee or Chicago was $12. Steerage rates dropped from $10 to $6. Break bulk cargoes—those items in barrels, boxes, and bales—saw a more significant decline of 54 percent for light freight and a stunning 85 percent drop for heavy freight, from $1.50 to just 20 cents per hundred pounds. Not all of this can be attributed directly to the propeller. The expansion of business in terms of volume—both westward-bound passengers and bulk freights such as wheat and salt—as well as increased demand, prompted overly aggressive shipbuilding. More bottoms drove transshipment rates down. Schooners accounted for the greatest percentage of the increased competition. Propellers gradually gained on side-wheelers numerically, mostly for bulk trade or the growing towing industry. In 1854 the former surpassed the latter in terms of tonnage carried.[35]

This last change was significant. The lightweight and compact power plants afforded by the propeller were ideal for tugboats, and they became the favored method of propulsion on these craft as the century matured. Invaluable in tight harbors or around silty obstructions, powerful tugs were essential to the high-sided steamers and packets when they were docking in wind. It was not unusual for tugs to deliver tardy passengers to a recently departed vessel—for a hefty fee. They assisted schooners up and down the long rivers, pulled them through crowded harbors, and were used to tow vast rafts of logs from lumbering rivers to large mill towns.[36]

CHAPTER 6

Maritime Politics

Apart from the physical innovations evinced by larger, faster, and more efficient ships, the Great Lakes marine industry adapted a number of organizational structures and business models that reflected increased commerce on the lakes. Professionalism was defined for owners and operators by law and contract. Market prices and changing cargo trends dictated vessel requirements, and the fleet expanded accordingly. Investment in the industry was high and demanded aggressive marketing and political attention.

Aboard ship, the strict adherence to maritime traditions was maintained. In the midst of the North American wilderness, disciplined and professional crews reassured passengers, but explosions and other accidents were a constant fear. In response to a number of high-profile steamboat incidents, the governments in both countries began regulating the industry. In the United States, this came as early as the Steamboat Act of 1838. In its effort to reduce fatal boiler failures and poor navigational practices, the federal government mandated licensing for masters, pilots, and engineers. This codified the professional craft within the system.

In British North America, the first initiative to regulate steam craft occurred in the province of New Brunswick in 1843. Similar legislation was adopted in Upper Canada in 1851, with inspectors assigned at Quebec, Montreal, Bytown, Kingston, Hamilton and Niagara. Under this act, machinery inspection was carried out every six months, with hull inspection annually. In 1859, laws across Canada were consolidated, and nine years later Parliament passed the first of many national steamboat acts. Because relationships between the Canadian provinces evinced little of the political rancor found among the not-so-united states to the south, the advancement of internal maritime improvements, like surveying and lighthouse construction, often anticipated demand.[1]

In the United States, maritime professionals supported efforts by government agencies to license and control all skilled positions. Despite some resentment among investors, conscientious vessel operators—many of whom were captains—embraced the public relations opportunity. Advertising fliers, schedules, and posters prominently featured a captain's name associated with his boat. Officers on crack steamers and packets were the first to adopt formal navy blue uniforms. Similarly, engineers dressed like the gentlemen of the vessel. Despite regional efforts, it would be forty years before executive-level steamboat men would form the American Association of Masters, Mates and Pilots and the Marine Engineers Benevolent Association (MEBA).

In an attempt to consolidate control of trade on the Great Lakes, American investors formed an association of steamboat owners in 1834. Eighteen members, representing $600,000 worth of vessels and generally interested in Chicago or Milwaukee business, committed to cooperative efforts that encouraged their interests, coordinated schedules and routes, and ensured that each vessel would share the profits of the burgeoning trade equally. There was little trouble making money; the *Black Rock Advocate* noted that the transfer of merchandise in 1836 was up by 70 percent over the previous year, and canal tolls increased by 50 percent: "[A]ll those [forty-seven steamboats] in service are in full employ during the navigating season, and at no former period have their profits been so great as during the past year."[2] Despite the optimism expressed in newspapers around the lakes, reality came in the form of the Crash of 1837. This downturn was caused by the bursting of a speculative real estate bubble and the subsequent suspension of specie trade. Projects around the region, including the construction of new towns, railroads, canals, and ships, ground to a halt. Even the organization of vessel owners dissolved.[3]

Fortunately, the influx of pioneers continued, and business rebounded sufficiently by 1839 to encourage formation of a second steamboat association. By the following year, forty-eight steamships were included in the organization; the ships ranged in size from 150 to 750 tons and represented a cumulative investment of $2.2 million. In 1841 the schedule out of Buffalo offered six first-class ships completing fifteen round trips per week to Lake Michigan ports. In an analysis developed for Captain W. G. Williams of the US Army Corps of Engineers, James

L. Barton estimated that business between Chicago, Milwaukee, and the East totaled $301.8 million.[4]

The grandeur of the steamers offered marketing opportunities that were not lost on the vessel owners. They nurtured positive relationships with the press, and editors around the lakes maintained a steady stream of superlatives and positive discourse. Typical is a narrative from the *Black Rock Advocate* quoting the *Detroit Advertiser*: "Of the vessels now on the stocks, and to be finished in readiness for the lake, the ensuing season, fifteen are steamboats of the largest class, and will probably compare to advantage with those of any waters in America." Also from the *Detroit Advertiser*: "For the last season, the business on the Lake has far exceeded the capacity of the shipping, notwithstanding the great increase of the latter. The disproportion will be probably quite as great next season. At such a time the construction of such a vessel as the *Illinois* cannot fail to be equally profitable to the owners and the public, as well as creditable to our city."[5]

Of course, newspapers were just as quick to report disasters, but positive press created a balance, particularly outside the region. News tidbits and travelogues published on the East Coast were reprinted in Europe, affording immigrants an affinity for the lakes and certain vessels. Reputations were cultivated within the immigrant community, and tickets for voyages across Lake Erie were often purchased before families cleared customs in New York, Boston, or Quebec. Speed and renowned accommodations were modest incentives for people who were anxious to get to their new homes.

Also important in advancing the cause of Great Lakes navigation were the lobbying and communication efforts directed at eastern investors and national legislators. A letter from Barton to Robert McClelland, a US representative from Michigan, exemplifies the one-on-one approach. On a grander scale, there were more public demonstrations of solidarity. Business interests from the different cities around the lakes began to consider themselves as a whole, and the most impressive example of this resulted in what one observer called "Undoubtedly the Largest Deliberative Body Ever Assembled." In terms of colossal promotional events, what followed was effective.

In 1845 William Mosley Hall attended the Commercial Convention in Memphis, a bustling young river town about a day's journey south of his home in St. Louis. He traveled by Mississippi River steamboat, as trains would not be an option for several more years. Five hundred sixty-four delegates from fifteen southern states, as well as Illinois, Indiana, and Ohio, came to an event chaired by US senator John C. Calhoun of South Carolina. The primary intent was to promote Memphis or St. Louis as the eastern terminus of a rail system to the Pacific. Delegates from states along the Mississippi River system also encouraged efforts to secure financial resources for projects that improved the natural river highway to New Orleans. At this time 65 percent of western exports floated southward to market.[6]

As an agent for the Lake Steamboat Association in St. Louis, Hall promoted the business interests of Great Lakes shipowners. Vessel operators on the western rivers were just as frustrated as Great Lakes mariners with the lack of federal funds to address navigational hazards. Captains on all waters managed their vessels with poor charts, few visual navigational aids, and almost no regulation. Rivermen felt their way through poorly marked streams in unpredictable currents. Their foremost concerns were shifting sandbars and submerged logs and trees, known as snags, which easily and frequently punctured and sank even iron-hulled riverboats. Great Lakes sailors suffered the same poorly marked rivers and shifting harbor sands, but they also faced broad stretches of open water flowing over unknown reefs and rocky shallows. Both factions wanted surveys, dredging, and channel markings. The lake men wanted lighthouses, too.

Hall was encouraged by what he heard in Memphis, but a year later his hopes had faded. In frustration he exclaimed to dinner companions that there was "much interest in Lake commerce" from Connecticut to Buffalo to St. Louis. Colonel A. B. Chambers, editor of the *St. Louis Republican*, commented that "although the democracy of the country was generally opposed to improvements, [a] properly directed effort, irrespective of politics," would be backed by the press and would "arouse Congress to favorable action."[7] As Hall traveled to the east via the lakes, he discussed the strategy with other businessmen. In Detroit merchants and shipowners Oliver Newberry and Eber B. Ward were enthusiastic, and he found similar sentiments in Cleveland, Erie, Buffalo, and Albany, as well as Boston, Providence, Hartford, New Haven, and New York. East Coast merchants were most interested in capturing some of the tonnage that was flowing to New Orleans.

On September 28, 1846, an organizational meeting was held at the Rathbun Hotel in New York to plan a convention. Besides Hall, it included influential newspaper editors Robert Fergus and Horace Greeley of New York and Thurlow Weed of Albany. William Duane Wilson of Milwaukee was elected chairman of the event, along with officers Thomas Sherwood of Buffalo and E. D. Burr of Copper Harbor, Michigan. Hall recalled later that many cities were "anxious for the honor" of hosting the convention, including Pittsburgh, Detroit, Cleveland, Cincinnati, Buffalo, and St. Louis. The Missouri city actually sent out announcements listing it as host, but Hall favored Chicago and convinced the committee to that effect. The dates were set for July 5–7, 1847, the stated critical topic being the "high cost of freight and the tremendous loss of life and property on the Western waters last season."[8]

In the spring of 1847, a call went out for an assembly of "respectable citizens . . . of the various trades and pursuits of business" to attend and "not [fail] to appreciate its importance." In Boston "a public meeting was called . . . in which the boundless resources and fertility of the west was one of the themes," and its attendees were encouraged by Mayor Josiah Quincy to "send a delegation and a large one, to the Chicago convention" for the purpose of participating in the obvious advantages of trade with the West. The New York Chamber of Commerce "did not fail to appreciate the importance to the city of every improvement that imparts additional security" of river commerce, "as well as the benefit to be derived from concentrating public opinion—independent of party influence or interest—upon the great subject of internal improvement through the aid and instrumentality of the general government."[9]

Buffalo held a similar meeting where attendees emphasized that the trade "between the states," heretofore discounted, was important. They vowed that if Rochester was sending twenty-five delegates, they would send fifty. Similar delegate selection meetings in other cities and towns expressed similar sentiments. Michigan City, Indiana, a short trip from Chicago, declared, "[T]he people of the Lakes and Rivers are unjustly deprived of an equal participation in the protection and benefits of Government." On March 23, 1846, the *Chicago Weekly Journal* editorialized, "There is little doubt the west is neglected. Our rivers are suffered to meander over bars, and our Lakes [are called] goose ponds. In government expenditures the West must no longer be considered a foreign territory, . . . and her harbors and rivers must not be treated with sneers of derision."[10]

These meetings were indicative of an important social and economic sea change in America. For centuries people had looked elsewhere for help, be it to the Atlantic coast or Europe. Now enormous economic opportunities galvanize leaders on a local and national scale. They no longer viewed their problems as disparate or isolated. They began looking toward the Pacific and beyond.[11]

The philosophical and political debate over internal improvements had grown with the young nation. The core arguments were simple: (1)

states should not be made to pay for transportation improvements from which they gained no direct benefit; (2) expenditures that improve the business prospects of the nation, even if they are directed toward regional improvements, make the whole nation stronger. Democrats generally championed the first position; Whigs, and later Republicans, supported the latter. Federal improvements spending grew incrementally through the first six US presidential administrations, allowing Andrew Jackson to win on a platform opposed to any spending not critical to national security or international commerce. Despite his rhetoric, he outspent all before him. However, his successors, Martin Van Buren and James Polk, closed the tap to a trickle, and it was not until the 1880s that monies coming to the western rivers and lakes were proportional to their contribution to commerce.

Federal money was not entirely lacking. Spending on navigational improvements doubled nationwide between 1830 and 1837, totaling more than $9 million on rivers, harbors, and lighthouses and an almost equal amount on roads and canals. Regionally, roughly a third went to the Mississippi watershed, half to the Atlantic coast, and the remainder to the inland canals, rivers, and Great Lakes of the north. Much of this money was spent on surveys, dredging, and the building of more than thirty northern lighthouses by 1846. On October 28, 1831, a meeting in Detroit first explored petitioning Congress to survey the lakes and provide a ship canal at Sault Sainte Marie. Ten years later Washington appropriated $15,000 for the survey, subsequently allotting up to $200,000 a year to the Lake Survey Office in Detroit through 1882. However, the federal government resisted involvement in the Soo canal, improvements to the St. Clair Flats near Detroit, and the Michigan-Illinois Canal at Chicago between Lake Michigan and the Mississippi system, just as it had shied away from the Erie Canal.[12]

In this regard it is important to understand how citizens symbolically viewed the "united States." Historian Robert Wiebe has noted that America "neither affirmed nor denied the existence of a nation." At the Memphis convention in 1846, John C. Calhoun stated, "We are, in our confederation, a congregation of nations, of sovereign states, and on that feature our system depends." Similarly, the *Southern Quarterly Review* described a "constellation of states or nations." Events like William Hall's proposed convention were important steps in the process of developing an American national identity, coaxing the "parts" to appreciate the possibilities of the whole. Proponents of improvements applauded the nationalist aspects of the Chicago convention, yet it is clear that a conceptual chasm had not been crossed. Illustratively, it was the gathering of these nineteen "free and independent sovereignties" that was remarkable to the attendees.[13]

In August 1846, President Polk vetoed a harbors and rivers bill, which would have spread maritime improvement money around the country, from Florida to Wisconsin. Standing on boilerplate Jeffersonianism with a tenacity and focus not seen in his more flexible predecessors, Polk stated, "The Constitution has not, in my judgment, conferred upon the Federal Government the power to construct works within the states." Harbors, in his opinion, were integral to their respective states. If this did not lend sufficient urgency to the arguments of those traveling to Chicago, Polk added an exclamation point when he pocket vetoed a bill in March 1847 that would have funded harbor improvements in Wisconsin.[14]

Delegates began arriving in Chicago at the end of June, mostly aboard steamships. Railroads had not yet come to town, and the few existing roads were little more than muddy stage trails. Chicago's river was its harbor and major entrepôt. Silting and ice fought every attempt to build piers and keep the channel open. Essential to regional commerce, budget battles among the city, state, army engineers, and Washington over the shifting sandbar at the river's mouth resulted in several unsatisfactory and temporary solutions. Army engineers had extended the north breakwater from the Chicago River into Lake Michigan almost a mile, yet the channel required vigilant dredging to remain open. Arriving delegates pointed to this as a perfect example of the need for more federal harbor and river money.[15]

There is some uncertainty over the actual number of attendees or participants. Estimates published soon after the event cited attendance numbers from 4,000 to 5,000. Official delegate registration numbers vary from 2,054 to more than 2,400. The additional crowd was presumably comprised of writers, politicians, businessmen, scientists, scholars, and curious residents. Attendance figures for previous commercial conventions, when available, are usually in the hundreds, so even the lowest estimate distinguishes the Harbor and River Convention as the first truly large gathering of its kind. With typical understatement, Thurlow Weed referred to it as "undoubtedly the largest deliberative body ever assembled."[16]

The proceedings were carefully recorded and provide a template for a period called the "era of conventions." The first day involved a grand parade of floats, bands, fire companies, and artillery, leading the throng to a massive tent pavilion in front of city hall capable of holding 4,000–5,000 by numerous accounts, with many standing at the back. At least thirty visiting editors, almost equally representing both parties, were taking notes. Sources disagree on the number of states represented, but nineteen are listed in subsequent reports, with delegates named to committees. Speculatively, there were citizens of other states attending in an unofficial capacity; however, the official roster included Connecticut, Florida, Georgia, Illinois, Indiana, Iowa, Kentucky, Maine, Massachusetts, Michigan, Missouri, New Hampshire, New Jersey, New York, Ohio, Pennsylvania, Rhode Island, South Carolina, and Wisconsin.[17]

Over the course of three days, speeches were made and letters of support read from the podium. Committees forwarded resolutions, votes were taken, and memorials were eventually submitted to the US Congress. The tone was predictably in favor of internal improvements, but arguments differed based on party affiliation. Democrats favored a national security approach, the rivers and lakes being important militarily for defending commerce and property. Whigs stressed the international importance of trade to the country, often pointing out that the river and lake trade accounted for far more of the nation's gross commerce than that of eastern ports. Ironically, after lunch on the third day, with the convention officially ended, delegates gathered to spar over western railroad issues before heading home.

Arguably, the Harbor and River Convention had only nominal results politically. Another internal improvements bill was presented to the House of Representatives less than a year later, but it was procedurally stalled by a representative from Georgia and never came to a vote. It wasn't until 1852 that President Millard Fillmore, who had been a delegate in Chicago, sanctioned a pork barrel appropriation of over $2.2 million for rivers and harbors in 1852. In 1854, President Franklin Pierce vetoed another river and harbor bill, and this type of gamesmanship lapsed until 1870, when support dramatically shifted. Throughout the following decade, annual expenditures grew from $2 million to almost $13 million in 1882–83.[18]

The more immediate impact of the convention, from the standpoint of business and shipping interests on the Great Lakes, was the extensive exposure and favorable impressions afforded the region in the national press. While there were many fractured railroad and agricultural conventions, the Chicago rally was reported to have been a cohesive meeting and a tremendous success. Readers around the world were focused on the tremendous resources being developed in the North Country, from the fleets of steamers and schooners to the cargoes of copper, lumber, and people they carried. Commerce and population were expanding there as fast as any in the country.[19]

A body of influential promoters and businessmen spent several days together aboard the Lakes' premier steamships discussing the region and their role in the aggressive expansion of the West. The reports were frequent, a travel dialogue lasting for weeks filed from the decks of the *Baltic*, *St. Louis*, *Empire*, and *Sultana*, and including the highlights of Green Bay, Mackinac Island, Detroit, the Lake Erie Islands, and the Erie Canal, or in some cases Niagara and Montreal.

On the way to Chicago, *New York Tribune* owner Horace Greeley detoured an advance party of journalists and scientists up the St. Marys River to Sault Sainte Marie. In the *New York Herald*, a correspondent identified only as "Sponsor" disembarked in Northport, at the northern tip of Wisconsin's Door Peninsula, the entrance to Green Bay. On his tour southward, he described the "most beautiful country the sun ever shone upon," with broad, sandy beaches, lush rolling prairies, and sturdy towns along the lines of those seen in New England. Without mentioning Chicago's oppressive heat and persistent cholera problems, another correspondent extolled the fresh lake breezes, like nothing in New York, which could only be appreciated on a luxurious voyage on the lakes. The publicity generated by such articles on the front pages of New York publications, which were reprinted in England and other European countries, was pure gold.[20]

Thurlow Weed, the influential editor of the *Albany Evening Journal*, and two hundred other dignitaries chartered the steamer *St. Louis* for the return trip east. The group included Governor William Bebb of Ohio, congressmen Thomas Corwin and Robert Schenck of Ohio, and Thomas Butler King of Georgia, as well as a legislators, judges, and entrepreneurs from a dozen states. The captain agreed to take them wherever they wished to go for two dollars a person, bed and meals included. As they departed Chicago, they met and agreed to make several detours on the way to Buffalo in order to fully appreciate the freshwater seas they were sailing. The first stop was Milwaukee, where a number of passengers disembarked for an extended tour. Among them were Erastus Corning, an Albany Democrat and railroad pioneer; and *Courier and Enquirer* editor Charles King of New York, soon to be the president of Columbia College. Following a stop in Sheboygan, the ship toured Green Bay to the northwest, crossed Lake Michigan to North Manitoulin Island, and proceeded northeast to Mackinac Island. Most of the party went ashore to tour Arch Rock and Sugar Loaf and to "pic nic," while a group of forty men went off to the Carp River in the nearby Upper Peninsula, "intent upon beguiling and capturing the wary Trout." Unintentionally, they caught the height of a mosquito and black fly hatch, too. They returned "blood-besmeared" after a few hours, with a remarkable bounty of more than twelve dozen fish.[21]

"Solitude—vast and sublime solitude—is the striking feature of these mighty waters and these boundless woods," wrote Weed, contemplatively. Lake Michigan was larger than his home state and surrounded by undeveloped lands that could sustain "a population greater than that of all the New England States. And yet there are hundreds of miles of Coast [1,600 miles total], upon this Lake, whose waters float hundreds of Vessels burthened with millions of dollars, where the Government has not yet expended the first dollar for a Harbor!" Weed and his cohorts would continue to beat the drum for internal improvements, indicative of another favorable result of the convention. The good publicity and level of support from the wide number of states participating let westerners know that they had a "reliable body of colleagues in the eastern states."[22]

The party proceeded to Sault Sainte Marie, carefully wending its way upriver amid luscious scenery on a quiet and hot Sunday morning. Unfamiliar with the upper river and having no charts, Captain Wheeler went to anchor thirty miles below the village. Most of the passengers traveled in Mackinaw boats, handy fishing skiffs common on Lake Huron. Upriver in the village, they packed the town's two hotels. They saw two schooners recently dragged on rollers up the main street in order to reach Lake Superior and barrels of virgin copper waiting for wagons to carry them through the town to ships waiting below the rapids. Naturally, Weed editorialized about the lack of dredging, channel markers, and charts and punctuated his sermon with rhetoric about the government's lack of foresight in failing to approve construction of a short canal.

He admonished federal inaction again as the *St. Louis* passed through Lake Huron and into the St. Clair River, where it had to deal with congestion at the Flats. According to Weed, 10 percent of the 300 vessels that had passed the Flats by mid-July had to unload cargo into barges in order to pass. All were forced to anchor at night for lack of aids to navigation. After spending the afternoon in Detroit and enjoying an evening performance of the Christy Minstrels at City Hall, the entourage made stops at Sandusky and Cleveland. July 16 saw the *St. Louis* returned to Buffalo after a voyage of twenty-five hundred miles. In seventeen days, some of the nation's most influential people had come to appreciate the Great Lakes, and their impressions must have been enhanced by the sumptuous accommodations and service they received on the journey.

The quality and abundance of food were remarked upon in several narratives. An abbreviated list of victuals consumed, including only meats, gives an interesting insight into the logistics of running a steamship's galley for such an excursion: 16 quarters of beef, 9 calves, 60 beef tongues, 22 lambs, 11 sheep, 18 pigs, 600 chickens, 60 turkeys, 40 hams, 128 live lobsters, 600 pounds of fish (not counting the 6 wheelbarrow loads bought locally and the trout caught at Mackinac), 800 eggs, 3 barrels of corned beef, 2 barrels of pork, 4 cheese wheels, and a dozen kegs each of pickled oysters and lobster. The list of spirits and wines was, by Weed's own admission, equally exhausting and included 8,000 "segars."

Conversation was convivial, politics generally cordial, food served continuously, and the evening dancing enchanted. Nearly a third of the passengers were ladies, genteel and socially engaging. They lent the voyage an elegance that was likely not the norm but came to be the expectation of the traveling public. As competition grew, marketing and public relations proved increasingly important to the success of the steamship business.

CHAPTER 7

The Palace Steamer Era

ailing into the midcentury, the United States was a nation on the move. Americans looked in all directions to spread their formula of freedom and free enterprise. The northwestern border with Great Britain was finally agreed upon, and decisive military action in Mexico gained the Southwest. The country stretched to the Pacific Ocean, large, undocumented, and open for development. America's attention was suddenly whiplashed from looking hereditarily eastward across the Atlantic to gazing west toward the Pacific shore. Many were already looking beyond it.

In 1845 the editor of the Washington, DC, *Democratic Review*, John L. O'Sullivan, posited that North America belonged to the people of the United States "by right of our manifest destiny . . . which Providence has given us for the development of the great experiment of liberty and federative self-government entrusted to us." He shared the feelings of many Americans. Free from the stricture of aristocrats and monarchs, America was destined to be the "great nation of futurity."[1]

In an earlier editorial, Sullivan stated "[W]e are the nation of progress, of individual freedom, of universal enfranchisement. Equality of rights is the cynosure of our union of States."[2] Regarding progress, he was certainly correct, but within a decade the nation's young legacy decried his sincere assessment regarding equality, freedom, and union. Suffrage remained limited. Entire nations of Native Americans were relocated to western lands, with broad public support. Poverty in the immigrant slums of the industrial northern and middle Atlantic towns was growing into a grotesque disavowal of America's image of itself.

Most fractious to the United States—in public perception and political direction—was the issue of slavery. The Great Lakes region had a long history of legal slavery, under both British and US statutes. Following Michigan Territory's acceptance into the Union in 1837 as a slavery-free state, it became an important egress point for enslaved people attempting to reach the legal freedom offered in Canada. Enforcement of the law, or the lack of it, defined the liberality of the Great Lakes maritime community and in numerous cases proved advantageous to the fugitive and an overt political statement on the part of the shipowner or captain.

Uncertainty in the "border states" over the slavery question caused factional wars. Eastern migrants and European immigrants looked to the north and northwest, where politics was delineated and transportation cheap. Cities around the Great Lakes experienced the increased growth and prosperity that might be expected in a virgin land with boundless opportunities and resources. Demand for steamboats grew exponentially, and the vessels built between 1848 and 1856 mirrored the market. They were made to move many eager passengers and a panoply of baggage, freight, and livestock.

Thus positioned, vessel owners might conceivably have sacrificed luxury in construction, appointments, and maintenance to maximize efficiency and profits. Instead, the most convenient and modest new travel options were beautiful steamers, unsurpassed in any market around the world. The zenith of the Palace Steamer Era began with the *Empire State* and lasted a decade until it ended abruptly during the Panic of 1857.

The dedication to beauty exemplified in steamboat design can be seen in the aesthetics of the era. Architecture was in a highly classical phase, as were art and literature. Federalist and Greek Revival influences on American buildings were found in all regions. At the end of the first half of the century, science and rationalism were elegantly refining both schools of thought.

Mass media blossomed. The American population was among the most literate in the world, and it yearned for stimulation in the form of American literature, newspapers, magazines, lectures, and traveling shows. It was during this period that Walt Whitman wrote *Leaves of Grass*, Thoreau penned *Walden*, and Harriett Beecher Stowe published *Uncle Tom's Cabin*. Nathaniel Hawthorne, Henry Wadsworth Longfellow, Herman Melville, and Edgar Allan Poe had taken up the mantle from Washington Irving and James Fenimore Cooper and were in their most productive phases. American literature helped define the rapidly expanding nation and was admired by the foremost English writers, including Charles Dickens and Lord Byron.

Books became increasingly accessible as technology improved and publishing costs fell. Publishers found the magazine, or journal, format to be increasingly popular. As a "storehouse" of information, the magazine was a century old, but entrepreneurs developed it into a literary device. Maturin Ballou and Frederich Gleason began publishing *Gleason's Pictorial Drawing Room Companion* in 1851. In 1854 Ballou's name replaced Gleason's on the masthead. This self-described "literary mélange" carried elaborately illustrated fare that ranged from historical travelogues to slightly romantic morality plays. The successful formula prompted competition, and within a few years *Putnam's Magazine, Atlantic Monthly,* and *Harper's* were in business.

During this same period, theatre and live performance venues sprouted and flourished in large cities. Similar to American steamboats, new theaters emphasized elegance and comfort with refined seating and embellished interiors. Gaslights and limelights replaced candles and whale oil, improving illumination, though not safety or air quality. Stylistically and topically, Americans were trending away from European classics and toward newer situational material sited on the American continent, much of it freshly written. Stock companies in major cities and some western towns accommodated a steady stream of touring celebrity actors.

Music enjoyed the fruits of metallurgical and manufacturing improvements as band instruments became affordable. Communities across the country took pride in their local gatherings of saxhorns and euphoniums. Musical societies flourished. Pennsylvanian Stephen Foster and Louisianan Louis Moreau Gottschalk were early superstars of American music on both sides of the Atlantic. P. T. Barnum contracted Swedish vocalist Jenny Lind for an extensive tour, guaranteed $1,000 a night for 150 performances. Barnum, already known for promoting Tom Thumb, was a purveyor of the nation's most adaptable entertainment, the traveling show. Consisting variously of lectures, concerts, burlesques, and minstrel shows, a mixture of musicians, actors, and scholars journeyed to the edges of civilization.

Lectures enjoyed their greatest popularity during this decade and were actively encouraged by religious organizations. As a social activity, they were considered properly formal, inexpensive, and instructional, often delving into moral themes, including the slavery question.

Ultimately, American entertainment tended toward the sedentary. Most people were occupied in agriculture, husbandry, manufacturing, and housekeeping; seated recreation, be it in a church or theatre, was welcomed. Athletics were almost unknown, even in colleges. The wealthy enjoyed riding and fencing. Rowing was emerging as an activity in which men of modest means could engage. The very rich chased the America's Cup. Baseball was in its infancy.

Socially, Americans habitually retained an allegiance to French custom, idolizing idyll as a social convention (which often included a liberal use of alcohol and tobacco). Prior to the war years, travelers and foreign writers noted the unhealthy look of most Americans and the general dullness of their towns and cities. While complimenting the climate and environment, both European and American commentators blamed poor diets and apparent lassitude. One chronicler reported that, where possible, a buggy ride was preferred to walking even a short distance. This type of indolence was not the norm in the slums of New York and Philadelphia, but in the prosperous and proper hinterlands it was an inexpensive concession to propriety—and vanity.

The rapid transport of fruits and vegetables made possible by steamships and railroads soon transformed the continent's diet. In the 1850s the luxury of fresh seafood and a variety of dry goods was common in Great Lakes ports. The pleasant mix of elegant service, hearty food, and sedentary adventure at an affordable price made freshwater steamers most attractive. As refined living was understood to be healthy, this experience was at the top of many travelers' lists, both explorer and immigrant. During twenty years of optimism and transformation, steamships allowed thousands of passengers to experience the elegant dynamism that defined America in the minds of its citizens.

Large steamers were launched on the southern lakes in 1847. The *Ontario* was built by John Oades at Clayton, New York, on the St. Lawrence River. At 230 feet, it represented the new norm for a standard passenger lake steamer. The ship was popular for the U.S. Express Line and later the Ontario & St. Lawrence Steamboat Company. On Lake Erie, Bidwell & Banta splashed the *Baltic*, fitted with a power plant taken from the *Constitution*. The following year its boiler was replaced with one made by the J. D. Shepard Foundry of Buffalo, one of the early examples of frontier manufacturing on the Great Lakes.[3]

The *Empire State* was the first boat to reach 300 feet—less a foot. While only a handful of Great Lakes passenger vessels would exceed this length—most within the next few years—this ship is notable for another reason. It represented the first of several Palace-class hulls built in the wilderness, far from the established yards to the east. Nestled on the St. Clair River forty miles north of Detroit, the town of Newport became part of the Ward empire in the West.[4]

Newport in 1848 was the logical home for a burgeoning shipbuilding community. Most transshipment vessels passed within a few hundred yards of it. Like a service station on a busy freeway, Newport yards built and repaired ships until late in the century. The *Empire State* was the first of several large lake vessels constructed in this village. While Bidwell & Banta launched the *Keystone State* and *Queen City* in 1848, that firm no longer had a corner on the market. Further evidence of shipyard growth in the West was Reed's *Globe*, launched the same year by Burton Goodsell at tiny Truago, Michigan (modern-day Trenton). Located on the Detroit River about ten miles south of the city, it shared the advantages Newport had: ample access to ready resources and a substantial investment by Ward interests.

The following year Ward and John Wolverton floated the *Atlantic*, again at Newport. Also in 1849 the Ward-financed *May Flower* was launched at the yard of John Lupton in Detroit. George Weeks, at Oswego, splashed the *Northerner*. Closing out the decade, Ward and Wolverton partnered on the *Ocean*, build at a yard in Detroit. Throughout the rest of the palace steamer era, Bidwell & Banta would do most of the significant construction. In addition, Frederick and Benjamin Jones established a successful business in Buffalo and John English a similarly notable yard in Detroit. Construction of the *Western World* and *Plymouth Rock* resulted in two of the largest steamboats in the world at that time and further established Detroit's place in the new western economy.

This half-dozen years increased the passenger fleet greatly, with twenty hulls topping 240 feet. Several vessels described above illustrated the shift in building from eastern yards to facilities in the west. Yet each of these ships has a history that is similar: all were larger, faster versions of their beautiful predecessors; most served multiple owners and routes; and only five survived as passenger ships for more than a year or so following the Panic of 1857. The economic downturn marked the end of the first palace era, but it should not overshadow the decade preceding it. The grand years of the palace steamers embodied the lavish vision of wealth and extravagant speculation that inevitably resulted in a market panic. Historically, we must enjoy the grandeur without anticipating its demise.

It was an era of ever-greater feats, and steamboat operators strove to feed the public's interest in everything bigger, faster, longer, and grander. Speed was important, and increases of as little as a mile an hour were considered triumphs. Increases in length came in increments of 50 and one 100 feet. Increases in numbers of rooms and amounts spent on luxury could be easily interpreted.

Following the *Empire State* in 1848 was the *Keystone State*, the second-longest vessel on the lakes at 288 feet. It began as a long-distance boat, running from Buffalo to Chicago, but later sailed a variety of profitable routes around the lakes. Laid up in 1856, it reentered service four years later and was quickly pressed into service as a troop transport during the American Civil War. Dispatched from Detroit to Milwaukee to collect Union recruits waiting there, the vessel was in poor condition when it encountered a storm on Lake Huron. Thirty-three men were lost when it sank.

The *Queen City* and the *Globe* were also built in 1848. The former broke its arches six seasons later. It was repaired and sold to the Simcoe & Lake Huron Railroad to run in tandem with the *Keystone State* on the Collingwood to Chicago run. The latter survived numerous collisions and groundings and was converted to a propeller ship in 1856. This likely made the vessel more economical to operate, and it survived the Panic of 1857 only to have a dockside boiler explosion kill sixteen people in Chicago in 1860. The engine was salvaged, and the hull was converted to a mud scow.

Debuting in 1849 were the *May Flower* and *Northerner*. At 282 feet, the *May Flower* was among the elite, accommodating 800 passengers. Only 406 would find beds, according to one report. The finer rooms had canopy beds. Staterooms all had fresh water. The family suites were named for notable female authors.[5] Typical of the period, paintings adorned the salon walls.

Running on the North Shore Route for the Michigan Central Rail Road, the *May Flower* was a favorite. James Cunningham, a Detroit hobbyist, characterized the ship in a scale model and won a silver medal for his work at the 1854 Michigan State Fair. Unfortunately, the speedy runs along Lake Erie's north shore took their toll. The ship grounded several times, notably in November 1850 west of Buffalo and late in the season of 1851 on the shifting sands off Conneaut. In both cases, it was pulled clear by the USS *Michigan* and lived to serve another day. Pushing the edge of the season two years later, the *May Flower* struck a fog-shrouded beach at Point Pelee in November. Once again the USS *Michigan* was dispatched, this time into a "fearful hurricane." Its skipper described "a gale and sea, which after forty years at sea experience I never saw surpassed." The *Michigan* was nearly lost to ice and a Pelee reef; only the exertions of its large navy crew saved the ship, which remained active for nearly another century.[6]

The *May Flower* was lost on the last trip of the season to Detroit, battling ferocious headwinds. The ship was trapped on the sands of Point Pelee's sandy finger. Fortunately, its Buffalo-bound Michigan Central Rail Road route mate, the *Ocean*, came upon the scene and assisted in removing all of the *May Flower*'s passengers. Captain C. C. Blodgett returned speedily to Detroit with the stranded, who had little but what they wore. The city's citizens turned out with clothing and financial aid.

Despite valiant attempts by the USS *Michigan*, the *Ocean*, and the little *Pearl* to pull the vessel free, the forlorn *May Flower* was rapidly pushed up the rocky beach. Efforts to pump it clear failed. Over the next several months, its engines, boilers, and machinery were removed. The vessel owners had eschewed insurance and stood the loss. Recovery of the ironwork and furniture covered nearly two-thirds of the original investment of $120,000. Eber Ward purchased and repurposed the engines for service in his expanding fleet.[7]

Also built in 1849 was the *Northerner*, 240 feet, by George Weeks at Oswego, New York. Originally on the Oswego-Lewiston route for the Ontario and St. Lawrence Steamboat Company , it later ran for the U.S. Express Line and was active after the 1857 panic with the American Steamship Company. During the Civil War, the vessel was acquired by the US Army and sailed as a transport ship along the Atlantic coast. The year 1865 found it running between Baltimore, Maryland, and Richmond, Virginia; it was scrapped in 1875.[8]

The *Ocean* was launched in 1850 at Newport for the Ward concerns. At 245 feet, it sported paddlewheels 36 feet in diameter. It was placed into service for the Michigan Central Rail Road, replacing the *Empire* on the North Shore run with the *May Flower* and the *Atlantic*. It remained on that run for five years, with one notable exception. In the spring of 1851, the *Ocean* challenged the speedy reputation of the *Empire State*, a South Shore boat. A writer for the *Detroit Free Press*, identified only as "M. B.," enthusiastically stated, "The most thoroughly contested, exciting and spirited contest in a trial of speed between two steamboats which I ever witnessed on Lake Erie, terminated at Buffalo on Saturday morning last. The Messrs. Wards temporarily withdrew their unrivalled steamer *Ocean*, Capt. Willoughby, from the Michigan Central Railroad Line, and on Wednesday morning last, proceeded with her to Cleveland, for the avowed purpose of . . . testing her qualities for speed in a trial with the *Empire State*, Capt. Hazzard, which runs between Cleveland and Buffalo, and which hitherto claimed a superiority over every boat on the lakes."[9]

As mentioned earlier, steamboat "racing" was not publicly embraced by the participants, the press, or the general public, usually due to the dually stated concerns about safety and the public welfare. Yet people loved the rumors and spectacle. Future races might gain more historical notoriety, but the confrontation between the *Ocean* and the *Empire State* became the World Series of steamboat races, and not by accident. The Wards, by word and action, clearly established the challenge. The owners of the *Empire State* initially demurred, then abruptly sounded departure whistles and headed for Buffalo. Reflecting the intensity of its preparedness, the *Ocean* needed only four minutes to clear gangways, passengers, and dock lines, to enter the lake only a mile behind its rival. Positions held steady as engineers stabilized engines pressures and squeezed every safe ounce of push from their engines. The newer vessel gradually pulled away, beating the *Empire State* to Buffalo by half an hour on the generally half-day journey.

An immediate rematch was requested. The owners of the *Empire State* claimed that they had not been at optimum trim and were missing their skipper in the first encounter. On the return trip to Cleveland, the *Ocean* added five minutes to the victory margin. In an all-or-nothing bid, which by now had become big news along the lakeshore, the Wards accepted a final challenge from the owners of the *Empire State*. The shore of Lake Erie east of Cleveland was lined with spectators who watched the *Ocean* quickly pull away from the local favorite. Firing flares into the evening sky, the crew of the *Ocean* decisively claimed the title "Flyer of the Lakes" in a Corinthian three-race series.

In 1856 the ship was acquired by John Owen of Detroit as one of the early assets of the Detroit & Cleveland Steam Navigation Company. It replaced the *Cleveland* on a route shared with the *May Queen* and *Morning Star*, and later the *North Star*, from Cleveland to Detroit. In 1858, while many boats were being laid up or converted, the *Ocean* was refurbished . . . only to suffer a tough grounding in the Detroit River a year later. Rescued by the USS *Michigan*, it was converted to a lumber barge and survived until 1873.

Perhaps the most storied of the palace steamers is the *Lady Elgin*. Launched by Bidwell & Banta in 1851, this beautifully shaped 252-foot ship bore no titles for longest or fastest. Over its short career, the vessel served several routes, was owned by at least five entities, required an engine replacement, and suffered several navigational lapses—perfectly normal for the period. Then came the night of September 8, 1860.

Returning from Chicago to Milwaukee in the early morning, the ship was struck by the modest lumber schooner *Augusta* off Winnetka, Illinois. The schooner had the best of it, shearing the lightly built steamer nearly to its beam just forward of the paddle box. The ship sank rapidly, despite the frantic efforts of crewmen. High winds from the northeast created a confused sea and huge breaking waves along the shore, hampering the efforts of survivors and rescuers.

Many of the people on board had attended a lively pro-Union rally and the subsequent celebrations earlier in the day. They were tired or drunk, and mostly asleep. Potential rescuers ashore—college students and farmers—fought a dark night and deadly surf. By the best accounts, 302 travelers and crew of the 398 aboard perished within a short cruise of their homes. If accurate, these numbers suggest that the *Lady Elgin* was overloaded by a third.[10] This story has been well-documented in numerous articles, ballads, and manuscripts and is a particularly poignant story of a steamer disaster worth further exploration by interested readers. Two common points gleaned from all accounts were the facility with which the 130-foot *Augusta* carved into the *Lady Elgin*, exemplifying with deadly clarity the gossamer construction of the palace steamers, and the need for navigational regulation aboard Great Lakes vessels. The *Lady Elgin* disaster goaded a gradual increase in federal spending on lighthouses and life-saving facilities along the southern Lake Michigan shore.

The year 1852 brought launches of the magnificent *Southern Michigan* and the *Northern Indiana*, nearly identical vessels at 300 feet. Bidwell & Banta were riding a crest that also saw launches of the *Crescent City* and the *Queen of the West*, built for New York concerns, in 1853. Competition heated up as the F.N. & B.B. Jones yard, down the creek from Bidwell & Banta, splashed the sister ships *St. Lawrence* and *Mississippi* that same year. At 326 feet, both were a few feet longer than the *Crescent City*.

The *Western World* and the *Plymouth Rock*, commissioned by Ward interests and the Michigan Central Rail Road, were originally to be built at Newport (today's Marine City), on the St. Clair River. The contract was shifted to designer John English at the Joneses' Buffalo yard, and the ship was constructed under the supervision of Isaac Newton.[11] The new "Queens of the Lake" were launched in Buffalo in 1854, a full ten feet longer than any Great Lakes ship heretofore. The prelaunch publicity added another ten feet to that. It was unnecessary, as no other

Advertisement for the steamer *Western World*, c. 1856.
(Courtesy of the Detroit Historical Society Collection.)

passenger boat would surpass them until 1893. The owners had to bring a dredging unit in to clear the channel to the lake to ensure that the maiden voyage went smoothly.[12]

Amid the flowery journalistic rhetoric about these magnificent sisters, some remarkable facts emerge. Estimated costs were a quarter of a million dollars each, only slightly less than the bids to build London's Crystal Palace that same year.[13] The main salons were 248 feet long and 18 feet wide. The cabins that opened off of the salons were often connected to the outer deck cabins by sliding pocket doors, creating suites or "family rooms." Each ship had two elaborate bridal cabins. All 127 staterooms had a marble slab washstand, complete with water fed by gravity from large tanks on the upper deck. Lavatory facilities remained communal, and the large lounges—one each for men and women—served multiple purposes as dining rooms, sleeping quarters, and places of respite. In the days before Pullman railcars, pull-down bunks were standard on steamers. Each ship was capable of putting more than 500 guests in bunks, a standard that would close out the century.

Many of these amenities were the inspiration of G. S. Wormer, steward of the *Western World*, formerly of the *May Flower*. During construction most contracts were let locally, including those for lumber, furniture, upholstery, painting, plumbing, and glass. Cameron & McKay provided the hair mattresses, each weighing twenty-five pounds. The custom Allaire engines, noted in newsprint for operating so smoothly as to provide "remarkably equable and steady motion," were from the East, as were the joinery, carpets, fabrics, and other hardware. The two vessels rose together. The *Plymouth Rock* slid into Buffalo Creek on March 21, and the *Western World* followed on April 18.[14]

Customer service improvements included changes in kitchen management. Dining rooms were placed adjacent to food preparation areas, increasing the likelihood that food would arrive hot to the table. Silver, ceramics, linens, and flatware were imported from England or Ireland to enhance the dining experience. Washrooms for gentlemen and ladies were adjacent to their respective salons. Cool temperatures in the bilge created floating "cellars" for butter and beverages. The *Buffalo Daily Courier* noted, "It is astonishing to see the amount of iron used in the construction. Bulkheads, forming air tight compartments are made throughout the hulls, making them life preservers in every sense of the word."[15] In addition, each ship carried fifteen hundred Ray & Polletts patented life preservers, equal to their rated passenger capacity.[16] Further boosting profits, the vessels could accommodate up to twenty-five hundred tons of cargo.[17] Utilizing the finest technology available, the railroad steamers plying the Great Lakes had reached a spectacular zenith.

The vessels were placed in the care of two veteran captains. Charles C. Stannard took command of the *Western World*. Nearly two decades earlier, while traversing the depths of Lake Superior well offshore, he discovered an underwater mountain rising to within four feet of the lake's surface. A navigational hazard to even a canoe, this reef saw a lighthouse activated in 1882. Stannard's Rock, twenty-four miles from shore, was the most remote light facility in the US.[18]

The first master of the *Plymouth Rock* was Captain George E. Willoughby. In a society in which steamship captains bore celebrity status, he was renowned. During a short career he was skipper of the *Emerald* and the *London*, and the palace steamers *Ocean*, *Atlantic*, *May Flower*, and *Plymouth Rock* on Lake Erie, and the *Canada* on Lake Ontario.[19]

Passengers swarmed to him, and spontaneous resolutions were composed and published.

Of Capt. Willoughby it is unnecessary to speak, but we may say, that on the inland waters of the world, it would be impossible to

Great Western Railway.

INTERNATIONAL LINE OF STEAMERS

BETWEEN

HAMILTON AND OSWEGO

Touching at Toronto.

THE STEAMER CANADA

CAPT. G. E. WILLOUGHBY,

AND STEAMER AMERICA

CAPT. J. MASSON,

Will run daily, (Sundays excepted,) between the above named ports,

CONNECTING WITH DAY EXPRESS GOING EAST AND MORNING EXPRESS WEST

On the Great Western Railway, and

At Oswego with Express Trains to and from New York

Boston and intermediate places.

Fare $1.00 in advance of Lake Erie Route

BUT INCLUSIVE OF MEALS AND BERTHS.

Freight will be carried by these boats at moderate rates. For particulars see Steamboat Tariff.

·C. J. BRYDGES, Managing Director.

HAMILTON, 18th June, 1855.

Advertisement for the Great Western Railway steamers, 1855. (Courtesy of the Detroit Historical Society Collection.)

find a man, for general intelligence, friendly and genial spirit, and all gentlemanly and seaman-like qualities, more finely adapted to the duties and responsibilities of his situation.[20]

Similar sentiments about freshwater commanders were common in the printed records of the day. Noteworthy skippers were considered important to public relations efforts in newspapers, magazines, and the public eye. Captain Willoughby was at the peak of his career when he died at Quebec in December 1862 at the age of forty-two.

The massive building campaign during the mid-1850s provided the railroads with high-profile publicity, but the palace steamers overshadowed other well-appointed vessels. The vessels *Golden Gate, Garden City, North Star,* and *Planet* were all launched between 1853 and 1855 and would have been standout craft on any other waterway in the world. Service and amenities were comparably fresh and first class, and passengers enjoyed similar comforts. In 1856 the *Western Metropolis* was launched at Bidwell & Banta for the Michigan Southern Rail Road Company, effectively the last of the breed. Michigan Central Rail Road interests purchased the *Mississippi* that same year, and it underwent an extensive renovation before joining the big boats on the North Shore Line.[21]

Riding the largest palace steamers was an experience that relatively few people enjoyed. The *Plymouth Rock* and the *Western World* sailed for only three seasons. The former had a typical number of collisions and groundings. Its arches broke in 1856, and hull integrity gradually decreased. The latter also had numerous collisions, five alone in 1856, generally minor brushes in Buffalo Harbor.

In the spring of 1857, panic overtook American financial markets as an investment bubble burst. Real estate sales collapsed, and travel nearly came to a halt. Demand for freight cartage in both directions on the lakes dried up. As in earlier speculative crises, American ties to European financial systems had significant bearing, and reactive federal legislation and tariffs had much to do with the secession of southern states in 1861. In a more immediate sense, the Great Lakes states were hard hit by excessive speculation in railroad-related businesses: stocks, construction, crop futures, and land.[22]

A quick explanation begins with federal subsidies for railroad construction, which came in the form of land grants. Railroads had performed well in the early 1850s, setting more than twenty thousand miles of track and extending the lake route from Milwaukee to the Mississippi by 1857. Land offices prospered, selling increasingly valuable railroad land to local farmers and fresh immigrants. The number of banks doubled in some states during the decade, while regulations and reserves became increasingly inadequate. When the railroads failed to realize profits or pay promised dividends to stockholders, defaults tightened credit. American farms were producing in abundance, particularly in the western prairies, but European currency problems and international trade imbalances slowed the demand for American farm products. In the southern states, restrictive tariffs squeezed the cotton industry. In northern states, farmers living on devalued railroad lands grew bumper crops of wheat just as the European and eastern markets dried up.

The collapse began in Cincinnati, home of the Ohio Life Insurance & Trust Company, a New York deposit bank headquartered in the West. This highly respected institution borrowed heavily against growing railroad bond losses and finally folded in August. Nearly every market was rife with overspeculation, and banks in most large cities suspended specie payments by the end of September. Nationally, the fallout was severe. More than five thousand businesses were shuttered, from banks to corner bakeries. Millions were lost in railroad investments, with many more millions lost to declining land and commodity values and diminished credit.

On the Great Lakes, the effect of the 1857 crisis on the palace steamers was immediate. Of the seventeen largest vessels in service, nine were laid up before the season was over, and four more sat idle the following year. With the collapse of the railroads, the Michigan Central and Michigan Southern hulls remained dockside. The *Plymouth Rock*, *Western World*, and *Mississippi* were dormant until 1863, when they were repurposed as dry docks and their engines passed to other vessels.[23] Survivors included the *Western Metropolis* and the *Ocean*; each received extensive refits in 1857, but both were out of service by 1862. The *Northerner* and the *New York* were sold to the US Army for war supply duty on saltwater. Only the *Planet* retained the guise of a grand steamer until 1866.

By all measures, the first age of the palace steamer ended in 1857. Shipping companies stunned by the American Civil War scrambled to keep commerce flowing. The palace hulls languished throughout the conflict, and by 1865 the northern states' antebellum social and economic structures had been largely dismantled, much as they were in the Old South. Similar grandeur and innovation would not return to the passenger trade for several decades, as the steamship business realigned itself with a market and population that had morphed from frontier to heartland.

The legacy of the Great Lakes steamboats during this most exciting period in America's commercial history is that of a consumer product that filled a transportation need with stunning elegance and technological superiority. The palace steamers represent one grand step in the way Americans, Europeans, and gradually Asians viewed the nation and its travel accommodations.

PART II

Steam Navigation
from 1860 to 1900

CHAPTER 8

The Civil War Years

It is impossible to absolutely delineate the first stage of Great Lakes passenger steamboat traffic and the second. The 1857 crash almost instantly beached some of the most impressive vessels in the world and slowed the profitable flow of travelers from the East Coast and Europe. Following the financial bust, immigration in the United States fell from 428,000 in 1854 to 123,000 in 1858 and remained suppressed for a decade.[1] Meanwhile, the American nation became completely absorbed by the civil strife that was redefining the country. The Civil War began in 1861, and the nation that emerged four years later was a much different place than the fractured "constellation" that had existed before. Likewise, efforts to formalize the Canadian Confederation and federalize the political landscape to the north were gaining momentum in the early part of the decade. Thus, it seems logical to draw a line at about 1860.

While economic, political, and social factors affected great change in the business of steamboating, the technologies of communication, propulsion, and transportation changed little. On the Great Lakes, commerce carried on along similar steamship routes—in smaller, more efficient hulls—with hardly a hitch. Propellers gradually became more prevalent than steamers, and trains slowly spread across the region, while schooners remained the workhorse of the lakes for several more decades. It wasn't until after the war that eastern capital and western entrepreneurs entered a prosperous period of regional resource harvesting.

Prior to the war, young men learned the steamboat business as novice investors or deckhands and later brought the steamer industry to maturity. A new vanguard expanded on the work of Eber Ward and

Henry Gildersleeve, steering the industry until the turn of the century. Steamship companies ranked with railroads around the lakes in terms of reputation and efficiency, the hallmarks of marketing in a mass transportation economy.

The Great Lakes shipping system had always been an east-west operation, despite efforts at the 1847 Harbor and River Convention to shift traffic to the Mississippi River. Federal spending on railroads during the war allowed that transportation sector to recover and blossom after the 1857 crash. Not afforded the same fiscal priority, freshwater vessels sat idle until the war's demand for wheat and iron increased freight tonnage and troop movements escalated traffic.

The Civil War forced the US Navy into the steam age quickly. The success of the USS *Michigan* should have encouraged the service to consider iron-hulled steam vessels for all new builds. However, throughout the war steam remained an auxiliary to sail, primarily because of its heavy consumption of coal. The navy was among the first to adapt propeller technologies to warfare, albeit gradually. While initially successful, paddlewheel steamers had tragic flaws. The amidships region was highly susceptible to heavy arms fire. Paddlewheels were the obvious flaw, but a strike to the boilers on the lower decks or the rocker beam perched fifty feet in the air would be equally debilitating. Propellers were cheaper to build, fuel efficient, and more effectively armored, if not necessarily fast. Blockade runners out of southern ports favored speed, and the side-wheelers *Advance* (or *A.D. Vance*) and *Robert E. Lee* have entered naval lore. The fabled CSS *Alabama* was a propeller.

The first propeller warship in the US Navy was the USS *Princeton*, in trials in 1844. Known for his groundbreaking steam-driven propellers, naval architect John Ericsson created the entire power plant. He also designed a huge twelve-inch gun, one of two monsters that the *Princeton* could sustain. During a demonstration in Washington, DC, Ericsson's engine, propeller, and gun performed well.[2] In 1850 Congress appropriated money to modernize the fleet, which in 1853 included only eighteen steamers—some built, some acquired. Within six years, thirty vessels were added, eighteen with propellers. At the outset of the war, the North had forty-two commissioned vessels, the majority made for deep water and generally considered ill-prepared for shallow-water maneuvers.[3] The exception would be found on the western rivers, where steamboats were well-adapted to the vagaries of coastal trade. Even the prolific gunboats, heavy laden, were constructed with sandbars in mind.

Initially, the South had few naval assets. Nearly all the plantation trade was handled in British or Yankee bottoms. At the beginning of the conflict, each Confederate state fielded its own defensive fleet. The South named Stephen Mallory secretary of the navy to coordinate support for the dashing blockade runners, which were generally sponsored by private interests. The region had only one major foundry, the Tredegar Iron Works in Richmond. There were few shipbuilding centers in the South. One was the US Navy yard at Norfolk, quickly secured by Confederate forces at the outset of hostilities, as well as a small government yard at Pensacola and private shipyards in New Orleans. Comparably, the Great Lakes boasted several yards, and New England had dozens. While new vessels could be purchased from Europe, strategic southern ports were scarce; only ten had rail connections. The Great Lakes Basin had nearly twice that.[4]

Another US Navy problem related entirely to personnel. Until 1862 the highest rank in the service was captain. Commanders of squadrons were designated flag officers, allowing them to fly a personal pennant. They were often referred to informally as commodores, but within military hierarchy they remained captains. Ambitious career military men, seeing little chance for significant advancement, chose the army. With the advent of the war, upper-echelon naval positions were created.[5]

On the western rivers, command of vessel movements was ceded to the army by Secretary of the Navy Gideon Welles. Not wishing to deal with small gunboats and troop transports, Welles relinquished command of activity on the Mississippi and Ohio rivers to General George McClellan in 1861. Shipbuilding and acquisition, manning, and piloting were handled by navy staff members who reported to the army, at least until October 1862. Historians recognize that this management structure streamlined Union efforts in the region, but rancor between the branches of service limited its duration and effectiveness. Troops were moved to railheads and battles along the rivers by privately owned stern-wheeled steamships, typical along the river system. Several steamboats were purchased by agents of both the army and navy for conversion to gunboats.

On the Great Lakes, steamships played many roles during the Civil War. The USS *Michigan* represented the American naval command that remained with Welles. As the only designated warship on the upper lakes, armament aboard the USS *Michigan* was restricted by the Rush-Bagot Treaty of 1818 to one eighteen-pound cannon.[6] With the declaration of war, the vessel's chief duty was to bolster recruiting efforts in enthusiastic Great Lakes states. As the war progressed, positive sentiment in the North toward the conflict waned. Conscription rules became increasingly less popular. Efforts to enforce them were resisted, prompting concern over draft riots and sabotage. Commander John C. Carter received orders to use the *Michigan*'s impressive profile to intervene at Detroit; the mere presence of the vessel in a harbor became a significant deterrent to civil disturbance. At Buffalo soon afterward, the tactic prevented the destruction of millions of bushels of grain.[7]

The navy reinforced the USS *Michigan* with two twelve-pound howitzers in September 1863 and ordered the ship to Sandusky Bay, where more than two thousand Confederate Army officers were imprisoned on Johnson's Island. Those men knew that British territory—freedom—lay just a few dozen miles across Lake Erie. Following the Confederate invasion of the North, the Union War Department grew concerned with the vulnerability of Johnson's Island. By December, a dozen rifled naval cannon had been added to the *Michigan*'s deck.[8]

Officers of the USS *Michigan* received intelligence on several occasions regarding plots to compromise the camp at Johnson's Island. A few were credible. All were treated with the same vigilance. One plan nearly worked, involving the *Philo Parsons*. A small steamship just 136 feet long, it was among the vessels that took up the slack when the palace steamers retired. Owned by Selah Dustin, patriarch of a regional steamboat dynasty, the *Philo Parsons* ran a regular schedule between Detroit and the southern ports of Lake Erie, including Sandusky.

The controversial scheme—initially rejected by Confederate president Jefferson Davis but eventually enacted out of urgency—involved a two-pronged attack. An undercover agent was charged with compromising security aboard the *Michigan*. Simultaneously, an armed squad was to hijack a commercial American steamboat, using it to board the warship and assume command. Southern intelligence forces had approached sympathetic groups in the North, primarily a disaffected bunch identified as the Sons of Liberty as well as Canadian sympathizers. Encouragement from those quarters led the Confederate officers to assume their plan was viable, despite the fact that a similar effort had been exposed by the Canadian government a year earlier.

Confederate captain Charles H. Cole was tasked with the first half of the strategy—compromising the *Michigan*. Recently escaped from a different Union prison camp, Cole was anxious to assist his compatriots at Johnson's Island. Arriving surreptitiously in Sandusky in August, his strategy shifted quickly from simple bribery of the *Michigan*'s crew to coercion by means of alcohol. He became friendly with several officers and assumed that they could be lured as necessary.

Spearheading the second half of the plot was Confederate Navy

The steamer *Philo Parsons*. (Painting by Father Edward
Dowling, c. 1963, courtesy of the Detroit Historical Society
Collection.)

acting master John Yates Beall. A college-educated Virginian wounded
early in the war, Beall left the Confederate Army to become an agent,
raider, and saboteur. Like Cole, he had recently been released as part of
a prisoner exchange. Beall's task was to arrange for the boarding party,
the weapons, the timetable, and the vessel. By mid-September, he was
in Sandwich (today's south Windsor, Ontario) with two confederates.
Across the river his lieutenant, Bennett Burley, boarded the *Philo Parsons* at Detroit. It was a Sunday evening, and a tired clerk agreed to
Burley's request for a quick stop the next morning at Sandwich on the
way to Sandusky.

On September 19, the ship departed Detroit at the appointed time
of 8:00 a.m. At Sandwich, three dapper men boarded, seemingly a
sporting party joining Burley. An hour later the regular Amherstburg
stop saw several roughly dressed men come aboard, accompanied by a
heavy trunk. Amid the other passengers, there was nothing suspicious.

The captain, who lived on Middle Bass Island, departed the ship at that next stop, leaving it to his mate to finish the trip. After leaving Kelley's Island, Beall's men popped open the trunk filled with weapons and quickly gained control of the *Philo Parsons*. They locked passengers and crew belowdecks, while engineers and pilots did Beall's bidding at pistol point.

The vessel headed, as scheduled, toward Sandusky Bay. But instead of the regular stop, the side-wheeler stayed out of the bay, made a languid, long-distance reconnaissance of the area around Johnson's Island, and then proceeded eastward out of sight. The *Michigan* was stubbornly on station, and Beall had not received any indication from Cole as to the final viability of their plan. Discovering the *Philo Parsons* to be low on fuel, Beall ordered the ship back to Middle Bass Island for cordwood. While deckhands quickly replenished the supply dockside, another steamer arrived with the same intent. The *Island Queen*, a small inter-island steamer, pulled alongside the *Philo Parsons*, and Beall's minions were forced to promptly take control of this interloper. Crewmen were sequestered aboard the *Parsons*, while passengers from both vessels were sent ashore on condition of parole, sworn to attempt no communication or action for a day. Upon their departure, the *Philo Parsons* towed the *Island Queen* out into the lake and scuttled it, then turned its nose toward Sandusky Bay.

Under cover of darkness, the pirated ship ghosted past Marblehead Point at the bay's north-facing entrance. Confederate lookouts reported that the USS *Michigan* had been relocated to a more advantageous position, creating a better defense for both itself and the island. At this point, seventeen of Beall's nineteen coconspirators argued against further prosecuting the planned attack on the *Michigan*. In a hastily composed protest, they stated that it was generally believed that the plot had been exposed and could not succeed. Faced with this mutiny, Beall ordered the boat back to the Detroit River. Most of the two steamboat crews were landed on Fighting Island, and the *Philo Parsons* continued to Sandwich, flying a Confederate States of America flag from its staff. This frustrated act of defiance marked the only time that ensign flew from a vessel under southern control on the Great Lakes. Once the rebels had disembarked, the ship was scuttled at dockside.

In reviewing navy records of the entire escapade, it can be seen that Beall's thugs were instinctively prescient. An informer within the ranks of the Confederate operatives in Canada had communicated the exact details of the plan to American authorities. The military commander at Detroit, Lieutenant Colonel B. H. Hill, knew of Cole's attempts to

The steamer *Island Queen*. (Painting by Father Edward Dowling, c. 1963, courtesy of the Detroit Historical Society Collection.)

bribe officers of the USS *Michigan* and wired its captain, John C. Carter, "It is said the parties will embark to-day at Malden on board the *Philo Parsons*, and will seize either that steamer or another running from Kelly's [*sic*] Island."[9] Carter put his crew at battle stations and had Cole arrested and interrogated. Certainly, any attempt to take the *Michigan* would have ended in abject failure.

Union intelligence, unknown to Beall, doomed the venture from the outset. B. H. Hill even visited the *Philo Parsons* at its Detroit dock on the morning of the nineteenth and so trusted his informant that he decided to allow events to proceed as planned in order to capture the Confederates in the act. Additionally, Cole proved to be a dangerously incompetent agent who failed to gain the support of the *Michigan*'s crew and received no cooperation from local southern sympathizers. His prevarications misled his superiors and nearly caused a strategic catastrophe. It is generally accepted that, had it gone as planned, capturing the well-armed *Michigan* with pistols and bowie knives would have been the desperate act of desperate men. Following the action, most of the raiders escaped through Canada and returned to southern states. John Yates Beall continued his espionage in the North and was eventually caught and hanged as a spy.

The steamboat heroes of this story, the *Philo Parsons* and the *Island Queen*, survived. The former settled close to shore; the latter drifted onto a shallow reef as it sank. Both vessels were promptly raised and returned to service. The *Philo Parsons'* career was effectively ended by the flames of the Great Chicago Fire in 1871 as it sat at a wharf on the Chicago River. The *Island Queen* maintained its route between Detroit and western Lake Erie for a decade, was later converted to a barge, and succumbed to Lake Michigan in 1876.[10]

Passenger steamers played a significant role in the transfer of military assets throughout the war. Around the Great Lakes, men heading for military camps near railheads in Cleveland, Detroit, and Chicago reached these muster points by ship. Steamers also carried lumber, iron, copper, coal, and—perhaps most important—wheat to be used in the war effort. The Great Lakes Basin contributed a significant percentage of the grain and meat that the Union states consumed—civilian and military. As the war progressed, antidraft protests staged in towns of all sizes drew the attention of the USS *Michigan*, which was dispatched to areas of trouble, including Buffalo, Detroit, Chicago, Milwaukee, Houghton-Hancock, and Duluth, as well as numerous small towns along the shore. Additionally, private vessels were chartered to move militia into hotspots. The *Comet*, one of the earliest vessels of A. E. Goodrich's Steamboat Line (later Goodrich Transportation Company), left Milwaukee in the middle of the night to spirit federal troops to a riot on Washington Island. The same ship regularly took fresh recruits to Cleveland.[11]

One war-related passenger steamboat activity had roots dating to the 1830s. In many Great Lakes towns, steamers served as the final step for people traveling north to escape slavery. The Underground Railroad was an informal but highly active social movement intended to guide unfree persons to freedom. A loose network of sympathetic citizens assisted runaways with shelter, food, and transportation. In the rural North, where free blacks were rare, whites served as "conductors and station masters." In urban areas, free blacks formed Colored Vigilance Committees, which attended to railroad duties, often with the support of elements within the white community.

In the maritime community, abolitionist activities included both subtle and overt involvement. While records of illegal activities related to runaway slaves are rare, facts often support the apocryphal Underground Railroad legends that have survived. The *Railroad* had little to do with railroads. Most travelers ventured alone or in small groups and happened across friendly folks often by accident. Folktales describing the use of symbols, code words, songs, and quilted guideposts along the Underground Railroad have generally been shown to be localized phenomena. Safe houses, people hidden in hay wagons and basements, nights spent in swamps, and subterfuge that occasionally included steamboats—this was the Underground Railroad.

Initially, the objective for escaping slaves was to reach a sympathetic northern state. Refugees often blended into a local community. Southern slave-catchers found that the farther north they traveled, the less their requests for assistance were embraced or accommodated. In 1850 the Fugitive Slave Act made it illegal for judges, law enforcement officers, or citizens to assist escaped slaves and accompanied the law with stiff penalties. Amid draconian enforcement, even established free blacks in the north were no longer safe. Immediately, Canada West became the only true haven, and towns around the Great Lakes became important embarkation points. The border towns of Detroit and Buffalo were so close to Canada that in the winter people could run across the ice to freedom. Travelers moving up the various Ohio River tributaries found their way to Cleveland, Sandusky, and Toledo, where they boarded steamers. Some found temporary employment on the voyage to Detroit. Others were given private cabins in which to remain concealed. The opportunity to leave the vessel while it took on cordwood at Amherstburg, a small town at the mouth of the Detroit River, was seldom missed.

One typical tale of personal fortitude involved Captain Thomas Titus. Earlier in this volume, Titus was described as trying to save passengers aboard the flaming steamship *Erie*. Eventually, the captain himself was saved by his friend and black servant James. Despite the disaster, Titus remained highly respected and subsequently served as master of several vessels. One day, while loading the *Queen City* in Buffalo, a couple came aboard that had run away from a Major Curtis in Kentucky. Siblings George and Clara had ventured north through the Appalachian Mountains and found asylum in Oberlin, Ohio. From there they moved to the steamer docks at Buffalo and were taken aboard by Titus and disguised among the ship's crew. In a coincidence that must have caused consternation on the *Queen City*, Curtis, on the hunt with the notorious slave-catcher Bill Shea, boarded the steamship at a port midway, having exhausted his search and headed for home. When Curtis discovered George and Clara aboard, he taunted them and began pestering Captain Titus to put him and his charges ashore on the American side of the Detroit River. He offered money, which Titus refused, promising only to put Curtis's party ashore on American soil once they reached the river.[12]

Following an oft-repeated script, the *Queen City* was in need of fuel as it entered the river and put into the Amherstburg dock. A furious Curtis and Shea attempted to follow George and Clara as they departed the boat on British soil, but local abolitionists forced the slave-catchers to continue on their voyage. True to his word, Titus reportedly put Curtis and Shea ashore on an uninhabited island upriver—an American island. The *Queen City* continued on to Detroit.

Free blacks in the North were actively involved in transportation. Many of the porters and cooks on the steamships were black, and they engineered the transfer of thousands of people. William Wells Brown, a porter, claimed to have helped sixty-nine runaways reach Canada on Lake Erie vessels in 1842. George DeBaptiste, a leader in Detroit's free black community, purchased the steamship *T. Whitney*, which he managed as clerk, leaving navigation to Captain Atwood. It was not a large craft, purposely chosen to run between Sandusky and small river towns in the Canadian interior such as Wallaceburg and Chatham. The Civil War ended the flow of people heading to Canada for freedom and the need for the Underground Railroad. Once peace was declared, a semblance of daily routine returned to the lakes region.

CHAPTER 9

New Era, New Business Models

The transition between the antebellum and postwar steamboat industries was gradual and almost seamless. The men and companies that came to dominate the lakes after 1865 had their roots in businesses in the first period of development. This chapter will explore several of the dominant players through the latter half of the nineteenth century and how they became entwined with every facet of the region's history. With their origins in the first period of the steamboat age, these entities were the basis for businesses that controlled the lakes and survived through the industry's final period in the twentieth century.

Albert E. Goodrich had a career that personified this era. Born near Buffalo in 1826, his father was a hotelier and an early investor in New Buffalo, Michigan, on the southeastern shore of Lake Michigan. His uncle Captain Harry Whittaker was a shipowner and mastermind of New Buffalo's development. When the town became the western terminus of the Michigan Central Rail Road's line from Detroit in 1849, business boomed at the Goodrich Hotel. More than one hundred thousand travelers arrived in New Buffalo that year. Some folks stayed, and local land prices soared. Most pressed on to Chicago or Milwaukee, riding Ward Line steamers across southern Lake Michigan. The trip from Detroit to Chicago took about a day and a half—remarkable for the period.[1]

Young Albert Edgar, or simply "A.E.," learned the hospitality trade in his father's hotel. Drawn to the lakes, he secured a job aboard the *A.D. Patchin* in 1847, a vessel leased to Ward concerns by his uncle. Albert was soon elevated to clerk and later captain, serving aboard Ward's *Pacific*, *Traveler*, and *Cleveland*. Business was brisk in New

Buffalo until 1852, when both the Michigan Southern Rail Road and the Michigan Central Rail Road completed through-routes to Chicago. By 1853 a trip from Detroit to Chicago took less than half a day, requiring no transfers. The lucrative cross-lake steamship trade suffered immediately. The Ward Line consolidated its business on the eastern and northern lakes, leaving the Lake Michigan trade open to all comers.

Captain Stephen Clement leased four forlorn Ward vessels in 1855 and formed the Clement Steamboat Line in 1856 to serve Lake Michigan ports out of a base in Chicago. Several former Ward personnel invested in the venture, including A.E. Goodrich. Within months the itch of entrepreneurial adventure piqued the young man, and by the end of the year, he and another Clement investor, George Drew, had left the enterprise and formed what became familiarly known as Goodrich's Steamboat Line.

Drew and Goodrich leased another available Ward boat, the side-wheeler *Huron*, and secured dock space in Chicago, Milwaukee, and Manitowoc, Wisconsin. By the end of the Civil War, Goodrich had purchased the *Huron* and the propeller *Ogontz* and acquired the new steamer *Comet* from Ward's Newport (Marine City) shipyard. Later he purchased the *Wabash Valley*, the *Union* (engines from the *Ogontz*), the *Sunbeam* (engines from the *Wabash Valley*), and the *Lady Franklin*. These vessels were typical of the fleet that carried on after the demise of the huge palace steamers. Sturdy and compact at 154 to 170 feet, the Goodrich line's shallow-draft ships gradually increased in tonnage from 348 to 434—a fraction of the *Western World's* 2,000. Most Goodrich boats served the many small ports along the Wisconsin shore. The *Wabash Valley* ventured throughout Green Bay. The *Comet's* itinerary included Muskegon and Grand Haven, Michigan—soon a standard Goodrich run. The *Sunbeam* served the Lake Superior copper country for two seasons before being wrecked on the Keweenaw Peninsula.[2]

The side-wheelers proved to be more seaworthy vessels for that time. As business increased Goodrich, who bought out Drew's interest in the firm in 1861, took control of the four-year-old *Seabird* and the aging palace steamers *Planet* and *May Queen*—former Ward hulls. The *Planet* and *Seabird* generally served Lake Superior during its short season, as well as the Chicago and Muskegon routes.[3]

Entering the postwar era, Goodrich controlled most of the freight and passenger traffic along the western shore of Lake Michigan. The firm was incorporated in 1866 as the Milwaukee, Sturgeon Bay & Green Bay Transportation Company but almost immediately recovered its brand as the Goodrich Transportation Company. Goodrich wharves and

The steamer *Northwest*. (Painting by Seth Arca Whipple, 1883, courtesy of the Detroit Historical Society Collection.)

offices in Chicago and Milwaukee were well-established and familiar to the traveling public. The company's base of operations on the north side of the river in Manitowoc was the hub of Goodrich's steamboat empire and remained so for another half-century. Notably, the company was incorporated in Chicago and later in Augusta, Maine, while the official port of hail was registered variously at Manitowoc, Kenosha, and Duluth, based on various tax advantages. Albert and his family resided in Chicago after 1865.

During the war, Captain Goodrich established relations with Greenleaf S. Rand, the principle shipbuilder in Manitowoc. In 1865 Goodrich bought the steamer *Michigan* expressly for its engine, which he placed in the new Rand-built *Orion*. The year 1866 saw retirement of the *Planet*, the engines being salvaged for service in the new *Northwest* of 1867. After the *May Queen* was wrecked and then burned, its engines were placed in the steamer *Manitowoc*, launched in 1868, for many years the fastest boat operating between Milwaukee and Chicago. Notably, the *Northwest* was considerably larger than anything Goodrich had commissioned—or Rand had built—to date. A spectacular vessel of

1,110 tons, it cost the company $117,000 and was considered the finest on the lakes. Perhaps it was an overreach, for Goodrich sold the vessel a year later to Detroit interests. However, the selling price nearly netted him his initial investment and allowed him to control the beautiful ship during its maiden year for the cost of fuel and personnel.[4]

While Goodrich Transportation survived the war as lesser organizations failed, it faced a number of setbacks. The loss of the *Sunbeam* and the roughly twenty-nine people on board came only a few years after the *Lady Elgin* disaster. These events resulted in a natural wariness among the traveling public, which further disrupted commerce in the war years. With the gradual growth of railroads along the coast of Lake Michigan, the steamer trade was forced to be increasingly creative. Fortunately, Goodrich was firmly ensconced in the northern trade, where iron rails were slow to reach, and well set up in the cross-lake service, which was constantly fed by the rails. As an example of the northern reach of the railroads, while Milwaukee got service a few years after Chicago, it would be nearly twenty years before the iron trail reached Manitowoc. Similarly, rails reached Lake Michigan from Detroit in the early 1850s, but it would be decades before a north-south route connected the numerous important western Michigan harbors.[5]

In an effort to compete with rail traffic in the critical Milwaukee to Chicago trade, Goodrich's advertised a new overnight service in 1868. According to news reports in the *Milwaukee Sentinel*, the recently renovated *Seabird* would run from Manitowoc to Chicago, with stops at Milwaukee, Racine, and Kenosha, offering cheaper fares than the railroads. The ship left Manitowoc at 7:00 p.m. on April 8 and was scheduled to be in Chicago by midmorning the following day. To sweeten the deal, there were no charges for overnight stateroom accommodations.[6]

The *Seabird* carried 104 passengers as it approached Chicago the following morning. While off of Waukegan, Illinois, a porter carrying a scuttle of coals and ash he had removed from a cabin stove stepped to the rail and carelessly, perhaps sleepily, threw the mess overboard, into the wind. The coals blew onto the cargo deck below, landing in crates containing a highly flammable packing material known as excelsior—essentially fine wood shavings—the perfect kindling. Fanned by the breeze, flames quickly engulfed the recently painted woodwork of the *Seabird*'s upper decks. According to A. C. Chamberlain, one of two survivors, the fire's rapid spread made the lifeboats unreachable. Some passengers jumped overboard and were drowned, while others remained aboard and burned to death. The resulting publicity and litigation were tough on the company. The vessel was not insured, but the courts limited Goodrich Transportation's liability to the value of the vessel—$22,000.

The company took another hit, both financially and from a public relations standpoint, when the *Orion* was lost entering the harbor at Grand Haven, Michigan, in 1870, just two years after the *Seabird*. While everyone aboard was saved, the cargo and vessel valued at $70,000 realized only $24,000 from the insurance companies. Goodrich suffered again a year later when the company's Chicago offices, freight sheds, and docks were destroyed by the devastating fire that crippled that city. Albert's family and his company records escaped on the *Skylark*, but the beautiful new propeller *Navarino*, just six months out of the Rand yards, was aground in the Chicago River and burned to the waterline. Goodrich lost three-quarters of the craft's $60,000 cost and carried no insurance on the dock and buildings.

Goodrich Transportation survived nearly a decade before disaster struck again. The Ward-built side-wheeler *City of Alpena*, serving Grand Haven and Milwaukee in tandem with the *Muskegon*, was lost in a freak storm on October 16, 1880. Dozens of passengers and crew disappeared with the ship, leaving only wreckage and bodies along Michigan beaches. That same year, the company's *Oconto* was blamed for setting fire to much of the town of Green Bay. This public perception proved false—the Astor Planing Mill was responsible—but litigation continued for six years.[7]

It is unfair to lump these catastrophes into three paragraphs. Overall, Goodrich ran a safe and efficient fleet. A.E. Goodrich constantly upgraded and refurbished his vessels, hired respected officers, and offered reliable transportation to his passengers. The company continued to grow, at its peak running up to seven steamers on four routes daily. Greenleaf Rand built a succession of vessels for Goodrich, including the trusty steamers *Sheboygan* and *Corona* (engines from the *Comet*) in 1869, the *Muskegon* (machinery from the *Michigan* and *Orion*) and the grand propeller *Navarino* in 1870, the propellers *Oconto* (engines from the *Skylark*) and *Menominee* (engines from the *Navarino*) in 1872, and the *DePere* a year later. Rand partnered with Henry Burger to produce the paddler *Chicago* in 1874, again repurposing an engine from the *Manitowoc* (originally taken from the *May Queen*). The year 1880 saw the launch of the *Ludington*, an 842-ton propeller that ran in the Goodrich livery until 1897, when it was completely rebuilt and rechristened the *Georgia*, seeing Goodrich Transportation through to the end.[8]

Following Rand's death in 1885, the firm Burger & Burger constructed the 200-foot steamers *City of Racine* in 1889 and *Indiana* in

1890. Both vessels maintained the popular and competitive Milwaukee-Chicago night run for Goodrich for many years. The Manitowoc yard also fashioned the *Iowa* from the bones of the *Menominee*, adding new machinery. Among the largest of the company's vessels, they matched the style and luxury of any ship on the lakes and profited well from the World's Columbian Exposition at Chicago in 1893–94. To bolster the firm's prowess at this event, Goodrich had the *Virginia* and *Atlanta* built at Cleveland. The former, at 1,606 tons and 269 feet, was the largest ship constructed for the line, and later it became a saltwater yacht for Chicago chewing gum millionaire William Wrigley.

It is notable that not all Goodrich boats were built for the company. In 1867 Albert bought the assets of Martin Ryerson, a Muskegon lumberman who had been running the propellers *G.J. Truesdell* and *Ottawa* in competition with Goodrich boats. Under Ryerson, these vessels carried lumber and—almost as an afterthought—passengers at cheap rates. After complete refits at the Rand yard, both propellers featured accommodations that matched the high standards of the other Goodrich vessels. They became part of Goodrich's experiment, which began with the ill-fated *Seabird*, running as overnight boats with inexpensive fares and comfortable staterooms.[9]

Albert Goodrich was an astute businessman. His "night boats" proved popular, and this formula eventually became an integral part of the Goodrich business model. Goodrich was also one of the first to offer "moonlight cruises" in the 1880s. Besides being popular with younger Milwaukeeans for the bar and dancing available, these excursions produced revenue on evenings when the company's ships were inactive. Besides innovations in the shipping business, his investments in land in the rapidly growing Michigan ports of St. Joseph, Grand Haven, and Muskegon were also maturing. Albert and his wife Rosamond had a son in 1868—Albert W. Goodrich—a young man who would eventually take the reins of the family fleet. Albert Sr. survived until 1885 and continued to selectively purchase and sell vessels based on a keen instinct for popular passenger routes and a dedicated eye for what the traveling public needed. His early trade was largely in immigrants. Later trade became the families of those same new Americans, comfortably established in their new homes, who sought respite from daily rigors as tourists drawn to new resort towns along the lake.[10]

As in the previous era, there was money to be made in partnership with the railroads. In 1876 the Goodrich Transportation Company contracted to carry all the freight that reached the Pere Marquette railroad terminal at Ludington, Michigan. Termed break-bulk freight, it was taken from railcars and loaded onto vessels for the trip across the lake. Upon arrival it was reloaded into railcars. This inefficiency was addressed by 1892 with the introduction of rail ferries, but in the meantime Goodrich had reliable cargoes that kept its vessels profitable throughout the year. The line built the *City of Ludington* in 1880 specifically for this trade. Because of the year-round nature of the railroad business, Goodrich looked to the metal-hulled propellers being built by the Detroit Dry Dock Company under the aegis of renowned naval architect Frank Kirby. Goodrich took possession of his *City of Milwaukee* in 1881, and it was an immediate success. Combining sumptuous passenger salons and staterooms with plenty of freight capacity and a staunch ice-breaking hull, this became the template for the *Michigan* and *Wisconsin*, launched later the same year. When the powerful Pere Marquette railroad introduced its own vessels to the Ludington route in 1882, Goodrich quickly sold his new ships to the Detroit, Grand Haven and Milwaukee Railway Company for his investment cost, averting financial disaster.[11]

During most of this period, Goodrich was an active captain of his vessels. As age and illness advanced, he retired from the lakes, and later turned management of the business over to his longtime friend and fleet superintendent Captain Thomas G. Butlin. At the age of fifty-nine, he died at his home in Chicago, hailed by his contemporaries and the historian James L. Elliott as the creator of the "most prosperous steamship line in the history of the Great Lakes."[12]

The company carried on under the guiding hand of Butlin until 1889, when Albert W. was old enough to be named president. That same year the company took delivery of the *City of Racine*, a 220-foot steamer that served the company well until 1912, when it was rehabbed and renamed the *Arizona*. It was finally sold in 1925.

One of young Goodrich's ambitions was to have the finest fleet available when the 1893 World's Columbian Exposition opened in Chicago. To this end he contracted for construction of the propellers *Indiana*, *Atlanta*, and *Virginia*. The latter ship was a twin-screw vessel with an "ocean liner" profile: enclosed main deck, single promenade deck, pilothouse well forward, and a single smokestack about half to three-quarters of the ship's length from the bow. At 285 feet and nearly two thousand tons, the *Virginia* was a modern palace steamer hailed by some as the most elegantly appointed passenger vessel that flies the American flag. A few years later, a second deck of cabins was added to accommodate more passengers. While the US economy suffered a severe downturn in 1893, the Columbian Exposition kept the ships

A shattered walking beam aboard the *City of Milwaukee*, 1885. (Photograph courtesy of William McDonald Albums, Detroit Historical Society Collection.)

busy. Following that grand fair, the Goodrich boats' reputation, safety record, and quality helped the line weather the recession better than its competition. So solid was its balance sheet that Goodrich was able to purchase the renowned whaleback *Christopher Columbus* for use as a Chicago-Milwaukee day boat.

While there were changes ahead in the new century, the Goodrich Transportation Company finished the era as one of the two dominant passenger shippers on the Great Lakes, certainly head and shoulders above other passenger carriers on Lake Michigan. The outstanding leader to the east was the Detroit & Cleveland Steam Navigation Company, based in Detroit, generally called the D&C line. A proper comparison between the two companies will illustrate some interesting similarities and notable differences.

The similarities are many. Both were born as an extension of the railroads and maintained close relationships with that industry for many years while seeking and developing business beyond the tracks' inevitable encroachment. Both staked out steady and profitable routes and defended them against relentless competition by launching a string of the most advanced and luxurious vessels available, almost exclusively built in local yards. Both suffered financial setbacks and accidents but remained respected for exemplary fiscal and safety records over many decades. And both continually altered their business models to accommodate the changing needs of their passengers, surviving longer than nearly all of their rivals.

Unlike Goodrich, D&C did not prosper as the result of one man's vision and tenacity. Instead, it was the product of a succession of foresighted men. Albert E. Goodrich was a skilled "horse trader," purchasing, leasing, repurposing, and selling numerous hulls and engines, in addition to ordering a number of beautiful vessels built. The Goodrich Transportation Company ran a total of twenty-six ships over a sixty-seven-year history. The D&C fleets included only fourteen craft over eighty-two years, most built for the company and retained for many years.[13] Perhaps in greatest contrast, Goodrich remained an active captain aboard his vessels for most of his life. The leaders of D&C were land-based financiers, investors, and managers.

In his treatise on the night boats of North America, marine historian George Hilton, stated, "By mixed criteria of size of vessels, traffic density and longevity, the greatest of the night lines was the Detroit & Cleveland Navigation Company. It had the largest boats, the heaviest traffic, and save for the Old Bay Line, the longest survival of any of the major lines."[14] The birth of D&C came out of a series of business relations between Lake Erie shipowners and the Michigan Central Rail Road, beginning in 1850. Several vessels ran on the route through the 1850s as part of the Detroit & Cleveland Steamboat Line, including the ships *Southerner, Baltimore, Forest City, May Queen, Ocean,* and *City of Cleveland.* Most were Ward-related properties, but there were a number of partners, and the relationship between the two companies was cozy. Two new hulls were built by Campbell & Owen in Detroit, the

Advertisement for the D&C line featuring the *City of Mackinac*, 1885. (Engraving by the Calvert Lithograph Company, courtesy of the Detroit Historical Society Collection.)

The steamer *R. N. Rice*. (Painting by Robert Hopkin, 1873, courtesy of the Detroit Historical Society Collection.)

Morning Star in 1862 and *R.N. Rice* in 1867. These became the basis of the venerable Detroit & Cleveland Steam Navigation Company, but the start was rocky.[15]

Incorporated on April 18, 1868, two years after Goodrich, the stockholders of the D&C were the eleven men and one woman who held an interest in the *Morning Star* and *R.N. Rice*, led by Detroiters John Owen, Ira Davis, and Solomon Gardner. Within three weeks, the *Morning Star* collided with an iron ore-laden schooner and sank in Lake Erie. Twenty persons were reported drowned. The other craft was at fault, but that was little consolation to the families or to the uninsured vessel owners. With only the *R.N. Rice* to maintain the Cleveland-Detroit route, the company initially looked to charter a replacement for the *Morning Star*. In a move with strong public relations overtones, the D&C purchased the spectacular *Northwest* from the Goodrich Transportation Company. Both companies benefited: the latter added $150,000 to a meager balance sheet; and the former gained the flagship of the lakes, as well as a high-profile attraction.[16]

The calculation paid off. Despite a tough first year and the cost of insurance premiums, the D&C was able to pay a $1 dividend in 1870. The next two years were profitable to the point that it retired all its debt and even invested in mechanical upgrades to the *Northwest*, improving its reliability. The industry was out of its adolescence. Vessel owners and their customers expected punctuality, because speed was increasingly their primary advantage over rail travel.

The year 1873 brought financial storm clouds to the nation. Wall Street and eastern markets were in turmoil, and competition in the grain trade drove freight costs to less than profitable levels. Additionally, dock workers in Detroit and Cleveland successfully fought for wage increases the previous year that varied from 20 to 33 percent.[17]

Fiscal reality came to the Great Lakes in 1874, nearly halting shipping. Fortunately, the Sandusky and Cleveland runs remained profitable, if only barely. Not so fortunately, the engine in the *Northwest* had become unreliable to the point that it was a safety concern by 1875, causing the company to lose market share. Additionally, a brief price war on the Detroit-Cleveland run brought the round-trip price down to a dollar. This economic climate forced the company to replace the craft's power plant for $12,000, instead of commissioning a new iron steamer for $80,000, or a composite steamer—wood hull over iron framing—for $68,000. The refit included sprucing up the *Northwest*, and it was soon back in form, drawing excursion traffic—the increasingly familiar hint of a profitable new tourist trade being evidenced around the lakes.[18]

As the economy improved, the company weighed its position. David Carter assumed general management duties from John Owen in 1875 and suggested to the board of directors the following year that the company had the reputation of keeping abreast of the times. A considered statement, this could indicate to stockholders the company's place as either a technological leader or a reactionist competitor. Fate forced the company toward the former when the venerable *R.N. Rice* burned on the Detroit waterfront in 1877. Carter convinced his colleagues that the D&C would be best served by a program of modernization. Not all shareholders agreed or could afford the levy of $5 per share, and a large number of delinquent shares were purchased by John Owen, James McMillan, and John Newberry.

New shareholders were not unusual, and over the years rosters of the D&C board varied in number from three to fifteen. Yet the addition of the names McMillan and Newberry is significant. These two men, intimately associated through friendship and investments, controlled considerable lumber, railroad, and manufacturing interests in Detroit and throughout the Great Lakes region. McMillan eventually controlled the entire shipping company. He became a nationally prominent Republican politician and senator, ultimately responsible for the design and completion of the Mall in Washington, DC. This new association was a significant turn of fortune for the D&C line.[19]

The immediate result was an order sent to the Detroit Dry Dock Company for a fully iron built vessel to be named the *City of Detroit*. This ship, the first purpose-built ship for the corporation and one of the earliest all-iron steamers, served on the lakes for an incredible sixty-two years. Designed by Frank Kirby at 234 feet overall length, it shared familiar dimensions with lake steamers for several decades. Additionally, this hull established a tradition within the D&C family to name new launches for a port of call. The ship's success led to the launch of *City of Cleveland*, the flagship of a new venture aimed at Mackinac Island and, in conjunction with the Lake Superior Transit Company, onward to Houghton, in Michigan's copper- and iron-rich Upper Peninsula. The *City of Mackinac* was added to this route in 1883, and the Lake Huron Division (later the Mackinac Division) proved profitable for the line over three decades, primarily due to the growth of tourism.[20]

The Lake Erie side of the operation introduced the new *City of Cleveland* in 1886. Utilizing the nearly new engines of the *Northwest*, the all-steel ship cost the firm almost $214,000. It incorporated many of the innovations that made the first *City of Cleveland*—now renamed the *City of Alpena*—"the fastest boat in America" at more than twenty miles per hour.[21] Within three years, David Carter, manager of daily D&C operations, petitioned the board for a sister to the latest *City of Cleveland*. Christened the *City of Detroit II*, it replaced the first ship of that name. The older vessel was placed on the Chicago–St. Joseph route for a single season. While turning a modest profit, competition on southern Lake Michigan convinced the board to bring the first *City of Detroit* back to Lake Erie. Renamed the *City of the Straits*, it became a day boat running excursions from Cleveland to Put-in-Bay and Toledo.

Entering the final decade of the nineteenth century, the D&C was in a very strong financial position. Carter even received an inquiry from English investors regarding a possible buyout. Nothing resulted, but Carter was able to report gross profits in 1890 of more than $424,000, the company's best year to date. John Owen passed the presidency of the D&C board to newly elected Senator James McMillan seamlessly. With the unfortunate exception of the *City of Detroit II*'s rudder jam that same year, resulting in a collision and the death of one of its crewmen, the company was respected for its safety record, as well as its punctuality and comfort. Four of its five boats had been built in the last decade, helping to define one of the finest fleets running anywhere in the world.

This was no accident. Competition on Lake Erie routes was fierce. With more than twenty other operators vying for the trade along the south shore, quality of experience was important to passengers. Speed and punctuality were essential to freight agents. The D&C wanted the finest boats afloat and contracted naval architect Frank E. Kirby at the Detroit Dry Dock Company to create them. McMillan, like his predecessor Owen, was also president of this shipyard and the related engine works and carpentry shops, so the partnership was predetermined. Kirby came to Detroit specifically to manage affairs at Detroit Dry Dock and in the process created fast and functional ships. His myriad innovations will be discussed later, but in terms of the D&C steamers, he developed a template for some of the prettiest and most profitable side-wheeled vessels anywhere. His designs appeared on the Hudson River and Long Island Sound and were admired and imitated on passenger routes around the world.[22]

In 1892 General Manager Carter conceived a plan to further modernize the fleet. He proposed selling the *City of Mackinac* and the *City of Alpena* in order to partially fund the building of two newer, more efficient steamers for the Mackinac line. The board was rightly concerned that the surplus ships might fall into the hands of competitors. They were also leery of entering into direct and obvious competition with Cornelius Vanderbilt's New York Central Railroad running between Buffalo and Cleveland. Vanderbilt was a valued partner, owning an interest in both the Michigan Central and Lake Shore & Michigan Southern railroads.

The solution was singularly simple. The vessels were sold to Cleveland investors to form the Cleveland & Buffalo Transit Company, more commonly known as the C&B Line. The agreement included a noncompete clause, but, more importantly, the general manager of the new entity, Thomas F. Newman, had been a D&C employee since he was a boy and until recently was the manager of the company's Cleveland operations. He and David Carter were best of friends, and they established a cordial, cooperative, and profitable relationship between the two companies that was critical to their futures.

With the $270,000 received for the two steamers, renamed the *State of New York* and the *State of Ohio* in C&B livery, Carter needed vessels to service the Mackinac run quickly. After some frustrating delays—Kirby's was one of the busiest shipyards on the lakes—two new bottoms arrived from Detroit Dry Dock midseason 1893. Familiarly christened the *City of Mackinac* and the *City of Alpena*, the price came to over $564,000. With these fresh faces, Carter reinvigorated the Mackinac Division—the tourist line—and extended the route southward from Detroit to Toledo, on the Maumee River at the southwest corner of Lake Erie. For the additional three hours of steaming, this route established a daily connection to a new market of one hundred thousand residents, an active hub of railroad activity, and a source of cheaper coal for the hungry boilers.[23]

The new steamers arrived amid the excitement associated with the exposition in Chicago, but Senator McMillan was closer to the markets than most industrialists. He noted as early as 1890 that he felt "as if something had dropped." Money tightened, and revenues ceased keeping up with obligations in 1891, a portent of the coming storm. The company issued new stock, a popular buy even at 25 percent above par, which was mostly absorbed by active stockholders. It also took out an additional loan to cover losses and pay for the new steamers. The year 1892 saw passenger traffic up slightly, proving beneficial to the northern line. Freight was down, however, hurting the Lake Erie operations. Despite a 20 percent drop in earnings, the company paid its traditional 5 percent dividend. Soon afterward, in a strategy mirroring that of the bulk carriers, management announced temporary wage cuts of 10 percent.[24]

To boost revenue, Carter turned to Saturday night excursions, known to future generations as moonlight cruises. These inexpensive trips utilized the ships during a regular downtime. They had little impact on the housekeeping staff and proved to be quite profitable. Carter reported taking in $3,000 on a single late summer evening. The concept was popular, particularly with young adults. At fifty cents per person, these resplendent floating halls offered a romantic experience. The boats featured live musical entertainment, a boon to the professional musicians of Detroit. However, during the high Victorian era, dancing was not allowed. That would change during the Jazz Age.

Despite this profitable innovation, 1893 was a tough financial year. Besides obligations on the new steamers, the company built a new dock and freight sheds on its property at the foot of Wayne Street in Detroit. Fuel prices were affected by mining and railroad labor strikes, so Carter stockpiled a six-week supply of coal. The company was also invested in the Grand Hotel project on Mackinac Island. Notably, D&C suspended its August dividend payment, and the December dividend was reduced to 3 percent. The company was forced to borrow $84,000 to close out 1893.[25]

The only bright spots in 1893 were the new *City of Mackinac* and *City of Alpena*. Regarding them, Carter notes that they "have been found to be perfect in all that pertains to modern floating palaces, and they have already earned for themselves an unequalled reputation as such on our Lake Huron route. With these steamers we shall be able to take care of our growing tourist travel to northern resorts, which we have not been able to do the past few years." For the first time, passenger traffic became the bread and butter of the company, supporting the depressed freight side on the balance sheet. Business remained slow the following year and then recovered at a solid pace. The D&C came through the tough times with new ships, strong political relationships, and a respectable ledger. It was a good start heading toward the next century.[26]

Typical of the interdependency of the various transportation sectors is the schedule offered by the Star-Cole and Red Star lines based in Detroit. Founded in 1855 by Darius Cole and associates, the *Northerner* and a succession of ships served points in Lake Huron as far as Mackinac. By 1885 the partnership had refined its reach to concentrate on resort service along the St. Clair River to Port Huron and between the Detroit River and Toledo. However, its promotional brochure describes twenty routes taking the traveler from northern Ohio to California and British Columbia. Of course, this involved railroads, including the Great Western, Canadian Pacific, Northern Pacific, and finally Southern Pacific to San Francisco. On the lakes, partnerships included the D&C to Mackinac Island or the Northern Steamship Company to Sault Sainte Marie, Duluth, and Port Arthur (modern day Thunder Bay, Ontario). In a score of years, travel options had become reliably transcontinental.

Marketing of this type allowed relatively modest transportation companies—Star-Cole had a radius of only 110 miles—to throw a long shadow. The pan-continental pride evidenced in both the United States and Canada during this period was a tremendous hook. While the transcontinental trip to San Francisco cost $127.50 and was out of financial reach for most regional tourists, it was possible to travel from Detroit to Port Arthur, at the very edge of the wilderness, for only $27, meals included.

The new rival on Lake Erie, the Cleveland & Buffalo line, surpassed the expectations of both investors and competitors. It ordered two new boats in the 1890s—the *City of Buffalo* and the *City of Erie*. Both were classic Kirby paddlewheelers of about three hundred feet, elegant and fast. The smaller boats joined the partnership servicing the western lake basin. The *State of New York* joined the *City of the Straits* running from Cleveland to Toledo for the D&C. The *City of Ohio* was sent to Lake Michigan to run out of St. Joseph and Benton Harbor for O'Connor Transportation.[27]

These disparate business models were employed by the most successful Great Lakes passenger steamboat companies during this era, but there were other plans that proved successful in other spheres. Several companies ran smaller excursion steamers or belonged to the "mosquito fleet" of modest passenger boats that operated shuttle routes radiating from major ports. Others maintained a long-distance, end-to-end trade: Buffalo, Erie, and southern Georgian Bay on one end; Chicago, Duluth, or Port Arthur on the other. A familiar name continued into this period. The Ward Central & Pacific Lake Company was active to the north, surviving as Ward's Lake Superior Line over a decade after Eber B. Ward's sudden death in 1875.[28]

The Union Steamboat Company was incorporated in 1869 by Jay Gould and S.D. Caldwell, formalizing a railroad relationship more than a decade old. Under their aegis, it provided western connections operating in tandem with their New York & Erie Railroad Company. Typical of Gould, it began with a bang: he assembled the largest fleet to date. The company bought twenty-one screw steamers to operate a freight-centered route to Milwaukee and other western ports. Additionally, the board authorized the purchase of two new vessels. Union ships accommodated passengers generally on the upper of two decks and competed with D&C ships on Lake Erie. Propeller craft were profitable and efficient for the owner but offered passengers less commodious salons and less walking-around space, the two constant advantages that ships had over rail. Schedule and connections were an important consideration for Union passengers.

Gould eventually lost control of the Erie Railway, which merged with the steamboat company in June 1896. Successful afterward for almost two decades, the Union Steamboat line was affected by the Panama Canal Act of 1912, which mandated the separation of organizations controlling competing transportation routes. Apart from the railway, Union steamboats maintained declining operations until 1916.[29]

The Anchor Line's story is similar. Founded in 1865, the Erie & Western Transportation Company became the primary carrier for the Pennsylvania Railroad. The company, using ships leased from the Empire Line, maintained a daily departure from Erie to Milwaukee, Racine, and Chicago. Erie & Western also connected with the

Northern Pacific Railroad at Duluth. By the mid-1880s, the company adopted a red anchor as its marketing icon and thereafter advertised itself as the Anchor Line. Like Union Steamboat, this was essentially a freight connection for the railroad that coincidently carried passengers in comfortable style. Similarly, it was running a fleet of seventeen ships by 1894.[30]

The Anchor Line, active through the opening phase of the new century, gradually refined its fleet. It built passenger-friendly ships that incorporated the sleek physical profile of ocean vessels. The slab sides and narrow girth of traditional propeller packets easily distinguished them from the wide paddlewheel steamers. The Anchor Line was among several operators that chose this distinctive look, which eventually came to define companies. While there were exceptions, most companies chose to run either steamers or propellers. The Anchor Line ran propellers, and its later passenger ships were elegant.

The Canadian pedigree was similar but based to the north on Lake Huron's Georgian Bay. Geography allowed American vessels to complete a connection to the Atlantic via Buffalo. The Ontario landscape partnered with the railroads to create a favorable route from Montreal and Toronto to Collingwood by 1857. From there vessels sailed to Sault Sainte Marie and on to the growing towns of Port William, Port Arthur, and Michipicoten. After depositing their valuable supplies, barrels of grain and ore filled the holds for the return trip south, fruits of the great Canadian forests and plains. Other vessels served the many settlements of Georgian Bay and the North Channel, sailing north to French River and west through Little Current to the Soo.

In his book *Steamboats on the Lakes*, historian Maurice D. Smith notes the importance of maritime commerce to these villages.[31] At a time when much of the continent was becoming reliant on railroads, the inhabitants of northern lake towns remained heavily dependent on steamboats for several more decades. Except for telegraph communications in the larger towns, ships were the only tie to the outside world. Their regular visits were anticipated, reflecting a true frontier lifestyle that remained in some places until a decade after World War II. When winter ice finally formed and thickened, true wilderness isolation set in. The first vessel of the new season, perhaps arriving by mid-April, brought fresh supplies, visitors, and news. It was cause for celebration, and the captain who braved reluctant ice floes and tenuous weather often received a new top hat or gold-headed cane.

In 1873 Canadian rail tracks reached the lumbering port of Owen Sound, and trade was shared with Collingwood. The former gained ascendancy in 1884 when the Canadian Pacific Railroad (CPR) bought the Owen Sound line, having already ordered new steel packets for the route. The nearly identical sisters *Algoma, Alberta,* and *Athabasca* were built in Scotland, sailed across the Atlantic, bisected at Montreal for passage to the lakes, and rejoined at Buffalo. These ships had the distinction of being the first large passenger ships on the lakes lit by electricity. Within a year, other companies were following suit.[32]

Like the propellers of the Union and Anchor lines, CPR ships had the distinctive ocean liner physique. Notably, above the hold and main cargo deck were passenger accommodations located on a single promenade deck. Unlike the Goodrich-type twin-deck steamers, the single passenger deck offered a sleek impression to the viewer. When the *Algoma* came to grief on Isle Royale in Lake Superior, the CPR recovered its machinery and installed it in the *Manitoba,* launched at Owen Sound in 1889. Twenty percent longer than the sisters at three hundred feet, the *Manitoba* could accommodate three hundred passengers and served the company well into the next century.

As the railroads extended west across the Canadian prairies, this route remained important. The CPR had competition from the Georgian Bay Navigation Company, later the Great Northern Transit Company, and the North Shore Navigation Company, both based in Georgian Bay. When the Grand Trunk Railway reached Sarnia, Canada West, at the base of Lake Huron, another firm used that port as a departure point for the Canadian lakehead. Known locally as the Beatty Line, the 1865 partnership became the Lake Superior Line after 1870 and was incorporated as the North West Transportation Company of Sarnia in 1882. With a few exceptions, these companies ran propeller vessels of a lesser size than those of the CPR.[33]

Perhaps the clearest indication of trends in the passenger business can be traced to Minnesota mogul Jim Hill. His railroad empire included tracks running west from Duluth and east from Buffalo, making a Great Lakes fleet between the ports a natural extension of the business. Hill did not build the propeller packets favored by many of the through-carriers. Instead, when founding the Northern Steamship Company in 1888, he compartmentalized the business. Six ships carried nothing but cargo. Two ships carried only passengers. It seemed the ideal mix: the bulk and passenger businesses were very different, and packets were an imperfect combination of the two from the standpoints of scheduling, efficiency, and passenger comfort.

Hill's St. Paul, Minneapolis & Manitoba Railway, later the Great

Northern Railway, made a perfect partner on the northern end, supplying nearly a million bushels of wheat to the bulk carriers in its first year and more thereafter. To the south, Hill's Great Northern Elevator at Buffalo relieved the ships of their golden burden, and, with his connections to the Lehigh Valley and Erie railroads, sent the ships back laden with cement, tobacco, coffee, hardware, and farm implements—everything needed by growing towns on the Great Plains.

The *North West* and the *North Land,* launched in 1894 and 1895, respectively, became passenger favorites instantly. Gleaming white and handsome, they combined the sleek lines of the ocean liners with some distinctly Great Lakes touches: the pilothouse sat back a bit from the bow, and three impressive smokestacks stood in line along the hurricane deck (later reduced to two). The cabins were resplendent with a modified rococo decor, "striving for harmony of color and avoiding the vulgarity which comes with overloading ornament." Such sophistication was matched by a robust power plant that propelled the ships at over twenty-two miles per hour and lit more than twelve hundred electric bulbs—surpassing all other craft afloat on any waters.

The freight segment of the Northern Steamship Company was profitable, even in the worst economic times. Conversely, the "white flyers" lost money most of the time. Capable of carrying more than 400 passengers in 130 staterooms, the flagships each employed a crew of 147. The twenty-eight water tube boilers were state-of-the-art but required additional firemen and coal passers.

Typical of the reorganization that took place in the industry at the turn of the century, the *North West* and the *North Land* were reassigned to the Buffalo-Chicago route in 1901—a course already crowded with competition. More important, management sold the profitable freight business, leaving the Northern Steamship Company a perennially deficit-ridden passenger line. The ships made money but not enough to cover operational expenses like maintenance and dockage fees. When the *North West* caught fire in 1911 during a refit, resulting in the destruction of the cabins, the company released the intact hull and machinery for the insurance value. The *North Land* remained in service for five more years, but it was on the auction block by 1916 and scrapped by 1921.

It is hard to compare the failure of this passenger-only line with any other situation. Most vessels, even the finest passenger steamers, carried cargo. Increasingly, efficient cargo handling favored bulk carriers, and break-bulk contracts were being won by overland carriers. Steamers carried short-haul or express freight. It seems, in retrospect, that once the profitable freight arm of the company was sold, dissolution was inevitable. Yet about this time, a new shipper named the Chicago, Duluth & Georgian Bay Transit Company launched a passenger-only operation with two vessels, on essentially the same routes, with no direct tie to the railroads. Commonly known as the Georgian Bay Line, the company survived to close the era.

From a business perspective, the transformation of the nation during this half century was remarkable. From iron to steel. From telegraph to telephone. From dark to light. From travel travails to coast-to-coast-in-a-week—comfortably. The century closed on a much different travel market than existed in 1857.

CHAPTER 10

Changing Tastes and Technologies

Steamboat operators developed a spectrum of strategies to ad-dress specific changes in the business climate of the continent. Some organizations focused specifically on the passenger trade. Others created separate arms to handle passenger business and bulk cargoes. The majority relied on break-bulk freight and a predictable load of passengers for a profit.

The migrant trade was strong but gradually changed character. From a cargo standpoint, it was less frequently pioneers transporting everything they owned. In the 1870s and 1880s, European and American farmers knew that quality plows, harvesters, and housewares were available in their new homes. Skilled tradesmen, merchants, and scholars brought their cherished tools, but many of the finest and cheapest instruments in the world were being produced in America. The frontier character of passenger traffic gradually was replaced by steady commuter and tourist revenues that enhanced, but seldom supplanted, freight revenues.

Contemporary tastes, influenced by the elaborate ornamentation of the late Victorian era, were evidenced throughout the new generation of palace ships. Journalistic hyperbole matched earlier analysis, but the needs and tastes of the continental traveler in North America were changing, as were the demographics. Successful steamboat operators stayed attuned to shifts in travel patterns and catered to a changing clientele.

The late Victorian period peaked in the latter half of the century in the British Empire. The United States entered its Gilded Age. Both

The steamer *City of Cleveland*. (Painting by Seth Arca Whipple, 1888, courtesy of the Detroit Historical Society Collection.)

countries embraced the notion of empire. The British were adept at managing their worldwide assets, mixing firepower and diplomacy. Americans and Canadians looked to their western plains as the future sites of limitless farms and ranches and employed force in the pursuit of their perceived destiny. By the end of the era, North America had connected the coasts by rail, and immigrants continued to flow to the plains. Along with those people new to the West, there was a strong contingent of second- and third-generation North Americans following the relentless westward tug that had drawn their forefathers from New England to the Midwest, or from Nova Scotia to Ontario.

The Great Lakes saw growth from its farms and forests, too. American Civil War veterans often received compensation in the form of land in northern Michigan and Wisconsin. Much of the land was poor farming soil, either too sandy or too swampy, and after a few frustrating seasons these pioneers moved on or found work in the lumber camps. Lumbering in the Great Lakes peaked in the 1870s and 1880s, gradually moving north and west, leaving behind clear-cut counties and busted boomtowns. Steamboats brought the lumbermen in with their machinery and crews, loaded millions of board-feet for the haul to thriving lake ports, and helped move operations northward when the hills had been lumbered out.

Beyond the farms and woodlands, the greatest influx of workers went to the burgeoning cities and mining towns. Most were immigrants, often untrained and illiterate, looking for tough, simple, steady jobs in the fastest-growing industrial region in the world. Cities such as Buffalo, Cleveland, Detroit, Milwaukee, and Chicago sprouted smokestacks like weeds, each a proud symbol of relentless progress. The towns of Gary, Marquette, Sault Sainte Marie, Duluth, Houghton, and Hancock profited from their proximity to resources and rail lines. By the turn of the century, these municipalities found native English speakers in the minority. Northern mining towns absorbed Finns, Swedes, Italians, and Cornishmen. The great cities were flooded with Italians, Poles, Russians, and Slavs, as well as the familiar Irish, Scots-Irish, and Germans. These groups generally created thriving enclaves where English was not required, but encouraged. European traditions were largely eschewed, save for religious practices and familiar foods. Being an American was a dream for most, and American optimism and opportunity were embraced. It was left to later generations to revive the "old ways."

One result of industrialization and the Gilded Age was the opportunity for hardworking people to afford leisure time. Most laborers worked six days a week, but a relatively high standard of living created a middle class that had money for Sunday jaunts and short vacations. With a nod to the lassitude of previous generations, social norms in the late Victorian period favored idyll pastimes. Women, heavily clothed and petticoated even in the hottest weather, were encouraged to take their leisure. Sports, generally for men, included baseball, tennis, and rowing for the athletic. Fishing and shooting were popular for those at ease. Cycling, swimming, bathing, and boating came on strong at the close of the century. Leisure affinities resulted in the formation of clubs. These groups were formed around the various sports but also for those interested in singing, theatre, lectures, and education. Moral themes such as temperance and philanthropy drew followers, young and old. Club members often coalesced based on ethnic or professional familiarity. When they looked to sponsor an event, steamboats offered the premier social venue—affordable to all.

When leisure travel became popular, steamboat companies adapted. For decades they transported migrants and bulk cargoes. Gradually, the trade changed, and bulk cargoes were carried by specialized ships. Increasingly, passenger steamers catered to settled clientele traveling for business or pleasure instead of international tourists or migrants. Resort towns and picnic parks reliant on steamer traffic developed around the lakes. Often this was a day trade. Historian George Hilton has demonstrated that Lake Michigan steamboat companies were most successful if they could complete a port-to-port cycle of at least one round trip per day. Longer trips from Chicago northward to Ludington or Manistee, or southward from Milwaukee to St. Joseph or Michigan City, were not as popular. He also notes a paradigm shift in scheduling. Steamships originally set departure times based on daylight and navigational concerns. Gradually, schedules were adjusted to accommodate railroad arrivals. As this period evolved, the traveling public increasingly made choices based on departure and arrival times, and the carriers reacted accordingly.[1]

Marketing efforts were mounted to attract the traveling public. Advertisements appeared daily in newspapers touting speed, convenience, comfort, and safety. The diarylike travelogues of the previous period were replaced with professional travel guides, funded in part by advertisements for railroad and steamship companies serving the particular region. Additionally, steamship companies developed brand identities that included distinctive logos, exterior paint configurations, and smokestack colors. This began as early as the 1830s, when the steamer *Illinois* sported on its smokestack the silhouette of a native warrior with bow pulled to full extension. Following the Civil War, business leaders within larger organizations came to realize the power of regional and even national branding. For many years Goodrich boats were painted entirely white with a distinctive red stack. The D&C boats featured dark green hulls with buff-colored superstructures and the distinctive D&C script mounted between or atop the black smokestacks. Graham & Morton generally had black hulls and white cabins. Canada Steamship had regional variations. As boats were traded and sold, patrons used stack colors to identify the company. In every beach and harbor town, people scanning the lake could name passing ships many miles away by their profiles and stack markings.

Top-tier companies that could afford to build new vessels had the added luxury of creating distinctive profiles for their ships. Hilton identifies the "Goodrich look"—high-sided, compact craft that immediately conveyed a solid and safe impression. The D&C remained loyal to Kirby side-wheelers throughout its long tenure. Unlike most propellers, the side-wheelers retained a delicate, linear look, while the deck arrangement offered guests extended outside promenades; the *City of Detroit II* had roughly a quarter mile of exterior walkways on three decks in 1889. The Northern Steamship Company was among those that claimed the sleek, ocean liner look as its signature. The regular departure of vessels from local docks marked the time for millions of folks around the Great Lakes. The smart "lines-off" whistle of a scheduled packet or excursion steamer was a reassuring part of the daily soundtrack in harbor towns.

At the three-quarter-century point, there were upward of three thousand schooners moving iron, wheat, lumber, and coal on the lakes. Over the next few decades, iron-hulled steamers were adapted as carriers in the bulk trade. Wooden schooners by the hundreds, and later steam tugs towing schooner barges, helped close out the great lumber era. A few survived into the new century. Passenger steamers, long reliant on break-bulk freight, saw the nature of their profits shift. As early as 1893, the D&C's Lake Huron Division made more money on tourist fares than on freight. Lake Michigan carriers, dependent on seasonal fruit cargoes since their inception, increasingly tried to balance their books with the colorful allure of lakeside resorts.[2]

During this period, the appointments and outfitting of the passenger fleet became more refined, but the physical configuration changed little. Steamers remained more commodious than propellers, even as the latter became more common, particularly on the open northern lakes. Steamers benefited from the broad overhang of decking that protected the paddlewheels. This teardrop shape added hundreds of square feet of cabin and salon space on each deck. A ship like the *Darius Cole* was able to place washrooms, lavatories, and janitorial closets into these centrally located but loud and damp parts of the vessel's footprint. In exchange, rocker-beam paddlers gave up the middle portion of the boat for vertical machinery and smokestacks. This separated the salons and lounges into two distinct ends of the ship, each lined with cabin doors. If there was a third deck, it was nearly always a wraparound balcony, creating a multilevel grand salon. The third deck, again lined with cabin doors, was accessed via an appropriate grand staircase. Contemporary illustrations and photographs throughout the period show draped ivy and floral centerpieces adorning the tables and railings.

Propeller-driven vessels were different for a number of reasons. To a seasoned traveler, the throb of the engine, the thrust of the propeller,

Interior salon of the *City of Chicago*, c. 1890. (Courtesy of the Detroit Historical Society Collection.)

and the motion of the hull as it passed through the water were distinct from those of the side-wheelers. Propellers were often deeper keeled and generally more enclosed. Their narrow nature unencumbered by midship machinery allowed guests to enjoy one beautifully long main salon with dozens of cabins and utility rooms opening on to it. It was common for separate gentlemen's and ladies' cabins to be located on upper or lower decks. The common room bunking for overflow passengers seen in the first steamboat era became less popular and was a rarity by the 1880s.

There was no pattern for the placement of dining rooms in Great Lakes vessels. For ease of motion within the hull, dining salons were initially placed in the most stable part of the ship—on the cargo deck, often below the waterline. From an operational standpoint, dining rooms were intrahull utility rooms often aft and adjacent to the galley (kitchen) and adapted for sleeping after dusk. Dining rooms without windows can be tough places for people prone to seasickness. As the industry matured, architects improved the experience by elevating the dining rooms within the hull to improve ventilation. Some went a step further, offering window-lined rooms so that dining patrons could enjoy expansive views. This presumably enhanced the cruising experience and potential profits. Other ships created beautifully decorated dining spaces wedged into the bow with only portholes for daylight.

The future of Great Lakes ships—particularly passenger ships— took a tremendous turn in 1870 as the result of a chance meeting. Eber B. Ward, the shipping magnate profiled earlier, was returning to Detroit and he met young Frank E. Kirby. Kirby was returning to his Michigan home after studying naval architecture at the Cooper Union engineering school in New York. Ward must have seen Kirby's potential because soon afterward he gave him a job. It is probable that Kirby's talents would have led to a great career had this meeting not taken place. Yet the succession of events argues that the relationship between the two men sealed his fate. Ironically, this bit of serendipity occurred in the coach of a westbound railroad train.

Kirby was born to the lakes in Cleveland. His father Samuel was an entrepreneur who became involved in lumbering and shipbuilding in the Saginaw River region and moved his family there in 1863. Frank received his primary education locally but displayed an aptitude that suggested more formal training. While attending Cooper Union, he maintained a day job as a draftsman at two of America's premier ironworks, Allaire and Morgan. Eber Ward hired him at his Wyandotte, Michigan, steelworks, where Kirby stayed until 1882. Eventually Frank's brother Franz joined the firm, and the two produced the modest *Queen of the Lakes*.

Following Ward's sudden death in 1875, the steelworks was purchased by a syndicate that included Samuel Kirby. Two years later new investors came together to form the Detroit Dry Dock Company. Kirby was a partner. So was James McMillan, owner of the D&C and partner in an engine manufactory soon dubbed the Detroit Dry Dock Engine Works. This latter business had roots going back to 1852, as Campbell, Wolverton and Company, and later Campbell & Owen. The Detroit Dry Dock Company built vessels of all kinds, and Frank Kirby's genius touched them all. He is most associated with passenger vessels, particularly side-wheelers, but he also developed a variety of vessels for transporting railcars. These specialized craft were especially suited to icebreaking in northern waters, employing reinforced hulls with soft chines and movable water ballast to rock the ship. Particularly innovative was a system developed in concert with Captain L. R. Boynton

Naval architect Frank E. Kirby (*center*) at the christening of
the *Greater Detroit*, 1924. (Courtesy of the Detroit Historical
Society Collection.)

that mounted propellers at both bow and stern.[3] The forward screw
pulled water from beneath thick ice, allowing it to collapse under its
own weight before being parted by a spoon-shaped bow. The concept
proved so effective that Russian designers co-opted the technology for
their Baltic fleet. Detroit Dry Dock also built Kirby's flat-topped rail
carriers for the Detroit and St. Clair rivers service.

In terms of passenger ships, Kirby's mix of form and function allowed vessels sailing out of Detroit on routes between Buffalo and
Mackinac to have a distinctive and elegant profile. If output is any
gauge, he preferred wheeled propulsion, but he also built beloved propellers. Unlike the recognizable and enclosed form of Lake Michigan
or Lake Superior packets, Kirby's style emphasized maximum exterior
promenade decking that was visually sleek and horizontal, suggesting
speed and refinement. Smokestacks—an integral part of a vessel's visual identity—were carried in a number of configurations. The *City of Detroit* had a single narrow stack set nearly amidship. The *City of Detroit
II* had two pipes mounted behind the pilothouse athwartship or side-
by-side. The *Tashmoo* was immediately recognizable by its two smart
stacks, set fore-an-aft. The *City of Detroit III*, as well as the *Greater*

Detroit and the *Greater Buffalo,* displayed three. On all the lakes, only Cleveland's *Seeandbee* sported four giant smokestacks, rivaling anything on saltwater.

The Kirby side-wheelers gained a significant advantage when feathering floats, or paddle faces, were introduced for the first time on the lakes in 1880 aboard the initial *City of Cleveland.* Prior to this innovation, paddles were fixed and their faces set radially from the wheels' axis. The paddles, also called buckets, hit the water's surface at obtuse and unproductive angles and were effective for a relatively short period during their cycle. Feathering paddles were geared to self-cant and produce optimum output. Feathering increased thrust and efficiency while reducing stress on the machinery. Presumably, it also reduced the persistent "misting" that deck passengers endured on the windward side. Kirby's shop was able to successfully integrate into its designs smaller wheels turning at faster revolutions. Smaller wheels and wheel housings were visually less obtrusive, but they also increased available deck real estate. From a marketing standpoint, smaller wheels were indicative of the latest, most sophisticated technology.[4]

Kirby's yard became a pioneer in the development of steel-hulled ships. The transition from wood to iron to steel came in a number of steps. It was related earlier how the USLS *Abert* and the USS *Michigan* pioneered iron construction for military vessels in the United States prior to the Civil War. While cost-effective in the long run, the initial investment kept the technology from becoming widely adopted, preventing attractive economies of scale. It wasn't until profitable cargoes of ore, tremendously destructive to wooden holds, justified further development.

Initially, iron was only employed to build the internal skeleton of a ship, with wooden beams secured to the frame to create the hull. This type of "composite" construction produced a stiffer vessel and avoided the expense of rolling and riveting iron plates for the hull. However, even the best iron was less flexible and weaker than steel, which by the end of the century was to gain favor despite the expense.

The first all-iron ship on the lakes was the tug *Sport,* built for Eber Ward at the Detroit Dry Dock Company yard in 1873. The process proved successful, and Kirby undertook to build the *Brunswick,* a 235-foot bulk carrier. Enrolled June 11, 1881, at Detroit, it preceded the *Onoko* by a season. The former operated for a few months before being destroyed in a collision. The latter generally gets the nod as the first iron ship. Within eight years the steel-hulled *City of Detroit II* passed down the ways at the Detroit Dry Dock Company.

For comparison, the 234-foot composite *City of Detroit* cost the D&C $125,000 to fully commission in 1878. Four years later the company paid almost 20 percent more for the 203-foot, all-iron-hulled *City of Mackinac*. It was understood that a wooden hull was only expected to be viable for fifteen years; iron and steel were projected to be good for decades. By 1886 Kirby's team was commissioned to build an all-steel steamer, the second to bear the company's *City of Cleveland* moniker. With an engine purportedly repurposed from the *Northwest*, the vessel's costs were recorded by General Manager Carter as $214,000. Newspaper estimates placed the final total higher, suggesting that cabin and accommodations were extra.

The 1883 *City of Mackinac II* and *City of Alpena* are cited as the first vessels on the inland seas rigged with a mechanical bow rudder to assist pilots in the restricted river ports. In 1908 the *City of Cleveland III* advertised that "No other passenger steamer in the world has a bow rudder *operated by steam*."[5]

Kirby was first on the lakes to integrate electric lighting into his passenger ships through the *City of Cleveland II* project in 1886, although credit for introducing this innovation to the region falls to the CPR's *Algoma*, mentioned earlier, in 1884. By the 1890s, this innovation was wildly popular with passengers and increased the ship's visibility to shore-side observers.[6]

Frank E. Kirby's company was the most innovative organization on the Great Lakes, though not the only one. In Duluth a Scotsman created the *Christopher Columbus*, unique in the world, and likely the Great Lakes' all-time most recognizable craft. Nine-year-old Alexander Mc-Dougall arrived on the southern shores of Georgian Bay in 1854. Seven seasons later he began his maritime career as a deckhand and was a captain by his twenty-first birthday. After a stint in a Buffalo shipyard, he imagined a revolutionary vessel: a ship designed to sit low in the water with a radically rounded deck that earned the genre the nickname "whaleback." A seemingly cylindrical hull section was wedded to conical bow and stern sections. McDougall intended that, without hard gunwales and water-retaining flat decks, his configuration would allow the hull form to pass more efficiently through rough seas. Waves would pass over the deck, while cylindrical deck housings would enclose the cabins and machinery.

He formed the American Steel Barge Company in Duluth in 1889 and successfully built a propeller steamer and five barges with this radical, cigarlike profile. In 1891 the firm moved across the bay to Superior, Wisconsin, and produced another thirty-three hulls. The steamers

The whaleback passenger propeller *Christopher Columbus*, 1893. (Courtesy of the Detroit Historical Society Collection.)

proved seaworthy, and barges reportedly tracked well in tow, but all whalebacks were difficult to load and unload. The narrow deck hatches, resulting from the rounded deck, proved to be the ship's greatest deficiency.

However, the visual profile was a tremendous asset when McDougall developed the *Christopher Columbus*, the only whaleback designed as a passenger boat. The commission, from an entity that McDougall created as the Columbian Whaleback Steamship Company, had no trouble selling stock, and the owners included John D. Rockefeller. The conglomerate's anticipation of the crowds that eventually flooded Chicago's World's Columbian Exposition in 1893 proved a good bet. Over the stable hull were two sleek decks supported by seven ovoid turrets. As commercial profiles were increasingly important, the *Christopher Columbus* became the immediately identifiable symbol of progress and represented "space age" design in the era of Jules Verne and H. G. Wells. Launched after only three months of construction, it received preferential docking while running from downtown Chicago to the fairgrounds at Jackson Park. The builders promised room for five thousand passengers carried at twenty miles per hour and claimed it could load and unload them in less than five minutes. Eventually restricted to four thousand passengers, the craft and its crew made the seven-mile round trips in about an hour. By the time the ship was sold to the Goodrich Transit Company in 1894 for the Chicago-Milwaukee run, it is estimated that it had carried about two million passengers in a few months.

McDougall-built vessels were launched on all four North American coasts, as well as in Great Britain—forty whalebacks altogether. Most enjoyed long lives. The *Christopher Columbus* became an icon of the greatest North American "world's fair" of its era, well-recorded in the press and in the memories of millions as the ship-of-the-future. That prediction went unfulfilled, although the unusual profile was popular along the western Lake Michigan shore until 1933.

One experiment that proved less than successful was installation of a "Whittaker propulsion system" on the Goodrich steamer *Victor* in 1861. Little is known about the design, but it seems to have involved mounting a 10-foot propeller on either side of the craft's hull, where paddlewheels were normally situated. The propellers were vertically aligned abeam and oriented to exert thrust aft, as normally mounted stern propellers do. Each propeller had its own engine and boiler, but the Whittaker system was unable to move the ship faster than ten miles per hour—too slow to be competitive on any of the Goodrich routes. By law the ship was required to carry additional engineers for the second engine. Novelty was trumped by practicality, and by spring of the following year a standard beam engine and paddlewheels had replaced the fantastic power plant. As if to erase this failure from the public's memory, Goodrich renamed the ship *Sunbeam* and placed it on the Chicago-Superior route. The ship was lost in 1863 near Ontonagon, Michigan, with only a single survivor.[7]

At 274 feet and nearly two thousand tons, the D&C's *City of Cleveland* of 1886 successfully and competitively heralded the second palace steamer era. With the launches of the *North Land* and the *North West*, at nearly 360 feet, the steamboat business was closing the century on a high note. Meanwhile, Canadians and Americans were still finding their identity. With predominantly European roots, their immigrant populations had stopped looking across the Atlantic for their social and professional cues. They reveled in their new homes and strove to integrate themselves into the North American mainstream. Overall, the sacrifices required to start anew during the late Victorian period produced stalwart, driven, and very frugal people. Yet jobs paid well, and part of each budget was allocated for leisure and entertainment. This included, perhaps, a Sunday afternoon cruise or even an adventure to Chicago.

The Gilded Age had been good to the lake services. Thousands of vessels stayed busy, and iron ore cargoes grew as lumber receded.

Schooners became "consorts" in the tow of tugs and hookers, carrying more tonnage for less money. The switch from sailing craft to steam barges discounted the skills that many men had spent a lifetime honing. Trimming, reefing, and splicing became lost arts in less than a generation. This was not particular to the lakes. It happened on saltwater, too, but the Great Lakes represented a highly competitive market, and sail faded quickly. The schooners were not heavily built and soon became surplus. Men who were put out of work found kindred souls on the docks, and union activity, which began along Michigan's Saginaw River, would grow in the new century.

PART III

Steam Navigation in
the Twentieth Century

CHAPTER 11

A New Century Brings Change

Around the Great Lakes and around the world, the twentieth century came in with a bang. Recovery from the 1893 crash was nearly complete, and the national political tenor was balanced toward stable. The global economy experienced several years of upward growth, and the manufacturing engine was churning. The New Year in 1901 was rich with justifiable optimism and high hopes for the new decade. Century boxes were buried with messages for future generations. Detroit Mayor William Maybury asked in a typical manner:

> We travel at a rate of speed not dreamed of [in 1801]. The power of electricity has been marvelously applied, while compressed air and other agencies are now undergoing promising experiment.
> We travel by railroad and with steam power from Detroit to . . . New York City by several routes in less than twenty hours. How much faster are you traveling? How much further have you annihilated time and space, and what agencies are you employing to which we are now strangers?[1]

Technology altered the world in directions only dreamed of in children's books. Music embraced a new syncopation, dance and ballet were finding diverse expression, and publishers gambled on everything from industrial exposés to children's magazines like *American Boy*. Presidential politics became aggressive, shaking nineteenth-century norms, and new factions gained traction on the political landscape.

As if to define the chasm between the two centuries, the Victorian

Detroit passenger wharves on a busy day, c. 1910. (Photograph courtesy of the Detroit Historical Society Collection.)

era suddenly became the Edwardian. The frail icon, Queen Victoria, died on January 22, 1901. King Edward VII, a large and energetic man, came to symbolize the new era in Europe. Edwardian stylistic influences, in vogue for a few decades, had a progressive effect on dress, literature, theatre, and politics. Yet the economy relied on a rigid class code that rapidly dissolved after World War I in the century's second decade.

The United States also experienced sudden political change. President William McKinley, freshly into his second term, was in Buffalo attending the Pan-American Exposition. Only nine months after Queen Victoria's death, McKinley was assassinated while greeting people at a reception. He died eight days later. Vice President Theodore Roosevelt, scion of a wealthy New York family and a recent hero in the Spanish American War, assumed the presidency. During the recent election cycle, he had carried on a vigorous whistle-stop campaign and brought an ebullient style to the stump, which subsequent politicians emulated.

Success in the war with Spain through 1899 vaulted the United States into position as a world power. Big business and big money appeared to be guiding the ship of state, and, despite the political upheaval, Americans met the new decade with optimism. A new wave of immigration and steady growth in the consumer sector created a positive business climate. Yet within a few years, antitrust litigation, transportation competition, union agitation, and explosive industrialization changed the operating criteria for steamboats, especially on the Great Lakes. By the second decade of the century, the La Follette and Jones acts bolstered some segments of the nation's maritime economy but had long-term implications for freshwater operations.

The beginning of the century saw European powers forced away from colonialism, even as the United States was expanding its reach. British interests struggled through the second Boer War in Africa and faced challenges against their claims on the Indian peninsula and China. Americans quickly conquered Spanish holdings in two hemispheres entirely through naval finesse, previously the sole sphere of the British admiralty. During these first few years of the new century, political assassinations increased, Russia and Turkey were plunged into revolution, and working classes around the world struck for better employment conditions. Capital interests retrenched.

This was the decade in which Einstein and Freud defined relativity and sexuality, women demanded voting rights, and the National Association for the Advancement of Colored People was organized in America. Accelerating reactions to all events were new media—magazines, film, records, and radio—which generated robust consumer demand for entertainment and information. *The Great Train Robbery*, the first commercially successful American motion picture, debuted in 1903. The first baseball World Series was also held in 1903. The New York subway opened in 1904. Electric washing machines were introduced, and telephones became common in many homes and businesses by 1905. W. K. Kellogg signed his first box of corn flakes in 1906.

Developments in transportation were equally auspicious. Automobiles graduated from curiosity to sport to fad and gradually to commonplace. Steam and electricity were quickly outpaced by the internal combustion engine. In 1915 Detroit had already staked its claim as America's motor capital, boasting more than one hundred businesses involved in automobile manufacturing. There were hundreds more across the nation. Detroit and Ohio communities experimented with concrete roadways in 1911 and found them to be superior to asphalt or gravel. The Good Roads Movement, a concept developed by cyclists in the 1880s, was adopted by automobile enthusiasts. The Lincoln Highway, conceived in 1912 by Indiana entrepreneur Carl G. Fisher, founder of the Indianapolis Motor Speedway, and promoted by Henry B. Joy of the Packard Motor Company, was a national road from New York to San Francisco that was completed only a year later. It was a rough road, but it paved the way for Americans to conceptualize a national highway system.

Flying was introduced during this period, though it never became a serious threat to steamboats. Air travel was beyond the budget of most tourists until the 1930s and did not impact the commercial travel market until after steamboat travel had waned. However, flying melded with other emerging technologies to draw the public's attention away from the classic and toward the future. Over the early decades of the twentieth century, the grandest ships were, like railroads, glorious symbols of bygone days. The traveling public in many areas was reliant on steamships until the 1920s and considered them viable transportation options until after World War II. An industry that had long relied on freight revenues pivoted when passenger traffic became its prime business.

Three developments related to freight transfer stand out: the introduction of the commercial truck in about 1902, the introduction of the Ford Model T in 1908, and the invention of the semitrailer in about 1916. The history of the Model T is well-documented. Henry Ford made mobility affordable for most Americans. People began to travel long distances overland, perhaps twenty or thirty miles on a Sunday drive. It became a fad. Middle-class families and even the wealthy went auto camping. Only a decade before, such excursions were unthinkable. By 1906 *Bowen's Automobile and Sportsmen's Guide for Michigan* was available, offering maps by county, town information, and geographic features. Soon afterward, *Popular Mechanics Automobile Tourist's Handbook No. 1* offered plans and suggestions for camping, adding to offerings by Rand McNally and the various American Automobile Association affiliates.

Particularly important to steamboat operators was the introduction of trucks and semitrailers. Initially, trucks and trailers proved to be wonderfully efficient at getting steamer cargoes off of the docks and to their local destinations. However, as roads improved, trucks and semitrailers began competing for long-haul freight between ports, a battle that trucks eventually won. The *Marine Review* in 1906 noted, "Though the passenger traffic is increasing of late, it is more exacting than it used to be, and a steamer to be successful in the business must be a floating hotel, with an immense crew and a build that does not favor the carrying of much freight, even when the passenger traffic is light."[2]

Despite these challenges, the first fifteen years of the twentieth century saw a fleet of new ships launched on the freshwater seas. Frank E. Kirby had closed the previous century with his riverboat masterpiece the *Tashmoo*, built for the White Star Line, and he opened the

1900s with Graham & Morton's *Puritan*. The year 1902 was notable for the launch of four Kirby passenger boats: the *Greyhound* for Ashley Dustin; the propeller *Columbia* for the Detroit, Belle Isle & Windsor Ferry Company's Bob-Lo Island excursions; and two Detroit & Buffalo Steamboat Company workhorses, the *Eastern States* and *Western States*. Additionally, Northern Navigation Company launched the elegant *Huronic*. The year following saw splashes for Dunkley-Williams' the *City of South Haven*, the grand *Tionesta* for the Anchor Line, and the ill-fated *Eastland*. The year 1904 saw the launch of the *Missouri* for the Northern Michigan Transportation Company; 1905 brought the *Tionesta*'s sister ship, the *Juniata*; and 1906 brought the Detroit, Belle Isle & Windsor ferry *Brittania*, Lake Muskoka's iconic *Sagamo*, and the popular transient *Theodore Roosevelt*, which was owned by several companies throughout its career. Over the next nine years, eighteen iconic passenger vessels of this final era hit the water: the ships *City of Cleveland (III)*, *Keewatin*, *Rapids King*, *Hamonic*, *United States*, *Octorara*, *Alabama*, *Canadiana*, *Ste. Claire*, *Noronic*, *North American*, *Seeandbee*, *Put-in-Bay*, *Saguenay*, *City of Detroit III*, *City of Grand Rapids*, *South American*, and *Nevada*.

Then the building stopped. It wasn't until 1923–24 that the *Greater Detroit* and *Greater Buffalo* were built for the D&C line. Tremendous floating palaces, these two boats were the largest side-wheeled craft ever built, with a single exception: Isambard Brunel's *Great Eastern*, built a century earlier to lay the transatlantic cable. These were the last and the greatest. It is clear that when the century opened the steamship business was highly competitive but healthy. In 1915 the fleet peaked, a dozen years before the industrial wealth of the major Great Lakes cities reached its full potential. A number of developments converged at this point, which determined the future of the steamship industry.

Technology and communication continued to enhance the navigational tools available to mariners. In 1903 the American side of the lakes had a total of 446 lighthouses and beacons, 10 lightships, and 709 buoys. That same year, Canada installed 44 new lighthouses, 23 pole lights, and 9 new buoys. The Canadian Department of Marine and Fisheries managed Ontario lights after Confederation in 1863 and thereafter transferred them to several departments. The task was finally assigned to the newly formed Canadian Coast Guard in 1962. The US Lighthouse Service was merged with the US Coast Guard in 1939, a branch of the military that had resulted from the 1915 melding of the Life-Saving Service and the Revenue Cutter Service.[3]

The river steamer *Tashmoo*, c. 1901. (Courtesy of the Detroit Photographic Company Collection, Library of Congress.)

From a propulsion standpoint, engineers began experimenting with diesel engines, and by 1913 there were seventy-five ships worldwide sporting this type of direct propulsion, including four freighters on the Great Lakes. During that same year, a diesel-electric-driven ship, the *Tynemount*, was launched in England for use in the Canadian canal trade. This propulsion system gradually became the norm on the lakes but only as the coal vessels went to the breaker's yards. Replacing coal was too expensive for most, and nearly every passenger carrier retained its bunkered boilers and expansion engines until the end. Only the Georgian Bay Line cruise ships and a few excursion boats could boast the clean, soot-free experience of oil-fired boilers. In an effort to reassure the traveling public, fire suppression systems were installed on passenger ships, including fire doors and sprinklers.[4]

The most important safety technologies introduced to the world's maritime industry were wireless telegraphy and telephony. Available

The propeller *City of South Haven*, c. 1904. (Courtesy of the Detroit Historical Society Collection.)

commercially at the beginning of the century, radio signals allowed vessels to exchange important information with other ships and shore stations over ever-increasing distances. Advanced weather and hazard information instantly made maritime travel safer and more popular. Travelers felt secure with the ability to receive or send important news. The advent of radio was the first great electronic advance of the twentieth century across the globe, particularly for people at sea.

Experiments had been underway for decades on both sides of the Atlantic. The first practical, open-ocean applications occurred on naval vessels and were rapidly embraced by the premier passenger carriers of Germany, Britain, and the United States. The Italian scientist Guglielmo Marconi was able to secure patent leverage in Europe, and then in Canada and the United States. Marconi's early transatlantic successes took place at Canadian stations in Newfoundland and Nova Scotia. It was from Table Head, near Glace Bay, Nova Scotia, that the first transatlantic message was transmitted to Poldhu, Cornwall, on December 15, 1902.[5]

The government of Canada invested $80,000 in the Marconi station at Glace Bay and continued to invest in marine radio stations along the

The propeller *Juniata*, c. 1920. (Courtesy of the Detroit Historical Society Collection.)

coast, with six in operation by 1904. Marine insurers encouraged the investment. Safer vessels decreased the possibility of losses. By 1907 commercial traffic had been established and transatlantic communication by radio telegraph was routine. On the Great Lakes, in 1912, the Marconi Wireless Telegraph Company had a station operating at Port Arthur and the following year opened facilities at Toronto, Port Burwell, Sarnia, Midland, Tobermory, and Sault Sainte Marie, Ontario. Additionally, legislation passed in the Canadian Parliament that required vessels carrying fifty or more passengers between ports two hundred miles apart to install wireless equipment.[6]

On the American side of the lakes, representatives of the Marconi company spread across the region attempting to secure contracts with municipalities and private investors to build new broadcast facilities. Inventive forces throughout the region competed against Marconi patents, sharing "first-in" rights. It was an open field, and one of the most successful men in the vanguard was Thomas E. Clark of Detroit.

In 1902 Clark was involved in the first successful marine radio experiment, equipping a ferry that normally relayed passengers across

The ferry *Promise* broadcasting progress via radio telegraph while towing the unfinished hull of the *Greyhound* up the Detroit River, 1902. (Photograph courtesy of the Detroit Historical Society Collection.)

the river between Windsor and Detroit. The ferry *Promise* was tasked with towing the new steamer *Greyhound* from the Detroit Ship Building Company's Wyandotte yard upriver to the Detroit Dry Dock facilities at the foot of Orleans Street for final fit-out. According the *Marine Record*, the telegraphic receiving instruments were set up in the pavilion of the ferry company at the foot of Woodward Avenue: "From the time the boat left the dock at 7 o'clock until she arrived at Wyandotte, a distance on an air line of about sixteen miles, communication was kept up at intervals of a few seconds. The condition of the ice, the boat's progress, etc., being regularly reported of the entire distance."[7]

A month later the D&C's *City of Detroit II* tested a Clark wireless telegraph system, installed to great success by the Electric Service and Appliance Company of Detroit. On election night in 1906, Clark's company reportedly provided D&C customers with the latest midterm election returns. In 1908 Clark was broadcasting voice transmissions

The steamer *Seeandbee*. (Courtesy of the Detroit Historical Society Collection.)

from a promontory near Alpena to the *City of Alpena*, expanding his relationship with the D&C. Competition was fierce between the two largest corporate patent-holders: Marconi and inventor Lee DeForest. Clark soon joined forces with several other entrepreneurs to form the United Wireless Telegraph Company, based in Chicago, which secured contracts with Graham & Morton and others. Clark was swept into the tumult of the early radio business and shifted his focus to launching Detroit commercial station WWJ. Tracing its roots to an amateur station created by teenager Michael Lyons in 1922 at the behest of *Detroit News* owner William Scripps, today this station lays claim to being America's oldest provider of regularly scheduled commercial radio programing, albeit originally unlicensed. Clark was instrumental in developing its state-of-the-art technology.[8]

By 1909 all of the D&C boats carried registered wireless telegraph stations, as did Goodrich's *Virginia* and *Carolina* and Erie & Western Transit Co.'s *Tionesta* and *Juniata*. Over the next few years, most of the premier passenger vessels on the Great Lakes followed suit. Cargo carriers had less incentive to install expensive radio equipment, but

The steamer *City of Cleveland III*. (Courtesy of the Detroit Historical Society Collection.)

they clearly saw its advantages after the disastrous storm of 1913. With twelve ships and more than 250 men lost, another twenty-six vessels stranded, and dozens of hulls sustaining severe damage, the benefits of ship-to-ship communication and timely weather reports was reinforced. Without radios a captain's best guides were the flags at various shore stations—if they were close enough to see. Gale warnings might be seen from lifesaving stations, and primitive weather maps were available at ports or through ports like Sault Sainte Marie or Detroit. Of the hundreds of commercial bulk vessels afloat on the lakes, only two ships of the Shenango Furnace fleet—the *Col. James M. Schoonmaker* and the *William M. Snyder*—had wireless operators that could report the incredible conditions of November 1913. Because of radios, only one passenger boat suffered. Most of the bulk fleet didn't receive radio capability until the early 1920s.[9]

As evidenced by Clark's experiments with voice transmission in 1908, wireless telephones came on the heels of the wireless telegraph, but they were not widely known until after World War I. Telephone, or voice-to-voice radio, did not require a trained telegrapher, and, in the words of one promotional piece, "used in conjunction with the enormous existing land system of wire telephones, will make it possible for persons either on the shores of the lakes or hundreds of miles away, to talk with officers or passengers on any of the vessels engaged in the lake trade." Whether a business executive or vacationing mother, this reassuring connectivity raised the traveler's comfort level.[10]

CHAPTER 12

The Lake Cruising Experience

ourism was the life blood of the industry in the twentieth century. Initially, it involved day trips for those who enjoyed a little extra income and free time. As Americans became increasingly mobile, their affinity for travel created a new vacation industry. Elegant resorts and humble tourist cabins sprouted near mountains, streams, and lakes from Florida to Maine and west to Minnesota. The natural beauty and historical attractions offered on the Great Lakes—as well as the moderate summers—made the lakes themselves a draw. Steamship operators adroitly followed the trend and aggressively adapted to the market. Initially, some companies became financially involved in resort hotels and picnic parks, but few stayed that course. Most concentrated on providing a first-class cruising experience and transporting people between exciting cities, small cottage communities, or stark wilderness—wherever they wanted to go.

Ship design was refined to address clearly identifiable travel patterns, which fell roughly into four categories: excursion ferries, car ferries (both rail and auto), palace steamers, and palace propellers. Excursion ferries carried large numbers of people for a few minutes or maybe a few hours. Cross-lake rail ferries on Lake Erie and Lake Michigan served two purposes: they carried loads of about twenty-eight railcars or several dozen automobiles on their main decks and provided passenger accommodations on a cabin deck above. Of the pre–World War II fleet, only the *Pere Marquette 17* and the *Pere Marquette 18* offered substantial cabin accommodations. Most offered day-trip amenities such as lounges and viewing salons and a few private rooms. The term *palace* has been reintroduced here because the grandeur is reminiscent of the antebellum ships that first bore the name. These side-wheelers and propellers utilized their interior space differently but strove to give passengers elegance beyond what many could afford.[1]

Excursion ferries found their greatest expression along the St. Clair River north of Detroit. The *Tashmoo* was a favorite and exemplified the river excursion class. Sleeping quarters were unnecessary except to house the professional crew. Indoor and outdoor deck space was optimized to accommodate transient clients and day passengers. On the *Tashmoo*, the entrance lobby herded the masses up broad staircases to second- and third-deck salons lined with windows. Good weather or bad, passengers could enjoy the vast panoramas offered along the St. Clair Flats. Typically, riders sat outdoors on folding, wooden deck chairs faced outward. Families, societies, and school groups rushed aboard once the gangway was opened, claiming their favorite spots. By the time the ship departed, chairs were ranked two or three deep along the ship's rail on all three decks so occupants could take in the passing scene. The *Tashmoo* had private parlors available, but most riverboats and ferries simply offered broad verandas running around the rail on each deck. Some people liked sitting in the front. Others only sat in the back. Some sat in the sun, others out of the wind. And then, if there was a good band, everyone faced inward toward the dance floor.

By contrast, the Lake Michigan excursion ships and day boats offered large open areas within a slimmer profile. The *Theodore Roosevelt* exemplified the propeller excursion boats and was a variation on the *Tashmoo* style. When guests came aboard the *Theodore Roosevelt*, they entered the purser's lobby, which occupied the middle half of the main deck. Occasionally used to store light cargo—by now the profitable fruit cargos of past decades were going to the railroads—this space generally served as a common room for boarding and disembarking. There was a bar near the bow to serve the crowd and crew's quarters behind a bulkhead in the forecastle. Along the ship's centerline running toward the stern, twin grand staircases led upward to the spar deck. Venting for the smokestacks was enclosed within two steel-walled mechanical rooms aft of the staircase. Still farther back, another central enclosure created the upper portion of the engine room. Windows around its sides and back allowed passengers to observe the intricate, quadruple-expansion steam engine and watch the engineers at work. Under prime conditions, the 4,500-horsepower engine would drive the ship at an incredible twenty-four miles per hour.

Behind the engine viewing was an enclosed dining room, occupying about a third of the deck space. Centered inside the entrance doors to either side was a wide central staircase with a substantial balustrade and a handrail up the center, leading to the spar deck. To the back of the nicely paneled and painted dining area, at the very stern, was a mechanical room used for docking and emergency steering access. Just in front of that space were the food preparation closets, containing two refrigerators and two dumbwaiters connected to the galley on the deck below. The buffet was horseshoe shaped, with utensils and hot entrées to port, coffee and beverages to starboard, and salads, fruits, and desserts toward the back in the middle. Patrons sat at square pedestal tables that were bolted to the deck. Tablecloths prevented dishes and drinks from sliding if the boat rolled while underway.

Upstairs the spar deck was roughly divided into quarters. Occupying the aft quarter was the enclosed ballroom, a vast wood-floored public space where dancing and music entertained hundreds at a time. The orchestra occupied a small stage set into the half circle defined by the fantail. The room's vast windows, running from wainscoting to ceiling, could be pushed open from the bottom for ventilation or closed on cool or blustery days. Beneath the windows padded deck seats attached to the wall could be folded up or down as needed. Structural posts and vents were painted to blend with the metal beams overhead.

Forward of the ballroom was a long salon covering half the length of the vessel. Along the center were beautifully disguised mechanical rooms, as below, and the staircases led to decks above and below. Also in the center were public toilets and a prominent soda fountain. Upholstered benches lined the outboard walls of the salon, with small, American-hung windows placed at regular intervals for viewing and ventilation. At the forward end of the salon were candy and souvenir counters to either side of the grand staircase. Along both outer rails were outdoor deck spaces offering moderate protection from the wind and sun. A bench seat ran the length of the narrow walkway. Access to the salon was through doors at either end and in the middle. At the very front of the spar deck, occupying the final quarter, was the observation room. Enclosed in the same manner as the ballroom, the walls were lined with booth seating, and the deck was dominated by an octagonal bar.

Guests who ventured farther up the grand staircase, turning to the right or left in the ascent, found themselves on the promenade deck. True to its name, it was an open, covered deck that allowed travelers to wander the entire perimeter of the ship. Down the center, running nearly the length of the deck, was a continuous cabin house. Near the

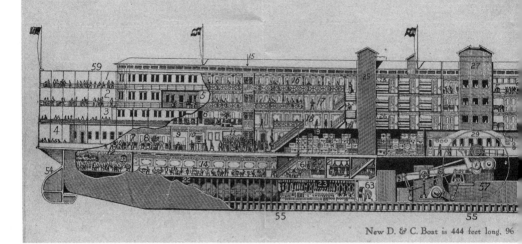

The Latest and Greatest Prod

STEAMER "CITY

In Commissi

New D. & C. Boat is 444 feet long. 96

KEY TO DIAGRAM

1. Upper Deck
2. Gallery Deck
3. Promenade Deck
4. Main Deck
*5. Private Veranda from Parlors
6. Grand Salon
7. Men's After Cabin
8. Ladies' After Cabin
9. Switchboard for 500 Telephones
10. Purser's Office
11. Grand Lobby or Social Hall
12. Venetian Garden Buffet
14. Grand Dining Room, Orlop Deck
15. Electric Passenger Elevator
16. Exterior Upper Deck Staterooms
17. Gallery Deck, Main Salon
18. Grand Stairway
19. Baggage Room
20. Pantry

21. Galley or Kitchen
22. Fresh Water Filters
23. Refrigerators
24. Writing Nooks
25. Washed Air Ventilator
26. Interior View of Stateroom
27. Engine Ventilator and Observation
28. Convention Hall
29. Engine Room
30. Cabin, Promenade Deck
31. Smoke Stacks, 75 feet high, 8½ feet wide
32. Stack Casing
33. Boilers in Fire Hole
34. Smoking Room
35. Upper Deck Staterooms
36. Luxurious Bridal Chamber
37. Bath Room with Shower
38. Interior of Staterooms

F CLEVELAND"

on 1908

ches wide and cost $1,250,000.00

39. Captain's Bridge	53. Electric Dynamo Room
40. Wireless Telegraph Station	54. Stern Rudder
41. Pilot's Quarters	55. Double Water Bottom, 1000
42. Captain's Parlor	Ton Capacity
43. Chart Room	56. Bow Rudder, with Steam
44. Music Room	Steering Gear
45. Wheel House	57. Triple Expansion Engine
46. Upper Deck, Forward	58. Dome Deck
47. Gallery Deck, Forward	59. Trunk Deck
48. Promenade Deck, Forward	60. Fire Place
49. 1000 Ton Freight Deck	61. Private Dining Room
50. Crew's Quarters	62. Ballast Water Tank, 100 Ton Capacity
51. Coal Bunker	63. Ventilating Engines for Washed Air
52. Steadying Tank to Prevent	
Seasickness	

Cutaway illustration of the steamer *City of Cleveland III*, 1907.
(Courtesy of the Detroit Historical Society Collection.)

bow was the radio room and sleeping accommodations for two radio men and eight bartenders. Aft of this were toilets for men and women, and still farther back were sixteen small staterooms for those who could afford privacy on the short runs from Chicago to Michigan City or Saugatuck. Permanent bench seating was provided along the rails and on more expansive decks at the bow and stern.

It should be noted that, similar to other passenger vessels, the *Theodore Roosevelt* went through many owners and structural changes. These descriptions are taken from plans drawn in 1936, toward the end of its career. Images of the ship over several years show that the ballroom and observation decks were initially open spaces protected only by canvas curtains. Additionally, the foredeck promenade was initially uncovered, and a Lido space on the aft boat deck was added for additional outdoor viewing. These changes were instituted as the traveling public matured in its tastes and expectations after 1906, when the ship was built. These expectations were fed by developments on the highly publicized ocean liners—the stunning *Lusitania* of 1907 was almost eight hundred feet long—but equally driven by the new breed of palace steamers on the lakes. The *City of Cleveland* of 1907, and later the *City of Detroit III* of 1912, defined the luxury that passengers came to expect.

A similar walk around the *City of Cleveland*, as with the *Theodore Roosevelt*, highlights the extent to which passengers were pampered and impressed. Of course, the *City of Cleveland* (later the *City of Cleveland III*) was a cruise ship, not an excursion boat, and this was clear from the moment its guests came aboard. At nearly 400 feet long, it was among the longest vessels ever built for lake service, only surpassed by the *City of Detroit III* (1912, 455.6 feet), the *Seeandbee* (1913, 484 feet), and the twins *Greater Detroit* (1923, 518.6 feet) and *Greater Buffalo* (1924, 518.6 feet). These all followed the general outline of the Frank E. Kirby boats built for the D&C and Cleveland & Buffalo concerns. Exploring the original layout of the *City of Cleveland* can, with minor variations, be an exploration of this entire design family. This boat boasted a number of firsts and deserves to be explored from stem to stern.

Walking downhill along Detroit's Wayne Street toward the D&C docks, pedestrians were generally high and dry on stone sidewalks about a dozen feet wide. Posts with electric lamps were reflected in large plate-glass windows on either side of the street. Dry goods, hardware, and grocery stores invited customers to shop. Above

each storefront, the panes of narrow windows were painted to advertise the businesses that occupied the upper floors: dentists, lawyers,
truss makers, piano teachers, and more. Stepping off of the stone curb,
pedestrians found a street made of rough asphalt beyond the gutter,
dusted with dirt, manure, and other detritus. Shipping houses, warehouses, and the bustling Wayne Hotel and Wayne Gardens signaled the
proximity of the waterfront and the busiest waterway in the world. To
the south, blocking the view of Canada across the river, were the broad
balconies of a four-story building, two huge smokestacks protruding
through the roof. Along the river, such smokestacks were not unusual.
The balconies were unique in this neighborhood, however, and identified this "building" as a Kirby-designed steamship, so immense that it
hardly moved in the current.

When designing a ship, Frank E. Kirby personally illustrated and
signed profile sketches for the investors to review. Stylistically unso-
phisticated as renderings, they are exacting and trustworthy as evidence of what Kirby thought represented the ideal commercial steamer. Airplanes were often included in his drawings, adding context and
association to his most modern creations. Typical Kirby ships had three
or four decks lined with windows and open promenade spaces. Kirby
ships appeared very lateral, giving them an illusion of speed.

The Wayne Gardens dancing pavilion put the ship into perspective
as one drew near. The Gardens was a steel-framed pavilion two stories
high with a peaked roof above and room for a thousand on the dance
floor below. The steel hull and planking of the sheer-sided *City of Cleveland* were painted black, as were most D&C boats. Above, the iron
posts and steel screening along the rail were glossy white, as were the
facing and trim of the upper three decks. The ship dwarfed the Gardens.

Excited travelers boarded the *City of Cleveland* through an entrance about halfway between the small paddlewheel box and the
rounded transom. Crossing the passenger gangway, guests left their
luggage with baggage handlers and stepped into an elegant entrance
lobby paneled in dark mahogany, with "pilasters and capitals in an-
tique gold and exquisite panels in marquetry" camouflaging the steel
bulkheads. The grand staircase led upward to the left, with a rounded
cavity in the ceiling that excited guests with views of the grand salon.
Just beyond was the polished filigree of the open passenger elevator to
the decks above, a D&C first and one of few on the lakes. Around this
lobby were offices and quarters for the purser, chief steward and chief
engineer. There was a bank of ten telephone booths available for long-
distance calls when the vessel was docked. To the right was a rounded

Frank E. Kirby's drawing for a proposed steamer for the D&C line, 1922. (Courtesy of the Detroit Historical Society Collection.)

alcove whose doors led to a ladies-only waiting room and toilet. Along the aft deck behind the ladies' cabin was a similar freshening-up cabin for men, accessed through exterior doors.

The lower deck, below the main deck, held a warren of living quarters for most of the staff, extensive housekeeping and provisioning storerooms, refrigerators, and the galley. To the rear of the kitchen was the main dining room and then the Venetian Garden Buffet. Decorated in an art nouveau style, the grand dining room featured oak sideboards, finished in a rich forest green, running the entire seventy-foot length of the room. Green floor tiles matched the cabinets throughout. White linen tablecloths were festooned with shining silver settings, reflecting light from the lanternlike "electroliers" hung above. Imposing newel posts flanked the stairway leading back to the main lobby.

A third of the vessel's length on this deck was allocated to eight Scotch boilers, coal bunkers, and a triple expansion, inclined steam engine made by the Detroit Shipbuilding Company. This deck's sole, or floor, was slightly below the waterline, but nearly every space had a porthole mounted at eye level, increasing ventilation and comfort during the summer months. Save for the dining room, most passengers never saw this deck. Likewise, the main deck was partly enclosed and meant to accommodate miscellaneous freight, generally crated items such as furniture and dry goods, loaded through various gangway ports along the ship's side. Crew's quarters, mess rooms, and storage closets lined the outer hull.[2]

The grand salon aboard the *City of Cleveland III*, c. 1907.
(Courtesy of the Detroit Photographic Company Collection,
Library of Congress.)

Convention Hall on the steamer *City of Cleveland III*, c. 1907. (Courtesy of the Detroit Photographic Company Collection, Library of Congress.)

Passengers proceeded from the purser's lobby up the grand staircase into the sumptuous grand salon. First-time visitors might find the visual experience overwhelming. Here, in the middle of a ship, was the grandeur of Versailles. The eye passed upward over three stories of balconies, receding as in a theatre. Elaborately carved railings complemented stunning cornices, moldings, and statuesque nymphs in a Louis XVI style. Oriole windows, mirrors, and large paintings visually enhanced and defined the upper levels. Heavy pearl gray Wilton carpets ran nearly the entire 390-foot length of the ship on all interior decks. Sculpted with moldings, the walls were painted with an ivory enamel, and the lofty ceiling, arching above two ranks of clerestory windows, was inset with broad oval panels painted pearl gray to echo the carpets below.

The Detroit & Cleveland Navigation Company printed an extensively illustrated brochure that ran to more than sixty pages, touting its new flagship. The description reads, "Scattered about [the grand salon] are luxurious settees of soft cushions, old rose colored and supported by frames in old gold, a color blend which is observed through the whole scheme of decoration. . . . Here are dainty carved desks and chairs in a cozy setting of more rich mahogany, carved screens and mirrors and softly shaded electric lights." The walls of the promenade deck, gallery deck, and upper deck were lined with doors leading to private sleeping cabins. Each bore an ivory-toned ceramic plaque with a room number and a beautiful brass door handle deeply stamped with the D&C logo. Into the keyhole went a heavy brass skeleton key bearing the cursive D&C insignia, with an attached brass medallion indicating the room number. Even-numbered cabins were to port, odd to starboard. Overall, there were 342 staterooms of different sizes and configurations. They all offered exposure to the grand salon or a window with a view; only the upper deck offered both. Each room boasted running water, a small sink with mirror, an intraship telephone handset, electric lights, an automatic fire alarm, and a fresh air ventilation system. All the beds on the boat were set transversely to the keel.[3]

Most rooms were modest, painted a gloss white with over-under mahogany bunks. The lower mattress was wider than the upper, offering a step, although a ladder was provided. A small, single-legged seat could be folded down from the wall if needed. The basin was in the corner, with a porthole or window above it for fresh air. Standard staterooms along the inner ring opening onto the grand salon were nearly uniform in size and amenities: slightly deeper than a six-foot bed, with enough room to open a door—roughly eight feet square. Windows of frosted glass opened onto the hallway that serviced the outward-facing rooms and took in the natural light that filtered down to the hall from clerestories set in the upper deck.

Those staterooms lining the outer edge of the boat came in a variety of configurations. A few were like those described above, but the majority of the standard rooms were "sistered" with an adjoining one: the bunks in one room would be outboard, and in the next room the bunks would be inboard. By means of this arrangement, each had a door opening onto the hallway and a window opening onto a lake view, as well as the standard amenities. It should be mentioned that the standard features—telephone, sink, fire alarm, and filtered and cooled ventilation—were only available in the finest hotels ashore. To later generations, such accommodations came to be considered spartan, particularly compared to midcentury motels and hotels offering en suite bathrooms, picture windows, and larger beds. Yet in 1907 small rooms were adequate, as people generally wandered the ship and enjoyed the public spaces.

The twenty upscale parlor rooms were beautifully decorated and contained standard-size brass bedsteads and deluxe mattresses. The walls were paneled and painted with murals of flowers. The ceiling was coved, inset with filigree, and also carried the flower motif. Each parlor had an adjoining bath or shower. (For most passengers, toilet facilities remained communal, with lavatories and water closets in cabins amidships.) The eight largest parlor rooms were set directly above the main gangway. They could be paired as suites, each with a private balcony and thickly upholstered settee.

At the front and back of the long salons on the promenade and gallery decks were bowed or bay windows, with doors to either side leading to relatively small fore-and-aft viewing areas. Narrow, crew-only walkways on both decks followed the outer rails, connecting bow and stern.

Those interested in the finest views proceeded up any of a number of stairways to the upper deck. Ten lifeboats dominated the outer deck amidships. To the front and back were wide areas where chaise longues and chairs could be arranged as guests wished. The center cabin house ran from the captain's quarters beneath the bridge to the afterdeck. Cabins for the mates, pilots, radio operators, and radio gear had exterior egress, while the passenger cabins immediately aft were accessed from the interior upper balcony of the salon. These cabins were much like the inner-ring cabins just below them but with a lake view. Amidships on the upper deck was a large social cabin surrounding an elegantly disguised vent stack. Windows lined the port and starboard sides of the room, dubbed Convention Hall, offering a view twenty miles in either direction from fifty feet above the lake's surface. As in the main lobby, dark woods framed the windows and defined the arched ceiling. Upholstered wing chairs were spaced around substantial mahogany tables, and padded benches lined the room. Two carved, beshielded lions guarded the stairway, over which Neptune and his seahorse minions commanded a roomwide mural. Floor tiles set in a checkered pattern and heraldic shields below the clerestory windows gave the hall the feel of a men's club. Indeed, that part of the cabin was dedicated as a smoking room, socially considered a male-only activity.

Separate rooms, called writing nooks, were reserved for ladies on each deck. A portion of the forward salon on the gallery deck was dedicated as a music room, with a piano and, in a few years, a Victrola. There was a large bookstore located on the promenade deck to address guests' reading, stationery, and souvenir needs. Closets, lockers, and storerooms on each deck supplied a brigade of parlor maids, cabin maids, porters, waiters, and cooks.

Technological innovation in pursuit of customer comfort and safety defined the construction parameters of the vessel, which was built under the direction of Frank Jeffrey, general manager of the Detroit Shipbuilding Company. Comfort, of course, was addressed with every padded chair and air-conditioned stateroom throughout the craft. However, the most important feature installed to provide passengers with an exemplary travel experience was something they never saw. Set amidships forward of the coal bunker was a steadying tank capable of holding one hundred tons of water. This extra bulk, in conjunction with the two tons of ballast that could be pumped into the ten compartments of the double-bottomed hull, served to steady the ship in rough seas. Promotional material all but guaranteed that seasickness was a thing of the past.

From a safety standpoint, the double-bottomed hull also served to allay sinking in the event that the ship grounded badly in the shallow channels and harbors in which it operated. Perhaps the most significant improvement in the public's mind was the automatic sprinkler system for fire suppression installed throughout the boat. Coupled with the automatic fire alarms installed in every stateroom, the D&C line far exceeded what the US Coast Guard required of steamboats in order to put the traveling public at ease. Fire-related accidents in the twentieth century became rare, with the awful exception of the *Noronic* tragedy in 1949, discussed later.

Palace propellers, like the steamers, were being built with modern equipment and accommodating public spaces. Radios were installed, fire systems were included, and lifeboats were added. Ships of the Canadian Pacific Railroad, the *Keewatin* and the *Assiniboia*, were beautifully decorated in a manner more restrained than the D&C's newest vessels. The carpets kept beautifully upholstered furniture from sliding in rough seas. Flatware and china in the dining room bore the line's insignia, the silver was polished, and the parquet floor gleamed. Elegant mahogany accented every room, just not as much of it. Similarly, the Anchor Line's trio—*Tionesta*, *Juniata*, and *Octorara*—were tasteful and rich but did not resemble Versailles. The *Noronic* surpassed its Northern Navigation Company fleet mate, the *North West*, to become the longest Great Lakes propeller in 1915 at 362 feet (by comparison, the 1912 *City of Detroit III* was 455 feet). The Georgian Bay Navigation Company's *North American* and *South American* offered the lakes' most streamlined and understated interiors, surviving on the appreciation of traveling on a ship, not a floating eighteenth-century French palace.

The lower profiles of propeller steamers offered only one level of open balcony in its grand salons, similar to those in some of the smaller paddlers. Staterooms were configured much like the inner ring of rooms on the *City of Cleveland*. Special parlor rooms were included to accommodate bridal parties and more particular guests. No matter the interior, the real attraction of a Great Lakes cruise was the maritime experience and the majesty of the lakes themselves.

S o what did people come to see?
    In the opening years of the twentieth century, the continent's natural beauty moved the populace in both the United States and Canada to embrace the expansion of a national and provincial park system. Americans and Canadians understood, based on the tremendous leaps west in the previous few decades, that the frontier was not impermeable to civilization. Those who could afford it made a priority of traveling to enjoy the finite wilderness—while it lasted. The Great Lakes offered myriad opportunities to be surprised and enraptured, at a price that was within the reach of many. The four-day round trip from Detroit to Mackinac Island cost $7.00, including cabin and meals, or about 1 percent of Michigan's median household income in 1910. A century later, by comparison, the equivalent percentage of a Michigan worker's salary could not buy two nights at the island's Grand Hotel, including two meals.[4]

Affordability was a principal draw. Then there was the majesty. Any discussion of the region naturally slides into a string of superlatives. Its physical features are diverse, encompassing a number of climates and soils, from temperate woods and prairies in the south to the deep and rocky boreal forests in the north. The Great Lakes Basin, defined by the watershed that eventually sends water into the St. Lawrence River, covers more than 295,000 square miles.[5] When complemented by tracts outside the watershed that depend on the Great Lakes, the commercial basin becomes much larger. The five lakes have 94,250 square miles of surface area. In concert with hundreds of thousands of inland lakes and streams, the system represents 85 percent of the continent's freshwater.[6]

In geological terms, the region's surface features are both new and ancient but always stark and dramatic. A molten sea of lava five hundred million years ago gradually became a shallow saltwater sea. Whales swam where woolly mammoths later wandered. Polar ice caps several miles thick poured a frozen mass southward five separate times over several millennia. Each Ice Age sent massive glacial fingers to scour through the softest, most pliable rock strata. Harder basalt and granite layers forced the solid, frozen chisels to yield, but not before leaving their mark. The glaciers' southern advances stopped at a line scribed on the land just below the lower reaches of Lakes Erie and Michigan and drawn westward nearly to the Rocky Mountains. As each onslaught waned, various rivers and lakes were formed to hold and divert the receding waters. Early formations of Lake Michigan and Lake Erie drained to the south through the Mississippi River. After the last advance, Lake Erie was the first to take its current form roughly ten thousand years ago. Lake Ontario found its shores about four millennia later, fed in part by the nascent waters of Lake Huron. The northern lakes gradually filled out about the time that Rome was founded. Around their shores lay alluvial detritus ranging from rock debris to highly fertile soils and loam. Below the lakes surface are the remains of mighty rivers and waterfalls rivaling those of Niagara.

Each of the lakes was left with distinct characteristics and features to catch the adventurer's eye. Lake Superior is the deepest at 1,332 feet. Ancient rock formations line the entire coast, southern outcroppings of the Laurentian Plateau, which underlies central and eastern Canada. Dramatic cliffs formed by mineralogical panoply ranging from weathered limestone to solid basalt offer mariners few natural harbors or friendly beaches. Superior's 31,700-square-mile surface occasionally freezes shore to shore during the winter, clearing sometime in June for a brief summer. Snow flurries fly through the pine forests again in September. Towns along Superior's southern edge usually get more than a hundred inches of snow each year. Twice that is an average winter in some areas. The northern shore gets less snow and even less sun. Historically, the lake's surface temperature averages 40°F, but at a depth of 100 feet it hovers just above freezing.[7]

The voyage around the lake was popular, but there were few ports on the north shore. Fishing clubs and modest gold-mining towns prompted occasional steamers to stop. But most of the traffic ran between Sault Sainte Marie and the western ports: Munising, Marquette, Houghton and Hancock, Eagle Harbor, Ontonagon, Ashland, Superior, Duluth, Two Rivers, Grand Portage, and Port William/Port Arthur (eventually renamed Two Harbors). This northern voyage was rugged and rustic, but it held elements of the same northern allure that captivated writers and artists heading to Alaska later.

At the other end of the spectrum is Lake Erie. Like Superior, Erie can be rambunctious. Southernmost, it is also the shallowest with an average depth is 62 feet, and much of it is shallower. The prevailing winds in upper central North America usually blow from west to east. Since Lake Erie has the same orientation, prolonged gales over this shallow basin make Erie the lake with a short fuse. The natural harbors are shallow river mouths and deltas spaced periodically along the south shore. The north shore enjoys almost no secure shelter except for two significant, marshy dunes—Point Pelee and Long Point—which project far into the lake. Many vessels have been surprised by their low but dangerous silhouettes. A number of islands in the western basin provide both shelter and navigational obstacles. Located a few hours from Cleveland, Detroit, and Toledo, the Erie Islands became a huge tourist draw. This archipelago was a destination for all but the largest Lake Erie steamers. On the southern mainland were resorts along Cedar Point and Sandusky Bay. Farther east, Erie, Buffalo, and Port Colborne were major ports. Port Dover, Maitland, Port Stanley, Monroe, Lorraine, and Ashtabula supported modest fishing and shipbuilding enterprises.

Lake Ontario has a geographic orientation similar to that of Lake Erie but is vastly deeper. The smallest of the lakes in surface area, it is second only to Superior in average depth at 283 feet. Its shores share elements of its Laurentian birth with the northern lakes, yet the temperate climate associated with the lakes allows vineyards and orchards to flourish throughout the lowlands. There are a number of natural harbors, and to the east the Thousand Islands lie at the head of the St. Lawrence River, one of the continent's premier archipelagos. At the western end, between Lake Erie and Lake Ontario, runs the Niagara Escarpment. The final southern projection of the Laurentian Shield, this ridge of dolomite rises about 200 feet from the surrounding bedrock.

An observer in space could trace the Niagara Escarpment as it stretches in a crescent to the north and west, through the Bruce Peninsula, Manitoulin Island, Mackinac Island, the cliffs at St. Ignace, Wisconsin's Door Peninsula, and the midcontinental moraines. The eastern end tracks down into the Finger Lakes of New York, but not before allowing the Niagara River to carve a magnificent gorge and breathtaking falls into its face. Niagara Falls has remained among America's premier tourist attractions for two centuries. To the north across the lake sits Toronto, formerly called York, Canada's largest city. St. Catharines is the Lake Ontario egress of the Welland Canal. Mississauga and Hamilton are western industrial and rail ports. Far to the east lies Kingston, longtime home to the Canadian government fleet on the lakes, as well as the Royal Military College and Queens College, established in 1841.

Sackets Harbor, Oswego, and Rochester are historic towns along the southern New York State shore.

Lake Michigan's surface area places it as the fifth-largest lake in the world, and number three among the Great Lakes. Running in a north-south arc for three hundred miles, the lake sits laterally to the prevailing winds. It has an average depth just four feet shy of Lake Ontario's at 279 feet. Perhaps the least rocky of the lakes, this basin has a perimeter of sand and clay. To the west and north, final evidence of the Niagara structure fades through the Door Peninsula and inland moraines. The eastern and northern shores have the world's largest freshwater dune system, stretching up the coast from the lake's base to the Upper Peninsula. Besides creating an exquisite beach recreation environment, this well-drained soil extends up to a hundred miles inland, encouraging agriculture in a temperate lakeside location. These factors result in the region's two most important economic drivers: tourism and significant fruit and vegetable production. The importance of these markets to the steamship industry was discussed at length in the previous section, but it should be noted here that, while farm freight gradually abandoned the steamships for railcars and trucks, the tourism radiating from Chicago and Milwaukee held strong throughout this final era. Seasonal resort towns were firmly established as summer destinations for generations of Americans. In the early twenty-first century, Michigan is the most populated of the lakes, with large metropolitan areas to the south and recreational homes lining its perimeter shoulder to shoulder.[8]

Lake Huron features the most diversity in many regards. At its southern end, sand beaches complement a moderate climate, and proximity to major lake ports encourages population growth. Goderich, Bay City, and Alpena are among the few good harbors available, and they thrived building ships and transshipping wheat, produce, lumber, and cement cargoes. Saginaw Bay is the westward slash that gives Michigan's Lower Peninsula its distinctive mitten shape. The bay is broad but shallow, and its orientation, aligned with the prevailing westerly breezes, causes it to agitate quickly. North of Saginaw Bay, the lake broadens, arching toward the Straits of Mackinac, where it meets the outflow of Lake Michigan. To the east and north, the massive Georgian Bay represents a sea unto itself. Dotted with tens of thousands of rocky islands, these waters lead to the northern Algonquin Highlands, part of the precambrian rim that constitutes the Adirondack Mountains and New York's Finger Lakes far to the east. North of the broad farms and forests of Manitoulin Island, Georgian Bay meets the North Channel. Running to the west for one hundred miles from Little Current to the St. Marys River, this waterway offers protection from the open lake. Its wide surface is scattered with hundreds of atolls and reefs, and carved into the ancient cliffs are fiords and rock harbors with hearty cedars, spruce, and fir sprouting defiantly from the barren, mossy cliffs. Canadian steamers serviced small ports along the north shore, including Killarney, Gore Bay, Blind River, and Thessalon. The area offered true wilderness for campers, hunters, and anglers but accounted for a small segment of the Lake Huron tourist economy. Most were going directly to Mackinac Island.

An important element of any destination excursion is the anticipation created by promotional material. It was during this period that cards, posters, slogans, and brochures appeared that were not issued by the steamship companies. Municipalities and entertainment venues began to aggressively advertise themselves to the traveling public. Chambers of commerce were formed in towns around the lakes to promote their affinities to a national audience. For almost a century, Niagara Falls and Mackinac Island were the premier attractions. In Michigan in 1908, Alpena was touted for its fishing and Cheboygan as the gateway to the extensive inland waterway regarded by some as home to the finest fishing anywhere. In addition, "No summer resort or watering place on the continent can boast of purer air, fresher breezes or better hotels." Sault Sainte Marie, the Pictured Rocks, Keweenaw Peninsula, and Porcupine Mountains remained popular in steamship literature.[9]

During the first few decades of the twentieth century, advertising matured and extended into new venues, including movie theaters, streetcars, and billboards. The graphic arts became tied to powerful marketing campaigns. Visual literacy became as important as verbal literacy. Automotive advertising set the standard starting around 1910, with travel, tobacco, health and beauty products, and cereals birthing a new industry. New agencies were formed that aggressively embraced the science of advertising. Revolutionary printing techniques allowed photographs and multicolored illustrations to be produced inexpensively.

An important result was the growth of the postcard industry. Color images—generally a black-and-white photograph imposed over appropriate block-color tones—became available for a few cents. Postage was a penny. Five-by-three-inch pictures of landmarks and cityscapes, parks and steamships were mailed to friends and family members around the country with best wishes and "Wish you were here" inscribed on the

Cruise line advertising, 1924. (Courtesy of the Detroit Historical Society Collection.)

back. Some were produced by small-town photographers, others by huge outfits such as the Detroit Photographic Company, which operated studios worldwide. In each case, these postcards were the best advertising the travel business could hope for.[10]

Steamship lines invested heavily in advertising. Whether in magazines or city directories, they bought prominent ad spaces and filled them with handsome graphics that combined the romance of the north woods experience and exemplary passenger comfort. Competitively, steamships had trouble matching the status, speed, innovation, or possibilities conjured up by automobiles. In advertising jargon, cars were sexier. Autos, and later airplanes, were the future. Trains and steamships were passé.

Arguably, while buying daily print spreads, steamship industry advertising remained old-fashioned. Itineraries and timetables occupied valuable advertising real estate. The names of owners, general managers, and captains were listed, a throwback to the antebellum era. Through the 1930s, the quality of the vessels took center stage. The people-having-fun theme was not popular until the 1950s, perhaps too late.

Instead, the companies emphasized modern amenities, natural wonders, and the relaxing nature of a cruise, essentially the same line that had been pitched for a century. It is telling that, as early as 1908, the D&C adopted a message of "slower is better," declaring, "It is a pity that we are as a people in such a hurry. Who is the happier or wiser, or morally better to-day by reason of more speed?" This strategy would be reliable for a few decades, as people sought a return to simpler times. It also signaled an admission that the transportation world was changing and the steamboat industry had unresolvable physical limitations and dwindling resources.[11]

CHAPTER 13

Sailing into a Head Wind

The Great Lakes passenger industry opened the century with new vessels, premier safety equipment, and a very professional array of steamship companies. They recognized gradual changes in their customer profiles and reacted by relying less on freight profits. Several companies did not make that transition, but through consolidation, partnerships, and attrition the survivors emerged on a solid footing. Yet the industry was to face a number of business and marketing challenges that hit its bottom line hard. A perfect storm of events can be identified as contributing to the end of the steamboat era. Disasters, politics, and business trends, all in the middle of the century's second decade, significantly hampered the industry until its demise.

In 1911 D&C line decided to expand on the success of the *City of Cleveland* with the larger *City of Detroit III*. It was grander and more ornate, including an English-style pub, an extensive ladies' lounge, and the elaborate oaken Gothic Room, replete with an imported English leaded glass window and a pipe organ. The *"D-III"* was launched on May 30, 1912, just six weeks after the RMS *Titanic* sank. The loss of the "unsinkable" ship shook the public's confidence in touted marine technologies and resulted in a review of safety regulations in both Great Britain and the United States. Great Lakes shipyards pressed on with the 1913 launches of the *North American*, the *Noronic*, and the majestic 484-foot *Seeandbee*. In November of that same year, a cyclonic storm hit the Great Lakes region. Twelve freighters sank with all hands—more than 230 men—and dozens more ships were stranded or badly damaged. Contemporary newspapers carried large headlines and

The steamer *City of Detroit III*, c. 1912. (Courtesy of the Detroit Historical Society Collection.)

extensive coverage of the losses. Fortunately, only one passenger ship, the Northern Navigation Company's steamer *Huronic*, was caught in the maelstrom. Driven "on the sands at Shelldrake" reef, the ship was pulled clear with no noticeable damage. Radio communication aboard the passenger fleet had given those skippers an advantage over all but a few freighters.[1]

This event brought images of shipwreck disaster again into the mainstream media and before prospective customers across the nation. Resorters traditionally stopped traveling the lakes by the end of September, so some observers may have dismissed this disaster as the result of late-season misjudgments. Passenger boardings at Chicago the next season, as reported by the Army Corps of Engineers, enjoyed a modest increase over 1913. Milwaukee traffic was up by 66 percent, the peak year of ridership from that city for the next decade. The Chicago figures, while good, were 40 percent lower than the pre-Depression peak of 1,622,314 in 1911.[2]

The summer of 1915 was the kind that resort owners dread. June and early July were cool and damp. Daily fare revenue was down. Only the company- and club-sponsored excursion business remained steady. And then that market suffered a catastrophe.[3]

The morning of July 24 was typical of that season. There was a soft rain falling as employees of the Western Electric Company gathered on the wharves of the Chicago River for a daylong picnic scheduled in Michigan City, Indiana. Early birds wanted to be on the first boat to depart so as to not miss a moment of this company-sponsored outing. The Indiana Transportation Company was contracted to handle the estimated seven thousand passengers and had augmented its fleet with three chartered vessels, including the *Eastland* from the St. Joseph–Chicago Steamship Company. The *Eastland* was designated the first boat to leave, and by 7:30 about twenty-five hundred people had boarded, anticipating a quick, comfortable ride. There was no wind, so the lake would be calm. As dock lines were cast off, with hundreds of friends and family members watching from shore, the ship suddenly rolled away from the dock onto its port side and sank.[4]

Such an event was unprecedented, but in hindsight there were warnings and red flags. The *Eastland* was top-heavy from the moment it hit the water at the Jenks Shipyard in Port Huron. It tended to list easily—leaning to one side or the other—and efforts to counter lateral buoyancy with port or starboard ballast tanks occasionally resulted in severe counterlists. This reputation may have resulted in the boat being leased to Lake Erie routes for a few seasons before returning to Chicago. Efforts were made to alleviate the problem, but the ship remained hard to trim and "crank" when under way. Prior to fit-out in 1915, several tons of cement were added to an upper deck as fireproofing and reinforcement. In July three additional lifeboats and six life rafts—weighing several additional tons—were added to the top deck in response to new governmental regulations. The Western Electric group was the first large crowd the *Eastland* had carried since this refitting. Prior to departure, engineers began standard ballast flooding procedures. The loaded vessel began listing and quickly became unstable. The ship was thirty-eight feet wide, rolling in twenty feet of water. When it settled almost half remained above the surface.

It would have been difficult under ideal circumstances to evacuate a crowded ship in less than five minutes. The *Eastland* was on its side, flooded with fetid, opaque river water. Many passengers were trapped below. Others were thrown free. Many of those who cleared the wreck could not swim, either by training or due to the encumbrance of clothing. Rescue efforts were immediate, both from shore and from tugs, yachts, and lighters in the river. However, hundreds had been trapped belowdecks, and many more were drowning in the river. Within a few minutes, more than 840 people died, the greatest loss of life among all Great Lakes maritime disasters. When cutting torches breached the exposed starboard hull plates, where air had been trapped, a few dozen people were pulled to safety. After weeks and hundreds of hard-hat dives, most of the bodies were recovered. Warehouses were used as morgues. The news out of Chicago was grim.

The incident virtually stopped excursion and vacation travel on the Great Lakes and put a number of Lake Michigan carriers out of business. Passenger numbers for 1915 were half those of the previous year, having collapsed during the usually profitable August period. Steamship companies struggled to regain the public's confidence. One operator, endeavoring to prove the stability of its vessels to a now-wary public, piled sandbags equivalent to a full load of passengers on its upper deck and did figure-eight maneuvers at full speed in view of the Chicago waterfront. Carriers to the east had an easier time of it. The Canadian carriers had exemplary records. The D&C and C&B lines offered relatively new side-wheelers, noted for their stability. The *Eastland's* operators, the St. Joseph–Chicago Steamship Company, closed after the season and disbanded. The respected Indiana Transportation Company, liable as the charter company, immediately laid up its vessels in Michigan City, beyond Chicago's jurisdiction, and never ran them again.[5]

Almost an afterthought, but certainly a natural disaster for steamboat operators, was the flu pandemic in 1918–19. A virulent strain of influenza erupted in America and Europe, radiated outward globally, and then rebounded back again. Millions of Americans were stricken, more than six hundred thousand fatally; worldwide, tens of millions died.

Federal health authorities reacted quickly and effectively. One initiative was a public service advertising campaign that cautioned people not to gather in large groups or frequent public spaces. This message was tough on restaurants, theaters, hotels, and public transportation. Steamships were especially affected, as they were essentially floating hotels, with restaurants, theaters, and all. Coupled with the disruptions of World War I, the flow of passenger traffic, which had recovered in 1916, was depressed through the next two critical summer seasons.[6]

Steamship company executives and investors dreaded natural disasters, but they addressed safety issues with technologies and public relations. Political storms were a different matter. Union and labor activists were pressuring management to address wage issues and working conditions. Following the *Titanic* disaster, reactive and defensive legislation in the form of the La Follette Seamen's and Jones acts would gut profits and opportunities for Great Lakes carriers. Despite active lobbying efforts in Washington, the outcome of these political machinations were largely beyond their control.

Unions for sailors were among the last to formalize. Unlicensed Great Lakes mariners generally spent most of the year among a handful of similar low-wage workers. The perception of insubordination could carry stiff repercussions in any Admiralty Court. Arguably, sailors were among the last major labor groups to pass out of indenture.[7] Seamen were off the boats for only two months during the winter. The opportunities for organizing and rallies were few. During the nineteenth century, thousands of schooners were manned by crews of five to eight, often hired in the same small coastal town. Steam propellers gradually replaced schooners by the hundreds. While they employed the same crew as three schooners, their capacity and speed put a dozen out of business. Thousands of sailors were left "on the beach" looking for work. On the beach, that's where they could organize.

The first maritime labor group to exercise political clout was the longshoremen. These fellows loaded and unloaded boats, traditionally an occasional position with little remuneration and no security. The first organized labor actions began to take place by the 1870s, with union locals formed in the Saginaw Valley sawmills in 1870 and in Chicago in 1877. In addition, dock men took localized action in Detroit and Cleveland as early as 1871.[8]

Union activities among longshoremen were formalized on the Great Lakes in 1892. Delegates from ten local unions—lumber handlers from around the lakes—formed the National Longshoremen's Association of the United States. By 1895 the addition of Canadian workers had prompted a name change to the International Longshoremen's Association. Henry E. Hoagland stated that "by 1899 almost every man working on the Lake Erie docks was a member of that organization."[9] In 1902 the name changed again to the International Longshoremen, Marine and Transport Workers' Association (ILMTWA). The organization claimed more than one hundred thousand members, half located in the lakes region, with a demographic representing more than forty shipboard occupations. The ILMTWA eventually became the International Longshoremen's Association.[10]

The ILMTWA was not the sole maritime organization on the Great

Lakes. In contrast to the labor faction was the Lake Carriers' Association (LCA), formed by American vessel owners and operators in 1885 and reorganized in 1900. The LCA was an effective clearinghouse for navigation and weather information, and it served to establish standards and practices for professional mariners. Its members used their political influence to promote legislation favorable to navigational improvements—charts and dredging—and to prevent the passage of legislation detrimental to their interests. They also worked in concert to provide a united front in the face of growing labor demands. They were successful in their efforts to improve harbors and channels, but the owners' relationship with labor was a mixture of victories, losses, and draws. An immediate success was the breaking of a fledgling sailors' union in 1890.[11]

In 1912 sailors from both the deck and the engine room united to form the Lake Seaman's Union, which included wheelsmen, lookouts, deck watchmen, deckhands, firemen, oilers, water tenders, and coal passers. Maritime labor organizations outside occupational boundaries operated with a series of loose agreements between the various segments of the shipping industry. These relationships worked well and required relatively few strikes to reach agreements. Most unions operated at a very local level, with individual units dealing with local issues and owners. This gave the lakes' labor climate an element of flexibility. Most carriers attempted to abide by the LCA guidelines and make agreements with individual locals. But the various unions' lack of cohesion gave management a decided advantage, and it increasingly ignored union demands and forced open shops. Laws and conditions generally favored employers. Picketing was interpreted as an illegal disruption of the peace. Because of the many new immigrants, strikebreakers were easy to hire.[12]

Much of this grassroots union energy came to be associated with the political and social philosophies that defined the Progressive Movement in the early part of the century. Often identified with campaigns to eliminate child labor and exploitation in industry, progressivism represented a broad spectrum of reform-minded citizens advocating for the downtrodden, including young women, farmers, immigrants, and seamen. In the maritime world, progressivism was personified by Robert La Follette, a senator from Wisconsin. He vehemently attacked monopolies and addressed workplace issues, and was considered a radical even by many progressives. Senator La Follette began his crusade in 1910, attempting to close loopholes in earlier bills and add further statutes regulating living conditions and manning requirements. La Follette's initial legislation passed the Senate in 1913 but failed to pass in the House of Representatives.[13]

Finally, the Act to Promote the Welfare of American Seamen in the Merchant Marine of the United States was signed by President Woodrow Wilson on March 4, 1915. It became known variously as the La Follette Bill, the Seamen's Act, and the La Follette–Wilson Seamen's Act of 1915. In addition to provisions adopted from previous bills, it codified seamen's rights regarding safety, wages, and working conditions. It was to be the standard for all seafaring nations, with provisions included to protect all sailors.

After the *Titanic* disaster, ships were mandated to carry more lifeboats, and regular drills were to be held. The act required that 75 percent of a ship's crew understand the language spoken by the skipper, reflecting nativist elements of progressivism but arguably a commonsense precaution. There were specific rules regarding staffing levels, hours, and pay. Stipulations of the act forced companies to carry an expanded payroll through the winter, greatly increasing operating costs. Far more important, the onboard watch schedule was changed from two 12-hour watches to three 8-hour watches, necessitating a 50 percent increase in the crew complement.[14]

For the sailor, perhaps the most welcome part of the new law expanded forecastle space to no less than 120 cubic feet per man. Bunk dimensions were expanded from about 10 square feet to 16. Washroom space, regular fumigation, and onboard "hospital" facilities were mandated. Dietary improvements increased daily water rations by 25 percent and doubled the butter allowance. Rules for paying sailors were also written into law.[15]

As the legislation's names indicate, it was designed for sailors. Only the lifeboat provision addressed the safety of passengers. No part of this bill favored shipping companies or masters. They were forced to drop routes, redesign and renovate ships, and relinquish control over hiring and firing that captains had enjoyed for centuries. The Shipping Act of 1916 stifled foreign competition by requiring US-flagged vessels to be built and owned by American companies or citizens. This became of preeminent importance with the passage of the Merchant Marine Act in 1920, commonly called the Jones Act, which mandated rules governing coastal trade in US vessels. Even this legislation had some favorable provisions for seamen, offering legal grounds on which to collect damages for injury or negligence.[16]

Through all of this political distraction, the passenger carriers had attempted to keep a low profile. Correspondence between presidents

of the various passenger lines was common regarding wage negotia-
tion and the employment of "union men." However, particularly in Detroit, they faced an increased labor shortage created by the "great demand by auto people, who are paying better salaries." When the union
confronted the Lake Carriers' Association and Pittsburgh Steamship
Company in 1909, 1910, and 1912, the passenger vessel owners settled
quickly. The season was too short to dally.[17]

Despite concessions that hiked wages by 15 to 20 percent, further
job actions took place sporadically in 1916 and 1917. Longshoremen
in different cities and sailors employed by different lines struck inde-
pendently, with varying degrees of success. Because of the war, arbi-
tration was referred to the US Shipping Board in Washington, DC. In
a letter to American Steamship Association secretary W. M. Brittain,
D&C general manager Augustus Schantz proclaimed, "The Lake Carriers were whipped before they entered the conference, and if you leave
matters to be arbitrated by the Shipping Board, you will lose out, as
everything in Washington seems to be in favor of organized labor."[18]

The most onerous of the Seaman's Act provisions, from the carriers' perspective, was the one dealing with manning requirements. A
regulated formula dictated a certain ratio of passengers to crewmen,
and the ratio diminished at the beginning and end of the season, the
busy freight seasons. Passenger vessels with moderate capacities and
little freight were penalized because they could not afford enough able-
bodied seamen to match passenger capacity limits. As a result, ships
like the *City of Alpena* and the *City of Mackinaw*, rated to carry 700
persons each, were limited to 162 passengers and crew.[19] These boats
served many Lake Huron ports, and under the extant conditions, if the
ships were filled to rated capacity after just a few stops, they were
forced to bypass subsequent ports until sufficient passengers disembarked. This practice left customers waiting on the docks for ships that
never came. Ships forced to bypass ports due to full passenger comple-
ments were considered unreliable, which virtually destroyed the northern freight business. In each of the next two years, the Huron Division
lost $30,000, and in 1921 the D&C shut it down.[20]

Ratification of the Panama Canal Act in 1912 prohibited railroad
ownership of any common carrier on water where the railroad might
compete for traffic with the water carrier. Despite appeals to the In-
terstate Commerce Commission, shipping lines were forced to divest
themselves of railroad assets by 1915. This did not affect any of the
large passenger carriers, but the Erie Railroad Company's Union

D. & C.

DETROIT
STEAMERS

UNFAIR TO
ORGANIZED LABOR

All Other Passenger Boats
Are O. K.

LAKE SEAMEN'S UNION

A strike flyer specifically targeted the D&C line, 1917.
Courtesy of the Burton Historical Collection, Detroit
Public Library.)

Steamship Company and the Pennsylvania Railroad's Anchor Line were Great Lakes casualties. Comments made by H. C. Snyder, assistant general freight agent of the Erie Rail Road, in 1916 prompted an opinion in a trade journal to the effect that "the commission had driven innumerable steamers from the Great Lakes and has proven itself a costly experiment to the interests that were so aggressively instrumental in effecting the separation."[21]

Unfortunately, the growing number of passengers over the previous decade created an ironic public relations problem. Regulations had not been developed regarding the discharge of effluents into the water, be they engine oils or sewage. Cities around the lakes were major offenders, but so were the steamers. Like many small towns, ships drew drinking water directly out of the lakes, with only rudimentary filtration and no treatment. Additionally, like many cities, they dumped their sewage directly in the water. Both operations might happen while at the dock or in the open lake.

It was widely assumed that the immense amount of water the Great Lakes represent would dilute the pollution. But as these vessels plied the same routes day after day, particularly in shallow Lake Erie, it became a problem. During fiscal year 1913, sixteen million people took passage on the lakes, generally traveling along the same routes. The *Detroit Free Press* in 1914 reported hundreds of cases of typhoid fever, or typhus, among lake seamen, not counting the passengers. Stories of severe stomach ailments, coupled with the possibility of seasickness and stormy catastrophe, played poorly in the press.[22]

By 1920 the landscape of the lake passenger market had changed drastically. Natural disasters and legislation were contributing factors, but market conditions in both the United States and the Dominion of Canada had been affecting the industry for more than a decade. Notably, the *North West* caught fire in 1911 while undergoing a refit, resulting in destruction of the elegant cabins. The Northern Steamship Company released the intact hull and machinery for the insurance value, and it was converted into a bulk carrier. State-of-the-art sixteen years before, the ship was now redundant. Its fleet mate and sister ship, the *North Land*, remained in service for five more years but was on the auction block by 1916 and scrapped by 1921. A major carrier on the Chicago–South Haven route, the Crawford Transportation Company, was out of business by 1912. Indiana Transportation Company's long history simply ended with the *Eastland* disaster.

The Graham & Morton Transportation Company, dating to 1877, was a formidable competitor on the south end of Lake Michigan. Reincorporated in Indiana in 1902, it suffered through boom-and-bust cycles common to seasonal fruit crops and resort traffic. The company fell into receivership in 1915, was reorganized by 1921, and merged its assets into the Goodrich organization in 1924. This improved Goodrich's fleet and followed manager Harry Thorp's policy of acquiring significant rivals. However, this and subsequent purchases adversely effected Goodrich's financial agility.

The Chicago, Racine & Milwaukee line, which had progressively been the Hurson Transportation Company and later Barry Transportation, was the first major acquisition by Goodrich's Thorp. Others followed, including the lease of the *Theodore Roosevelt* in 1927, which proved unprofitable on a couple of routes. The Benton Harbor Transit Company came aboard in 1929, and soon afterward West Ports became a name partner. Goodrich–West Ports gained a near monopoly on Lake Michigan.[23]

Others remained independent. The Michigan Transit Company, successor to the Northern Michigan Transportation Company, was in receivership by 1927 and proposed a merger with Goodrich on nearly any terms. Goodrich did not absorb it, and it folded by 1931. Other stalwarts were the Wisconsin & Michigan Transportation Company and the Pere Marquette line, both mid–Lake Michigan rail-related carriers. Negotiations with Thorp proved unsatisfactory, which proved prescient. The two eventually merged as the Wisconsin & Michigan Steamship Company in 1934 and survived for many years. In the meantime, although Goodrich controlled most passenger and packet routes on the lake, its balance sheet was unable to support its debt, and in December 1932, its trustees petitioned the court for bankruptcy protection. Goodrich–West Ports ceased operations in July 1933.

The Hart Transportation Company, formed in 1905 from the litigated remains of the Hart Steamboat Line, ran a number of smaller steamers north into Green Bay, Mackinac Island, and the Soo. Within six years, Hart was selling off boats. Cliff Hart died in 1913, leaving a business suffering declining traffic revenues and increased staffing requirements as a result of the Seaman's Act. Its ship the *Sailor Boy* was mustered to a Lake Superior route in 1916, and the *Bon Ami* ran freight as required. The year 1917 gave the ship only two good months of resort traffic, and 1918 boardings were down, too. At the end of the season, the *Bon Ami* was destroyed by fire, and the company was dissolved.[24]

The Chicago & South Haven Steamship Company, formed in 1909 from the Dunkley-Williams Transportation Company's assets, was able to offer cross-lake service for half the cost of the railroad. But it fought to keep from losing passengers to the interurban trains, themselves only a few years from extinction. After loss of the fast *City of South Haven* to the Shipping Board during World War I, management had increasing difficulty keeping its *City of Kalamazoo*, *Glenn*, and *Petoskey* busy, and the company ceased scheduled traffic after the 1926 season. While it continued to operate through 1940 with occasional excursion-only voyages, it is notable that its regular schedule was abandoned during the glory years of the 1920s prior to the Great Depression.[25]

The Holland & Chicago Transportation Company, formed in 1892, sold its routes and assets to Graham & Morton in 1901, which in turn sold to the Crosby Transportation Company in 1916, whose assets trickled to West Ports. Regular service to Holland was discontinued in 1931.[26] The Chicago & Manitowoc Steamship Company, running one of the most reliable routes on the lakes, survived as long as the D&C, mostly on the strength of its popular ship, the *Theodore Roosevelt*.[27]

Of course, this disillusioning scenario was not particular to the Great Lakes. On the East Coast, the Hudson River Day Line from New York to Albany operated from 1863 until 1948. The Maine Railroad suspended its steamer service in 1931. The New England Steamship Company began eliminating routes in 1920 and suspended all routes between New England and New York by 1937. Most organizations did not survive World War II. One exception was the Chesapeake's Old Bay Line. Officially named the Baltimore Steam Packet Company, founded in 1840, it survived on tourism until 1961.[28]

A small number of Great Lakes companies made successful mergers. Canada Steamship Lines (CSL) became a fully integrated shipper of bulk and package freight and a provider of passenger services, absorbing most of the Canadian maritime commerce. The entrepreneurs who consolidated the CSL between 1910 and 1914 included an aggressive contingent of Canadian promoters, among them James Playfair, Christopher Furness, James Carruthers, James Norcross, and Roy M. Wolvin, as well as a number of British investors.

The entire operation included four separate networks: the saltwater routes radiating from the St. Lawrence River to points around the Atlantic, Great Lakes canalboats and bulk freighters, passenger and package-freight carriers on the Lake Ontario–Montreal route, and packets on the Detroit–Lake Superior routes. Much like the D&C line, the company held interests in a shipyard and foundry and was heavily invested in large hotels in Murray Bay and Tadoussac. All vessels, both propellers and side-wheelers, adopted the red, white, and black smokestack insignia of the Northern Navigation Company, one of eleven companies brought under the CSL umbrella and representing more than one hundred vessels. Historian M. Stephen Salmon suggests that "conservatism, coupled with their ties to the major banks and stock promoters, made it almost inevitable that the industry would be caught up in the merger mania that was sweeping the Canadian economy."[29]

To the east, the CSL's rapids-running excursion boats from Prescott to Montreal and Tadoussac were both practical and exciting. A cruise past majestic islands and mountains was far more comfortable than a comparable automobile trip. It also offered the perspective of proximity; the beauty of the St. Lawrence Valley and the Thousand Islands was very close and intimate.

The Northern Navigation Division offered a much different experience. In many regards the group operated as an entity unto itself within the CSL organization. It was the only CLS division whose vessels did not have overlapping routes and shared harborage. It offered long-distance tourist cruises and vital communications links to remote frontier towns. Passenger vessels on the eastern route were known as the Great White Fleet; a few sported black hulls, but most were painted entirely white. Steamers and propellers on the northern route were black along their enclosed main decks, and often on the upper deck, and then white above—a typical Great Lakes look. Also setting it apart from the St. Lawrence Division were trips that offered open-water adventures, out of sight of land on both Lake Huron and Lake Superior.

From a passenger carrier standpoint, the Northern Navigation Division's assets— the *Hamonic, Huronic,* and *Noronic*—were modern, first-class boats. They provided a critical railroad link from Windsor, Detroit, and Sarnia to the "lake head" at Port Arthur and Fort William, as well as Duluth/Superior. Two large ferries attended ports from lower Georgian Bay north to Killarney and west to the Soo. Two agile old rapids runners—*Rapids King* and *Thousand Islander*—tried to service the prosperous inland Ontario farm towns of Chatham and Wallaceburg, but the narrow, winding, shallow streams prevented the route from being feasible for CSL. All the lesser services were discontinued by 1929, but the trio of large boats continued in operation for several years. The CSL proved resilient.

Another successful consolidation project came in the wake of the forced divestiture of steamship assets by the railroad interests in 1915.

It resulted in an American company named the Great Lakes Transit Corporation, based in Buffalo, and a Canadian company named the Great Lakes Transportation Company, Ltd., based in Midland, Ontario. M. L. White and James Playfair were the respective managers. The American organization was formed from the thirty-three nearly new packets formerly operated by four railroads.[30]

Only three of these ships carried passengers, but these near sister ships were ship-watchers' favorites. The *Tionesta*, built in 1903, served the company well until 1940, when it was scrapped. The youngest, the *Octorara* of 1910, was with Great Lakes Transit until 1943, when it was sold to the US Coast Guard as a floating barracks and later served as a ferry in the western Pacific. The *Juniata* is still with us at this writing. It remained in the Great Lakes Transit fleet until 1940, when it was sold to the Wisconsin & Michigan Steamship Company to serve the cross-lake traffic between Milwaukee and Muskegon. Rechristened the *Milwaukee Clipper*, it received an extensive redesign that transformed its 1905 profile into a modern "mini–ocean liner." The public spaces of its interior creatively mixed the palette of mid-century modern styles, a dramatic break from the palace propeller style that was its heritage. In active service until 1970, this craft is a player in the final chapter.

Lake Erie, the smallest Great Lake, carried an immense amount of passenger traffic. A significant portion was controlled by the D&C line. The Cleveland & Buffalo Transit Company was organized in 1892 to compete between the two named cities. A few years later, the D&C formed the Detroit & Buffalo Steamboat Company as a competitive maneuver. By 1913 D&C interests had merged the Detroit & Buffalo boats under the D&C flag and improved relationships with Cleveland & Buffalo Transit. Such business acumen, of necessity, allowed the McMillan interests to play on to the end. On the upper lakes, Canadian Pacific Railroad steamers *Assiniboia* and *Keewatin* ran from Port McNichol to the lake head until the late 1960s, and a few smaller vessels continued to provide short-run excursions and ferry service.

It is important to note that a significant number of passenger boats went out of commission during World War I and the Roaring Twenties, when the economy was riding high and when disposable income was on the rise. This shift has long been ascribed to the advent and explosive growth of internal combustion vehicles for personal and commercial use. The steady decline in ridership mirrors the growth of auto sales, particularly when the Ford Model T went into mass production after 1910. Restrictive regulation was the bane of steamboat operators. Competition and increased labor costs simultaneously removed opportunities for profit at a time when margins were growing thin. Only the most attractive "cruise" routes survived the depressed 1930s. While it didn't last long, there was some grand fun still to be had. And, as so many passengers noted on the postcards they sent home, "It was a beautiful sunset."

Conclusion
The Final Years

The literature for this period, across several media, is far deeper than for any previous era. These vessels operated into the days when cameras became easy to use, mass-marketed novelties. Onboard snapshots, personalized postcards, fanciful marketing images, and promotional movies bring this era to life. Earlier days are captured in sketches and paintings, and gradually in dockside photo portraits, but the boats are static and the people posed. This final chapter is preserved with "movies," showing vessels in motion and active passengers enjoying the experience. A trove of published biographies, fleet monographs, and reminiscences, as well as extensive newspaper coverage, documented these decades well.

All reports agreed. Life on the lakes was grand. An increasingly mobile population had more disposable income than at any time in history. So how could the business erode so rapidly, as was evidenced in the previous chapter? Admittedly, the trade faced competitive head winds through the 1960s. Automobiles, particularly after World War II, became the way people traveled. Alternative freight options became more efficient. Entering the Space Age, steamships were quaint and expensive, with legacy costs that included constant safety upgrades, prime wharf leases, and taxes. Despite warm sentiments and revered cultural status, the passenger steamship industry could not survive, at least not in the glorious guise it maintained in the early decades.

The fade was gradual.

Entering the 1920s, despite declining margins, the D&C line had money in the bank. Following a profitable year in 1921, the company

The steamer *Greater Detroit*, c. 1924. (Courtesy of the Detroit Historical Society Collection.)

announced that it was planning two new ships, the large and luxurious *Greater Detroit* and *Greater Buffalo*. Those plans were delayed for reasons described by Superintendent C. L. Perkins: "It would not be advisable for us to build steamers now with the Seaman's Law in effect." However, two years later the company chose to proceed with construction. The project's cost—$6.8 million paid in cash—was justifiable considering the increased freight and passenger traffic generated in the growing cities and towns around the lakes. The decade was a boom time for building, manufacturing, retail, recreation, immigration, and migration—and, by extension, shipping.[1]

In hindsight, this investment bears review. Despite contraction of the overall Great Lakes passenger excursion business, the D&C kept to its strategy of fielding the finest vessels. With these launches, there was no question about that. The two ships were physically impressive—the longest side-wheelers in the world. Painted in D&C black and white, they were nearly two city blocks long and four stories tall. Indoors, they were as elaborate as the *City of Cleveland,* only more so. The deck layout was that of most Kirby steamers, with large salons and thousands of feet of outdoor promenades. The 625 staterooms were a bit larger, and the public spaces for up to 2,127 passengers offered variety, from nurseries to movie theaters. By 1930 the amenities throughout the fleet included barber shops, beauty salons, a tailor's shop, laundry facilities, libraries, daily newspapers, and activity rosters. Activities included "mile marches" around the deck; one circuit of a 450-foot steamer was almost 1,000 feet, or a fifth of a mile. On boats of the Canada Steamship Line (CSL), this full-ship tour was led by a highland piper in full regalia. Aboard others it might be a Dixieland band. This tradition lasted into the 1960s, but getting there was tough.

The Great Depression spread across the world's financial markets in 1929–30. Soon afterward, the manufacturing engine slowed. The large industrial towns of the Great Lakes region were hit particularly hard. For nearly a decade, people in the lower and middle classes no longer had the funds available to spend on steamboat excursions. Overnight trips, still within the reach of the well-to-do, saw a decrease in boardings. Shorter excursion routes took up some of that trade and weathered the storm.

The *Greater Detroit* and the *Greater Buffalo* represented the apex of the Great Lakes palace steamers. A declining fleet of boats survived the Depression and enjoyed renewed demand as a result of World War II. Maritime traffic grew in proportion to government ration limits placed on gasoline and tire purchases, as well as the volume of traffic on the railroad system. With soldiers given priority on the rails, vacation travel on trains was patriotically discouraged. Passenger steamships suffered no such stigma. The enhanced incomes of millions of factory workers throughout the Midwest helped the D&C enjoy increased passenger traffic. The D&C line was able to keep six ships in constant motion, despite a shortage of coal. In 1945 the line moved enough freight to realize a modest profit.[2]

Fortunes were not so good for the Cleveland & Buffalo Transit Company. In 1924 the company bought the aging *City of Detroit II* from the D&C line, renaming it the *Goodtime,* and simultaneously strained its finances. The Depression and increasing competition from trucks and railroads, along with destruction of the *City of Buffalo* by fire in 1938, caused the company's bankruptcy and liquidation in 1939. Its magnificent paddler the *Seeandbee* was sold into the war effort and came into the navy as the aircraft carrier USS *Wolverine.* Cabins were sheared off and a flight

THE GOTHIC ROOM

Once a smoking lounge on the D&C Steamer City of Detroit III, the Gothic Room has been restored to its original grandeur in the Dossin Great Lakes Museum at Detroit.

The City of Detroit III was built in 1912 and scrapped in 1956 at Detroit.

Color Photo by Harry Wolf

A PERRIN PRINT

Perrin Souvenir Distributors, P.O. Box 370, Northville, MI 48167
Phone (810) 348-8260

Donky "A tour from city of NY
* Detroit"

Reclining

chandler

POST CARD

PLEASE DO NOT WRITE BELOW THIS LINE. SPACE RESERVED FOR U.S. POSTAL SERVICE.

Made in America

K20723

deck was installed above the main deck. Pilothouse and smokestacks were mounted to starboard. The D&C's *Greater Buffalo* was similarly altered to become the USS *Sable*. As the only two side-wheeled aircraft carriers in the US military, they did admirable training duty on Lake Michigan during the war and were scrapped soon afterward.[3]

According to George W. Hilton, the interlake operators were stimulated by the war and benefited from postwar "See America First" appeals to those who might otherwise have gone to Europe for vacations. With excursions to Niagara Falls and Mackinac Island, the D&C fleet was popular during the war but struggled with high labor costs and the difficulty of getting good coal. After controlling the line for seventy years, the McMillan family sold to George Kolowich in 1947. Despite declining passenger revenues, the new owner made plans to refinance and refit the fleet and concentrate on the freight trade.[4] Considering the types of ships he bought and trends in the passenger business, it was not long before the new management was retrenching. A wartime lawsuit over the *Greater Buffalo* was finally settled in the company's favor for $2.6 million. On the downside, the City of Detroit insisted that the D&C relinquish its dock space at the foot of Wayne Street in order to clear land for the new Civic Center. It awarded the owner half a million dollars in condemnation fees, and the message was clear: the city was reshaping itself in a modern mold, and the steamers were no longer welcome on the land they had owned for decades at the heart of the waterfront. It is a ready metaphor for public sentiment. A new generation looked to the Jet Age, even for their automobile designs. Changing attitudes determined that there was no place in this vision for gaudy leviathans employing a propulsion system unchanged for almost a century.[5]

The D&C ceased running after the 1950 season and entered liquidation in 1951.[6] It began scrapping the *City of Detroit III* soon afterward. Much of the woodwork was bought by an Ohio investor and later sold to the Stouffer's restaurant chain and a few businesses on the East Coast to be used as architectural accents. The Gothic Room was preserved and installed at the Dossin Great Lakes Museum in Detroit, the only example of Great Lakes steamboat gothic still in existence. The other vessels had more abrupt and practical endings. The *Greater Detroit*, painted white in its final years, was towed with the *Eastern States* into Lake St. Clair and set ablaze as a public spectacle. The years of paint, varnish, and dry wood fueled an immense pyre, and when the flames died, only the salvageable steel remained. The *City of Cleveland III* caught fire accidently while being scrapped at a Windsor dock, the ultimate result being the same.[7] The *Western States* was relocated to

Tawas City, Michigan, in 1955 as a floating hotel and was purposely burned a few years later prior to scrapping.

Canada Steamship Lines, which removed the *Huronic* from passenger service in 1930, kept its liners *Hamonic* and *Noronic* busy throughout the war traveling between the Detroit River and Lake Superior's Port Arthur and Duluth. The *Hamonic's* career ended abruptly in what could have been a disaster on the scale of the *Eastland*. The ship was ignited on a Friday at about 8:30 a.m. by a wharf-side warehouse fire in Sarnia. Quick thinking by the captain, crew, and numerous skilled bystanders allowed more than three hundred people to escape. Only one person was reported lost.[8]

This left the *Noronic* to continue for the CSL until 1949. On a September afternoon, having completed the Detroit-Duluth season, the ship was wending its way eastward to join the CSL fleet for winter layup. At about 6:00 p.m., it docked at the Queen's Quay in Toronto. A large number of passengers departed for downtown restaurants and shows. Those who stayed behind were treated to a gourmet meal and other entertainments. By midnight most guests were asleep in their staterooms. Only seventeen crew members were aboard at about 2:30 a.m. when a guest, retiring for the night, smelled smoke. With the help of a young bellman, the source was discovered in a linen closet. The ship had 56 fire extinguishers and 43 hydrants with hoses. Don Church, the passenger, and Garth O'Neill, the bellman, employed both methods with little effect. Further alarms and fire suppression systems failed, and within a few moments the vessel was hard ablaze. The Toronto Fire Department responded with 20 vehicles, including aerial equipment and the fireboat *Charles Read*, but it proved ineffective against the compartmentalized steel decks of the *Noronic*. In the end, nearly 120 people died and 14 bodies went unrecovered. Rumors of sabotage swirled around both fires aboard the *Hamonic* and the *Noronic*—it was a time of Cold War security concerns. Regardless, it marked the end of the CSL's interest in Great Lakes palace steamers. In the Eastern Division, the river runners *Richelieu*, *St. Lawrence*, and *Tadoussac* were all retired by 1966.[9]

The Canadian Pacific Railroad's freshwater passenger fleet lasted through the mid-1960s. The Northern Division stalwart *Keewatin*, sold for salvage in 1966, was purchased by preservationists the following year and saved. Exhibited for many decades at Douglas, Michigan, it was towed in 2012 to its old terminus, Port McNicoll, and is scheduled for restoration. The *Assiniboia* was taken out of service in 1968, drawn into a failed New Jersey restaurant scheme, and eventually scrapped.[10]

The Chicago, Duluth & Georgian Bay Transit Company, generally known as the Georgian Bay Line, was the last long-distance carrier to schedule large overnight cruises. Organized by Robert C. Davis in August 1912, the business model was meant to address a fractured passenger market. From the beginning the Georgian Bay Line stood apart. Davis wanted nothing to do with freight, the traditional lifeblood of his competitors. Instead he ordered a ship specifically for the passenger trade. Half a year later the *North American* was launched at the Great Lakes Engineering Works near Detroit. It was a graceful propeller with five decks top to bottom. The ship was well-received, and a slightly longer sister, the *South American*, debuted the following season. The older boat generally ran weeklong adventures from Buffalo to Chicago and its fleet mate from Buffalo to Duluth. Initially, the Georgian Bay Line boats called at ports along its namesake part of Lake Huron's shore; although the name stuck, the Georgian Bay routes were abandoned by the 1940s.

The *North American* and *South American* were fitted with oil-fired boilers and therefore emitted little smoke and no cinders. Every other grand steamer burned coal, with its related detritus. It was a prescient marketing choice by the directors, managers, and designers and proved its worth in operational cost savings. The Georgian Bay Line vessels boasted this cleanliness by sailing in completely white livery, waterline to radio mast. Their substantial smokestacks—not tall but full and raked—carried the black and ochre bands of the fleet (later black, red, and ochre).[11] With a complete focus on the guests, these boats offered a high level of service for a modest fare. While in no manner as grandiose as contemporary D&C boats, they evinced new trends in the cruise ship experience. Entertainment directors kept shipboard activities in constant motion. Slot machines and music recitals gave way to shuffleboard, sing-alongs, card parties, and dances. The young college students hired as stewards and waitresses staged impromptu musical reviews. The highlight of the season occurred when the boats met at Mackinac Island for the final time before going to winter layup at Holland, Michigan. Each vessel sent a cast to the "Crew Capers" finale held at the island's Grand Hotel. Dinner guests voted for their favorites, and trophies were awarded.

Headquartered first in Chicago and later in Detroit, the Georgian Bay Line was the only American steamship company to concentrate on the passenger cruise experience. A Goodrich boat's run to Mackinac might include a dozen Wisconsin stops. Michigan Transit might touch at eight Michigan ports. Middle-of-the-night cargo transfers were un-

The *North American* and *South American* in Chicago, c. 1950. (Courtesy of the Detroit Historical Society Collection.)

avoidable, and the schedules didn't allow for long layovers. The Georgian Bay Line ran from Chicago to Mackinac nonstop, overnight, and then allowed guests a leisurely four- or five-hour layover to explore and shop. There were similar touristy breaks at other destinations along the way. The line profited from its charter commitments in the spring, when high school seniors were rewarded with class trips. These were memorable and lively affairs that kept the chaperones and security personnel on their toes. Later, wedding season arrived. Thousands of couples began their honeymoons aboard the boats. A more sedate and intimate week, it nonetheless demanded more of the crew's attention.

The 450 guests were pampered by a small army of about 120 crew, both men and women. By some accounts, the crew had more fun than the passengers, becoming family over the years. Most anticipated the beginning of the season and stayed for many years, making jobs on these boats hard to get. Porters, waiters, bartenders, waitresses, and souvenir store personnel were seasonal workers scheduled as traffic demanded. Navigation, deck, engine, entertainment, and housekeeping staffs were long-term hires who often stayed for decades. A perfect example is Mary Lou McIntyre, who spent twenty-seven years as social director aboard the *South American*, only retiring when the vessel ceased operations in Montreal.[12]

Trouble for the line was clear in 1962 when Erwin Goebel was quoted in the *Detroit News* suggesting that he had received an attractive offer to sell the ships. "As a result," he said, "our offices were flooded with telegrams, phone calls and personal calls from persons who have enjoyed the Great Lakes from the decks of the ships." Management decided to open the season with one boat to test the waters. The scheduled run from Buffalo to Duluth between June 22 and August 25 was available in two-, five-, and seven-day cruises. An article in *Motor News* in 1963 commented, "[T]he story is told succinctly in the appearance of the 1963 summer cruise schedule of the Georgian Bay Line. The blue-green brochure is different this year. . . . For the first time, the folder lists only the itinerary and schedule of the S.S. *South American*, which will cruise the lakes alone this summer."[13]

The *North American* was sold to the Harry Lundeberg School of Seamanship in Maryland to be used as a dormitory, but it sank en route. When it became obvious—following the final trips to Montreal recounted in this narrative's introduction—that the *South American* was headed to Lundeberg to replace its fleet mate there was remorse, but little action. However, when the dormitory plan fell through, a flurry of activity resulted, all coming to naught. Between 1974 and 1992, Holland, Mackinac Island, Duluth, Menominee, and Detroit all mounted energetic campaigns to convert the ship into a hotel, restaurant, shopping venue, or nightclub attraction. Preservation funding and grantsmanship were almost unknown for projects of this type in the United States, and successive grassroots efforts failed. Communities raised $5 for every $5,000 needed, most coming from regional boat fans, but not local civic boosters. There were several outstanding obstacles. Townsfolk feared the project would fail, and the ship would become an eyesore. The cost of towing the boat back to the lakes exceeded its value as scrap metal. And every year the hulk sat unused the cost of renovations climbed. After efforts to promote it as a restaurant in Detroit failed, the ship was finally scrapped in 1992.[14]

When the last long whistle blew and the last guest departed, the Chicago, Duluth and Georgian Bay Transit Company laid claim to having carried more than a million people. Through a half century, each ship averaged about ten thousand people a year, reflecting near capac-

The Wisconsin & Michigan Steamship Company's refurbished *Milwaukee Clipper* (formerly the *Juniata*), c. 1955. (Courtesy of the Detroit Historical Society Collection.)

ity guest rosters over a twenty-week or longer season. This is an impressive record by any measure.

Great Lakes passenger ship experiences did not end with the Georgian Bay Line. Cross-lake service on Lake Michigan was supplied by a number of vessels, the majority of them railcar ferries with passenger accommodations that ran for a variety of railroads. While comfortable, these were not cruise ships. The last of that line, the *Badger*, still operated in 2015 as the last coal-fired ship in the United States. Environmental concerns that threatened its licensing for several years have been addressed.

The *Juniata*, originally built for the Anchor Line, was laid up in 1937 but went on to serve for more than three decades. Following consolidation of the Wisconsin & Michigan Transportation Company, the ship was rebuilt at Manitowoc and relaunched in June 1941 as the sleek and modern *Milwaukee Clipper*. Wooden upper decks were entirely replaced with a sleek steel superstructure designed by George G. Sharp, with a modern interior to match. The hull was painted a striking aqua green and sported a white superstructure topped with a substantial streamlined smokestack. It bore little resemblance to its 1910 roots and was unlike anything else on the lakes.[15] Ernie Pyle, the popular journalist, after riding in it during the first season, wrote, "This boat across

Lake Michigan between Milwaukee and Muskegon is the berries. It is brand new and looks like a Norman Bel Geddes version of the 'Boat of the Future.' It's so streamlined I'm surprised they ever get it stopped. It's a big thing, too, big as an ocean liner."[16] Guests were greeted on arrival by uniformed bellhops and car attendants. It is notable that, while similar personnel on other lines generally wore nautical-type uniforms of dark blue or white, the *Clipper*'s bellboys wore pillbox hats and fitted jackets more akin to staff at first-rate hotels.

The ship was rated to carry 900 people and 120 autos. Because the cross-lake trip took about four and a half hours, there were only berths for 110 passengers. Instead, the public spaces were enhanced to include a broad, upper sun deck, a large hall with an orchestra for dancing, a movie theater, and a children's playroom complete with a registered nurse. Refreshments and food were available in three lounges, a large dining room, and a combination soda bar and coffee shop. The refit included oil-fired boilers, so passengers enjoyed a soot-free outdoor experience. In 1951 the electronics were upgraded to include radar—a post–World War II boon to navigators—as well as ship-to-shore public telephones. Significantly, and a first on the lakes, all the cabins were fully air-conditioned. For travelers unsure about the maritime experience, this vessel offered more comforts than home.[17]

The company marketed itself specifically to the automotive set. For those taking a cross-country auto trip, the *Milwaukee Clipper* became an extension of US Highway 16. Advertisements encouraged travelers to save 240 miles of driving, compared to a congested drive around the lake through Chicago. In 1951 promoters said that business was so good that they were planning a *Chicago Clipper*, which would run on a triangle between Muskegon, Chicago, and an unnamed Michigan town. "It will be built as soon as world conditions are sufficiently stabilized to make such a venture possible and profitable," they said. In reality this venture morphed into the *Aquarama* project, meant to replace—not augment—the *Milwaukee Clipper*.[18]

Brochures published in 1949 by the Wisconsin & Michigan Transportation Company originally advertised "year-'round 'streamline' service." This was a bit misleading. The flipside of the pamphlet offered a schedule limited to dates between May 29 and October 1. The company maintained this twelve-week schedule until the early 1960s but then eliminated the first week and cut most of the September sailings, effectively reducing the operating season to two months. In 1970 its final year, a one-way fare aboard the *Clipper* was $6.75 per adult; children paid half. Each car was $11.50. A club berth (railroad style) cost $3.75

lower and $3.25 upper. A two-person stateroom for those who wished privacy was $9 night, $8 day. Basic passage for a family of four and an automobile was $31.75. By comparison, when Walt Disney World opened a year later an all-day Adventure Pass to the Magic Kingdom cost the same family about $20. The four-hour Lake Michigan adventure was not cheap.

Unlike Disney World, this adventure was real: watching autos being loaded, absorbing the atmosphere along a waterfront, enjoying the passing scenery, relaxing in a comfortable, moving yacht club. Of course occasionally the salon would pitch more than glide when the boat was in a midlake crosswind. And sometimes boats would be delayed by weather. Other times vessels encountered mechanical problems and returned without completing the journey. There was an uncertainty to sailing that did not fit the immediacy of the Space Age. As expectations went unmet, the ship's owners argued that the *Milwaukee Clipper* did not have the capacity to be profitable. In the early 1960s, the *Aquarama* was proposed as a replacement, but that plan never came to fruition. After the 1970 season, the route was discontinued, and the ship was put up for sale.[19]

It was purchased in 1977 and moved to Navy Pier in Chicago as an attraction that included acrobatic water-skiing shows, dining and dancing, and hotel accommodations. Milwaukee interests, whose harbor had been graced by both the *Juniata* and the *Milwaukee Clipper*, made a bid to buy it but were turned down. Chicago authorities evicted the boat in 1989, and it was purchased by investors from Hammond, Indiana, in 1990. Eventually it got in the way of a new casino at that port, and was towed to the Calumet River in 1996.[20] The Great Lakes Clipper Preservation Association brought it to Muskegon in 1997, where it has been a beacon in the world of steamship preservation. The *Milwaukee Clipper* is recognized as a rare, intact specimen of midcentury modern architecture and design. As an example of early-twentieth-century ship building—even with its second power plant—the *Milwaukee Clipper* was named 2004 Ship of the Year by the Steam Ship Historical Society of America. Perhaps the greatest compliment it ever received came from its longtime first officer, Captain Barney Van Dongen, who said, "She rides like a five-knot breeze on a July afternoon."[21]

The *Aquarama*'s name evokes the optimism that followed World War II, and this project was an ambitious attempt to enter a market out of which most companies had been starved. Muskegon business interests, understanding that the *Milwaukee Clipper* could not support the route, purchased an oceangoing, war-surplus C-4 tanker and towed

Promotional poster for the *Aquarama*, c. 1960. (Image courtesy of the McKee family, Detroit Historical Society Collection.)

it up the Mississippi and into the Great Lakes via Chicago. It arrived in Muskegon in September 1953 for an eight-million-dollar renovation. Less than two years later, the Michigan-Ohio Navigation Company debuted the dramatic transformation at Chicago's Navy Pier. Local papers carried advertisements for the "Aquarama Water Thrill Show," four performances per day, as well as dining and dancing.[22]

The business plan did not include hotel accommodations because there were no staterooms. Arguably, this was a strategic flaw, but the investors sought to emulate the *Milwaukee Clipper*'s success as the proposed *Chicago Clipper* or on a sympathetic route across Lake Erie between Cleveland and Detroit. Highway 16 ran from Detroit to Muskegon and was linked via the *Clipper* to Milwaukee. In the minds of North American travelers, it was one of many new highway options available after the war. On paper this was a most efficient route from the East Coast to the transcontinental northern route and its popular attractions such as the Badlands and Mount Rushmore. The iconic Wild West enjoyed a nostalgic resurgence during this period, which may have influenced travel options. Additionally, the ocean liner cachet attracted another affinity group.[23]

The *Aquarama* was a mighty ship. Its massive bow gave it credence, and amenities such as two elevators, several escalators, and a closed circuit television system put it among the elite of world cruising.

If the *Milwaukee Clipper* was streamlined, the *Aquarama* was futuristic. Capable of carrying 2,500 passengers and 165 cars, a promotional brochure described it as "a cruise ship the like of which has never sailed the Great Lakes."[24] After a year in Chicago, the ship went on a high-profile ramble, "visiting the various lake ports making short stops in each," and offering day and evening excursions for the curious. After this gypsy existence, the company finally established a direct Cleveland to Detroit route in 1957, headquartered in Detroit. Success depended on fast runs and quick turnarounds. The ship was to make three runs per day—one each way and a third to close the day. Without cabins, it did not run at night. With each leg taking five hours and twenty minutes, there was as little as twenty minutes allotted to offload thousands of people and hundreds of cars and then reload and depart. To facilitate this, the company built a complicated, twin-deck ramp and gangway, but twenty minutes proved unrealistic. On top of that, the *Aquarama*'s deepwater hull design threw a mighty wake, which was blamed for swamping fishing boats and ripping docks from riverside boardwalks. Complaints and lawsuits forced the ship to check its speed in the river. Further adding to its difficulties, management found that onboard facilities and staff had trouble catering to the large crowds needed to make a profit. Complaints of long lines and poor service forced the company to decrease the maximum capacity from 2,500 to 1,800. Adding insult to injury, the fare of $20 to $28.40 for a family of four, not including food, was considered an expensive one-way trip.[25]

While impressive to look at, the *Aquarama* was a difficult boat to handle. It had a single propeller spun by a modern, oil-fired turbine that could drive the boat at a respectable twenty-two knots. However, when maneuvering at slow speeds, the elevated bow and pilothouse forward was detrimental in a crosswind. This led to a number of high-profile accidents. While finishing its tour and preparing for a run to Cleveland in 1956, the *Aquarama* was unable to turn in the Detroit River and ran straight into the Windsor seawall. The following year, on its inaugural run on the Detroit-Cleveland route, it had similar problems. Later that same season, it was blown into the *Detroit News*' docks. In 1959, while departing the Cleveland wharf, wind caught the ship's nose, and it clipped the stern of the massive USS *Macon*. In 1962 it grounded entering the harbor at Cleveland, and when a drawbridge did not hoist fast enough, its stern mast snagged on a cable. The cable snapped, and the mast was severely bent. These accidents caused minor physical damage to the vessel but brought a flurry of publicity, which tarnished its reputation.[26]

By 1962 the owners wanted to put the vessel on the Muskegon-

Advertising brochure for the Georgian Bay line, 1960. (Courtesy of the Detroit Historical Society Collection.)

Milwaukee route to replace the *Milwaukee Clipper*. The City of Detroit did not renew the company's lease on the dock in Riverside Park and actually ticketed the vessel for trespassing. The Cleveland office of the owners closed.[27] On Lake Michigan, the dock space assigned to it in Milwaukee was not deep enough for the ship. The City of Milwaukee committed $700,000 to dredge the site. The company countered that offer by asking for a reduction in the $32,000 dock rental fee. Milwaukee port director Harry C. Brockel said, "There is an extent to the concessions we can make to get the Aquarama." In the end, the city rescinded its offer, and many *Aquarama* investors abandoned the project.[28] There were a number of entertainment-oriented plans that never materialized, and the ship sat in Muskegon Harbor for a quarter century. In 1988 it began a nomadic route to Buffalo, with stops at Sarnia and Windsor. It was stripped of its beautiful *arte moderne* interior at Windsor and later vandalized. When it finally reached eastern Lake Erie in 1995, little of its glory remained. A dozen years later, it was finally towed to Turkey for scrapping.[29]

By the 1960s, it was still possible to enjoy a maritime experience on the Great Lakes, but the opportunity was becoming increasingly rare. Counter to predictions, the opening of the St. Lawrence Seaway in 1965 did not attract an influx of passenger ships. Straits of Mackinac ferries ceased operations the day the Mackinac Bridge opened in 1957. The Detroit River ferries took their last runs in 1938, but the excursion boats *Columbia* and *Ste. Claire* continued their route to Bob-Lo Island until 1991. Besides the *Badger*, running Ludington to Manitowoc, Lake Michigan still has the *Lake Express* between Muskegon and Milwaukee and the *Emerald Isle* and *Beaver Islander* between Charlevoix and Beaver Island, Michigan. Lake Superior's long-distance boats, *Ranger III* and *Isle Royale Queen IV*, run from the Keweenaw Peninsula to Isle Royale. On Lake Huron, the Owen Sound Transportation Company, with roots in the nineteenth century, is still running the impressive *Chi-Cheemaun* and *Jiimaan* from Tobermory to Manitoulin Island, Ontario.[30]

Short-run ferries provide service to tourist attractions such as Mackinac Island, Green Bay islands, the Lake Erie Islands, Niagara Falls, the St. Lawrence River's Thousand Islands, the locks at Sault Sainte Marie, and Lake Superior's Pictured Rocks. Additionally, most large lake towns offer some type of water-based historical tour.

In the first two decades of the twenty-first century, the touring public has enjoyed accommodations aboard a number of well-adapted cruise ships. Regular callers have been the *Le Levant* and the *C. Columbus*, among others. These vessels carry 100 to 150 passengers and have graciously filled the demand for short tours of the lakes each summer before returning to the East Coast and Caribbean for the winter. They bear little resemblance to the large, sumptuous vessels of the palace steamer era, but they offer a level of comfort and accommodations demanded by today's consumers, and unimagined by earlier tourists. They are far more efficient, flexible, safe, and environmentally friendly than their predecessors—the welcome descendants of a once thriving industry.

Notes

Note: Articles and other documents consulted on the Internet were accessed between 2011 and 2014. For a list of abbreviations, see the beginning of the Bibliography.

Introduction

1. Curtis Haseltine, "An Era Is Ended," *Detroit Free Press*, October 24, 1967, DGLM VF.
2. This description is based on letters and memos in DGLM VF.

Chapter 1

1. Fred Erving Dayton, *Steamboat Days* (New York: Frederick A. Stokes, 1925), 1.
2. Ibid., 2–9. William Henry was not a man easily deterred. He had successfully developed a practical screw auger. The American Philosophical Society's *Transactions* of 1771 printed Henry's account of his invention under the title "Description of a Self-Moving or Sentinel Register." It was intended to regulate the flue of a furnace. The same publication recorded his thoughts about steam engine design in 1782.
3. Ibid., 8.
4. Ibid., 9–10.
5. Ibid., 10.
6. Ibid., 333–37.

Chapter 2

1. J. B. Mansfield, ed., *History of the Great Lakes*, vol. 1 (Chicago: J. H. Beers, 1899).
2. Edward W. Callahan, *List of Officers of the Navy of the United States and the Marine Corps from 1775 to 1900* (New York: L. R. Hamersly, 1901), http://www.history.navy.mil/books/callahan/reg-usn-p.htm. While usually referred to as a commodore, Perry only received that as an honorary title. He was rated a master commandant at the Battle

of Lake Erie and awarded his captaincy (retroactive to the battle date) in 1814. President James Madison conferred the honorary title in association with a diplomatic posting in 1818.

3. Anna G. Young, "Great beyond Knowing," pt. 1, *Inland Seas* 21, no. 4 (Winter 1965): 271. Young equated £17,000 to US$100,000. In 1814, £17,000 was the rough equivalent of US$1.5 million in 2014.

4. Walter Lewis, "The *Frontenac*: A Reappraisal," *FreshWater* 2, no. 1 (Summer 1987): 28–39, http://www.maritimehistoryofthegreatlakes.ca/Documents/frontenac/default.asp?ID=ss003.

5. Candidus, "Another Letter from a True Briton," *Kingston Gazette*, April 6, 1816, http://images.maritimehistoryofthegreatlakes.ca/7845/data?n=3.

6. Richard F. Palmer, "First Steamboat on the Great Lakes," *Inland Seas* (Spring 1968): 7–20, http://navalmarinearchive.com/research/pdf/in_seas_xl_1-7_sm.pdf; Mansfield, 587.

7. "A New Steamboat on Lake Ontario," *Kingston Gazette*, September 14, 1816, 3, http://images.maritimehistoryofthegreatlakes.ca/7860/data?n=4.

8. Ibid.

9. *Kingston Gazette*, May 24, 1817, http://images.maritimehistoryofthegreatlakes.ca/33152/data?n=13.

10. *Buffalo Gazette and Niagara Intelligencer*, August 6, 1816, http://images.maritimehistoryofthegreatlakes.ca/33167/data?n=17.

11. *Niles' Weekly Register*, March 29, 1817; Manuscript diary of Capt. Van Cleve, Buffalo Historical Society, cited in Barlow Cunningham, *A Century of Sail and Steam on the Niagara River* (Toronto: Musson Book Company, 1911), chap. 2, http://www.maritimehistoryofthegreatlakes.ca/Documents/Cumberland/default.asp?ID=c008.

12. *Sacket's Harbor Gazette*, quoted in the *Buffalo Gazette*, May 20, 1817, http://images.maritimehistoryofthegreatlakes.ca/33167/data?n=2. See also *Daily British Whig* (Kingston, ON), August 5, 1890, http://images.maritimehistoryofthegreatlakes.ca/33167/data?n=2.

13. "History of Steam Navigation on Lake Ontario," *Onondaga Standard* (New York), September 29, 1847, http://www.maritimehistoryofthegreatlakes.ca/documents/Cumberland/default.asp?ID=c008#p063; *Kingston Gazette*, May 24, 1817, http://images.maritimehistoryofthegreatlakes.ca/7886/data?n=3.

14. *Buffalo Gazette*, April 20, 1817, http://images.maritimehistoryofthegreatlakes.ca/33167/data?n=1.

15. *Kingston Gazette*, May 1, 1818, http://images.maritimehistoryofthegreatlakes.ca/57799/data?n=2.

16. Young, 268–69.

17. *Daily British Whig* (Kingston, ON), August 5, 1890.

18. "The Steamboat *Ontario*," *Ontario Repository* (Canandaigua, NY), August 9, 1817, http://images.maritimehistoryofthegreatlakes.ca/5084/data?n=1.

19. *Sacket's Harbor Gazette*, quoted in the *Buffalo Gazette*, May 20, 1817. See also "The Steamboat *Ontario*," *Ontario Repository*, August 9, 1817.

20. "Steam Boat *Ontario*," *Rochester Telegraph*, August 11, 1818, http://images.maritimehistoryofthegreatlakes.ca/35912/data?n=8.

21. "The Steamboat *Ontario*," *Ontario Repository* (Canandaigua, NY), August 18, 1818, http://images.maritimehistoryofthegreatlakes.ca/5087/data?n=12; "Steam Boat *Ontario*," *Rochester Telegraph*, July 7, 1818, http://images.maritimehistoryofthegreatlakes.ca/6612/data?n=15 ; "Steam Boat *Ontario*," *Geneva Gazette*, July 7, 1819, http://images.maritimehistoryofthegreatlakes.ca/35718/data?n=1.

22. *St. Catharines Journal*, August 9, 1826, http://images.maritimehistoryofthegreatlakes.ca/57871/data?n=18; *Buffalo Emporium*, June 25, 1827, http://images.maritimehistoryofthegreatlakes.ca/results?q=Buffalo+Emporium%2C+June+25%2C+1827.

23. "Steamboat *Frontenac,*" *Kingston Gazette,* May 31, 1817, and June 7, 1817, http://images.maritimehistoryofthegreatlakes.ca/33152/data?n=2.

24. Lewis, "The *Frontenac,*" n. 45. This figure is the equivalent of about $1.25 million in 2012 US dollars, per "Pounds Sterling to Dollars: Historical Conversion of Currency," http://uwacadweb.uwyo.edu/numimage/currency.htm.

25. *Kingston Chronicle,* April 30, 1819, quoted in Cunningham.

26. *Kingston Herald,* June 25, 1822, reported in the *Sandusky Clarion,* July 31, 1822, 2, http://images.maritimehistoryofthegreatlakes.ca/49128/data?n=1.

27. *Kingston Chronicle,* January 14, 1825, http://images.maritimehistoryofthegreat lakes.ca/33141/data?n=6, quoted in Lewis, "The *Frontenac.*"

28. "Fire," *Farmer's Journal & Welland Canal Intelligencer,* September 26, 1827, quoted in the *Cleveland Weekly Herald,* September 27, 1827, 3, http://images.mari timehistoryofthegreatlakes.ca/50737/data?n=1; *Buffalo Journal,* quoted in the *Cleveland Weekly Herald,* October 10, 1822, http://images.maritimehistoryofthegreatlakes. ca/58510/data?n=22; Lewis, "The *Frontenac.*"

29. Joseph B. Stuart, Nathaniel Davis, Asa H. Curtis, Ralph Pratt, James Durant, and John Mead were from Albany. Samuel McCoon, Alexander McMuir, engineer Robert McQueen, and shipwright Noah Brown were from the lower Hudson Valley.

30. William Hodge, *Papers concerning Early Navigation on the Great Lakes* (Buffalo: Bigelow Bros., 1883), 23.

31. Ibid., 27.

32. This description is based on plans drawn by Captain Joseph E. Johnson for the Museum of the Great Lakes, now in the collection of the Detroit Historical Society. The plans were also published as Joseph E. Johnson, "Plan of the *Walk-in-the-Water,*" in *Telescope* 2, no. 11 (November 1953): 4–5.

33. *Detroit Gazette,* August 14, 1818, http://images.maritimehistoryofthegreatlakes. ca/3228/data?n=10.

34. *Detroit Gazette,* August 21, 1818, http://images.maritimehistoryofthegreatlakes. ca/3230/data?n=48.

35. Mansfield, chap. 33; Hodge, 28–29.

36. *Kingston Gazette,* September 15, 1818, http://images.maritimehistoryofthegreat lakes.ca/7941/data?n=51.

37. Hodge, 36.

38. *Detroit Gazette,* August 28, 1818, http://images.maritimehistoryofthegreatlakes. ca/31046/data?n=53.

39. Hodge, 36.

40. Mansfield, chap. 33.

41. *Detroit Gazette,* August 28, 1818.

42. Ibid.

43. *Niagara Patriot,* October 6, 1818, http://images.maritimehistoryofthegreatlakes. ca/48177/data?n=52.

44. *Geneva Gazette,* May 12, 1819, http://images.maritimehistoryofthegreatlakes. ca/4571/data?n=1.

45. *Detroit Gazette,* May 12, 1819, http://images.maritimehistoryofthegreatlakes. ca/4571/data?n=27; *New York Mercantile Advertiser,* quoted in the *Detroit Gazette,* May 14, 1819, http://images.maritimehistoryofthegreatlakes.ca/3256/data?n=18.

46. *Detroit Gazette,* June 18, 1819, 3, http://images.maritimehistoryofthegreatlakes. ca/3265/data?n=19.

47. Ibid.

48. *Detroit Gazette,* June 25, 1819, 3, http://images.maritimehistoryofthegreatlakes.ca/3265/data?n=20; *Detroit Gazette,* July 9, 1819, http://images.maritimehistoryofthegreatlakes.ca/3267/data?n=12.

49. Hodge, 29.

50. That fare was the rough equivalent of $320 in 2010, and was about 66 percent the value of an airline ticket between the two cities in the early twenty-first century (http://www.measuringworth.com/ppowerus/).

51. *Detroit Gazette*, May 12, 1820.

52. *Detroit Gazette*, June 16, 1820, 2, http://images.maritimehistoryofthegreatlakes.ca/3295/data?n=14.

53. *Detroit Gazette*, August 4, 1820, http://images.maritimehistoryofthegreatlakes.ca/3306/data?n=35.

54. *Detroit Gazette*, November 17, 1820, http://images.maritimehistoryofthegreatlakes.ca/31879/data?n=9.

55. *Detroit Gazette*, April 20, 1821, http://images.maritimehistoryofthegreatlakes.ca/3320/data?n=2; *Detroit Gazette*, May 18, 1821, http://images.maritimehistoryofthegreatlakes.ca/3323/data?n=16.

56. *Detroit Gazette*, July 6, 1821, http://images.maritimehistoryofthegreatlakes.ca/3327/data?n=40; *Detroit Gazette*, July 13, 1821, http://images.maritimehistoryofthegreatlakes.ca/3328/data?n=41.

57. *Detroit Gazette*, August 10, 1821, http://images.maritimehistoryofthegreatlakes.ca/3329/data?n=50; *Detroit Gazette*, August 17, 1821, http://images.maritimehistoryofthegreatlakes.ca/3330/data?n=42.

58. *Cleveland Weekly Herald*, November 6, 1821, http://images.maritimehistoryofthegreatlakes.ca/47525/data?n=2. Accounts differ on the number of passengers aboard, ranging from about eighteen to almost one hundred. It is likely that, late in the season, the number was about forty. *Buffalo Patriot*, reprinted in the *Kingston Chronicle*, November 30, 1821, http://images.maritimehistoryofthegreatlakes.ca/8241/data?n=33.

59. Mary A. Witherall Palmer, "A Letter to E. C. Walker," in *Report of the Pioneer Society of the State of Michigan*, vol. 4 (Lansing: W. S. George and Co., 1883), 113.

60. Ibid., 112–15.

61. Ibid., 114.

62. *Marine Record* (Cleveland), October 25, 1883, http://images.maritimehistoryofthegreatlakes.ca/47525/data?n=9.

Chapter 3

1. Kerri Jansen, "Lydia Bacon: Army Wife, Intrepid Traveler," in *Border Crossings: The Detroit River Region in the War of 1812*, ed. Denver Brunsman, Joel Stone, and Douglas D. Fisher (Detroit: Detroit Historical Society, 2012), 113.

2. Alice Morse Earle, *Stage Coach and Tavern Days* (Detroit: Singing Tree Press, 1968), 196 (originally published in 1900).

3. Ibid., 85–86.

4. Peter L. Rousseau, "A Common Currency: Early US Monetary Policy and the Transition to the Dollar," *Financial History Review* 13, no. 1 (2006): 116; John Paris, "Fraud on the Frontier," in *Border Crossings: The Detroit River Region in the War of 1812*, ed. Denver Brunsman, Joel Stone, and Douglas D. Fisher (Detroit: Detroit Historical Society, 2012), 35–48.

5. Rousseau, 116.

6. Bertha Monica Stearns, "Philadelphia Magazines for Ladies, 1830–1860," *Pennsylvania Magazine of History and Biography* 69, no. 3 (July 1945): 207.

7. Alan Taylor provides the characterization of an "American oasis" and cites the assessments of territorial officials Augustus B. Woodward and William Woodbridge. Surveyor General Edward Tiffin's letter to Josiah Meigs, commissioner of the General Land Office, was based on a unanimous report submitted by a survey crew assigned to the Michigan Territory. The surveyors quit their work, citing "incredible hardships" and

"extreme suffering." As a result, two million acres of Michigan land that was supposed to have been set aside for war veterans was ignored. Tiffin referred to "swamp beyond description . . . extensive marshes . . . [and] extreme sterility and barrenness of soil" and recommended that the United States "abandon the country." Willis Frederick Dunbar mentions references in schoolbooks to the "interminable swamp" of the territory's interior. Woodford addressed unfavorable coverage of Michigan in eastern newspapers and recounted the unappealing depiction of the territory by Jedediah Morse, "the foremost geographer of his day." Willis Frederick Dunbar, *Michigan through the Centuries*, vol. 1 (New York: Lewis Historical Publishing , 1955), 156; Alan Taylor, *The Civil War of 1812: American Citizens, British Subjects, Irish Rebels, and Indian Allies* (New York: Alfred A. Knopf, 2010), 153–54. Edward Tiffin to Josiah Meigs, November 30, 1815, in *Michigan Pioneer and Historical Collections* (Lansing: Michigan Historical Commission, 1888), 10:61–62; Frank B. Woodford, *Lewis Cass: The Last Jeffersonian* (New Brunswick, NJ: Rutgers University Press, 1950), 108–9.

8. William Darby, *A Tour from the City of New York to Detroit: In the Michigan Territory, Made Between the 2d of May and the 22d of September, 1818 . . .* (New York: Kirk & Mercein, 1819), 10, 194, 201.

9. Henry Rowe Schoolcraft, *Narrative Journal of Travels from Detroit Northwest through the Great Chain of American Lakes to the Sources of the Mississippi River Performed as a Member of the Expedition under Governor Cass in the Year 1820* (Albany: E. & E. Hosford, 1821), 19, https://archive.org/details/narrativejournal00scho. Schoolcraft notes that the actual travel time was forty hours for the 160 miles covered, an average of four miles per hour. The speed was not exceptional, but the level of comfort is duly noted. His travel from Albany to Schenectady averaged more than five and a half miles per hour but was markedly less comfortable.

10. Ibid., 47–49.

11. Ibid., 64–113, quote on 98. Schoolcraft notes that the coast of the Michigan peninsula "presents no change of character worth of remark" and "serve to imprint a character of uniformity upon the scene." He notes that north of Fort Gratiot (Port Huron), the soil quality begins to deteriorate. Had he explored the Saginaw Valley he would have had more good things to say.

12. Maurice D. Smith, *Steamboats on the Lakes: Two Centuries of Steamboat Travel through Ontario's Waterways* (Toronto: James Lorimer, 2005), 32–37.

Chapter 4

1. William Hodge, *Papers Concerning Early Navigation on the Great Lakes* (Buffalo: Bigelow Bros. 1883), 37.

2. *Detroit Gazette*, January 11, 1822, 2, http://images.maritimehistoryofthegreat lakes.ca/3334/data?n=26.

3. J. B. Mansfield, ed., *History of the Great Lakes*, vol. 1 (Chicago: J. H. Beers, 1899), http://www.maritimehistoryofthegreatlakes.ca/documents/hgl/default.asp?ID=s007; *Erie Gazette*, December 22, 1821, http://images.maritimehistoryofthegreatlakes.ca/31879/data?n=9; Hodge, 39; "Launch of Steamer *Milwaukee*," *Buffalo Daily Courier*, June 3, 1859, http://images.maritimehistoryofthegreatlakes.ca/30725/data?n=92.

4. "Launch of Steamer *Milwaukee*."

5. Extract of a letter from Buffalo, dated February 20, 1822, to the editor of the *Utica Sentinel*, reported in the *Detroit Gazette*, March 22, 1822, http://images.maritime historyofthegreatlakes.ca/3339/data?n=2.

6. "New Lake Erie Steam-boat *Superior*," *Detroit Gazette*, May 31, 1822, 3, http://images.maritimehistoryofthegreatlakes.ca/3347/data?n=11.

7. Ibid.

8. Hodge, 40; *Cleveland Weekly Herald*, April 30, 1822, 3–4, http://images.maritime historyofthegreatlakes.ca/30724/data?n=15.

9. Mansfield.

10. "The New Steam-Boat," *Detroit Gazette*, May 31, 1822, 3, http://images.maritime historyofthegreatlakes.ca/3346/data?n=2; *Detroit Gazette*, May 15, 1822, http://images. maritimehistoryofthegreatlakes.ca/3347/data?n=11; *Cleveland Weekly Herald*, May 28, 1822, 3, http://images.maritimehistoryofthegreatlakes.ca/33930/data?n=2; *Detroit Gazette*, June 21, 1822, http://images.maritimehistoryofthegreatlakes.ca/3350/data?n=20.

11. *Detroit Gazette*, July 5, 1822, 2, http://images.maritimehistoryofthegreatlakes. ca/3353/data?n=3; Extract from a letter, dated Saut de St. Marie, July 13, 1822, quoted in the *Detroit Gazette*, July 26, 1822, 2, http://images.maritimehistoryofthegreatlakes. ca/3356/data?n=17.

12. Mansfield, chap. 34: 1821, http://www.maritimehistoryofthegreatlakes.ca/docu ments/hgl/default.asp?ID=s014; *Detroit Free Press*, May 10, 1872, http://images.mari timehistoryofthegreatlakes.ca/4054/data?n=18.

13. *Detroit Gazette*, August 22, 1822, 2, http://images.maritimehistoryofthegreat lakes.ca/3360/data?n=12; *Buffalo Journal*, cited in the *Cleveland Weekly Herald*, October 10, 1822, http://images.maritimehistoryofthegreatlakes.ca/58510/data?n=22.

14. *Detroit Gazette*, September 27, 1822, 2, http://images.maritimehistoryofthegreat lakes.ca/3361/data?n=32.

15. *Black Rock Gazette*, January 13, 1827, 3, http://images.maritimehistoryoft hegreatlakes.ca/2787/data?n=24; S. W. Stanton illustration, http://images.maritimehis toryofthegreatlakes.ca/790/data?n=25; *Buffalo Commercial Advertiser*, August 1, 1838, http://images.maritimehistoryofthegreatlakes.ca/21900/data?n=9; *Detroit Post and Tri bune*, April 7, 1884, http://images.maritimehistoryofthegreatlakes.ca/6086/data?n=32.

16. L. Klein, "Notes on the Steam Navigation upon the Great Northern Lakes," *Inland Seas* 48, no. 1 (Spring 1992): 54–55. This article was originally published in the *American Railroad Journal* on May 15 and June 1, 1841. It offers a most complete look at several operational aspects of a typical, well-run, early palace steamer.

17. Ibid., 49–58.

18. Figures were drawn from the website Measuring Worth, http://www.measuring worth.com/uscompare/relativevalue.php. An annual deckhand's salary, $180, had a labor value in 2012 of $37,000. The captain's $1,000 was the equivalent of $200,000.

19. Klein, 51. See also Maurice D. Smith, *Steamboats on the Lakes: Two Centuries of Steamboat Travel through Ontario's Waterways* (Toronto: James Lorimer, 2005), 36.

20. Anna G. Young, "Great beyond Knowing," pt. 1, *Inland Seas*, 21, no. 4 (Winter 1965): 268–69.

21. Ibid., 272.

22. Ibid.

23. Ibid., 273–74.

24. Ibid., 274–75.

25. Ibid., 275–76; Anna G. Young, "Great beyond Knowing," pt. 2, *Inland Seas* 22, no. 1 (Spring 1966): 29–34.

26. Richard F. Palmer, "Wreck of the Steamboat *Martha Ogden*," *Inland Seas* 55, no. 1 (Spring 1999): 5; *Oswego Palladium*, July 13, 1881, http://images.maritimehistoryoft hegreatlakes.ca/5265/data?n=11.

27. *Oswego Palladium*, April, 4, 1876 http://freepages.genealogy.rootsweb.ancestry. com/~twigs2000/vancleve.html.

28. Thomas W. Symons and John C. Quintus, "History of Buffalo Harbor," *Publica tions of the Buffalo Historical Society* 5 (January 1902): 239–85, http://digital.library. cornell.edu/cgi/t/text/pageviewer-idx?c=nys;cc=nys;rgn=full%20text;idno=nys343;did no=nys343;view=image;seq=3;node=nys343%3A2; Augustus Walker, "Early Days on the Lakes, with an Account of the Cholera Visitation of 1832," *Publications of the Buffa-*

lo *Historical Society* 5 (January 1902): 287–318, http://www.maritimehistoryofthegreat
lakes.ca/Documents/walker/default.asp?ID=c1.

29. *Michigan Pioneer and Historical Collections* (Lansing: Robert Smith & Co.,
1894), 21:341.

30. Samuel Ward died on February 4, 1854, according to family Bible records and other papers in the Ward Family Papers, BHC, http://dgmgenealogy.info/StClairPioneers/
ps02/ps02_265.htm.

31. Chuck Sterba, "An Early Great Lakes Shipping Giant," *Soundings* 50, nos. 1–2
(Spring–Summer 2010): 3–5, 16–17.

32. *Erie Gazette*, cited in *Detroit Post and Tribune*, August 17, 1881, http://images.
maritimehistoryofthegreatlakes.ca/5766/data?n=1.

33. *Milwaukee Sentinel*, August 17, 1841, http://www3.gendisasters.com/new
york/14801/silver-creek-ny-steamer-erie-fire-aug-1841-further-particulars.

34. Klein, 49.

35. Ibid., 53–54.

36. Mary C. Gillett, *Army Medical Department, 1818–1865* (Washington, DC: US
Government Printing Office, 1987), 50–51, http://history.amedd.army.mil/booksdocs/civil/
gillett2/amedd_1818–1865_chpt2.html.

37. Walker.

38. Ibid. Other accounts list one or two sick soldiers being landed. See Mary Porter, *Eliza Chappell Porter, a Memoir* (New York: Fleming H. Revell, 1892), http://openli
brary.org/books/OL7208554M/Eliza_Chappell_Porter.

39. Henry Wayland Hill, ed., *Municipality of Buffalo, New York: A History, 1720–
1923* (New York: Lewis Historical Publishing, 1923), http://www.buffalonian.com/history/
articles/1801-50/cholera32.html.

40. Diaries of George W. Jonson, vol. 1, 1833–37, held at Dartmouth College, Hanover,
New Hampshire, http://www.buffalonian.com/diaries/dofweek.html.

41. G. F. Pyle, "The Diffusion of Cholera in the United States in the Nineteenth Century," *Geographical Analysis* 1, no. 1 (September 3, 2010), http://onlinelibrary.wiley.com/
doi/10.1111/j.1538-4632.1969.tb00605.x/pdf. Studies analyzing the pandemic show that
there is no correlation between the timeline and ports along the steamship routes. In
1832 the strain arriving from the East Coast hit Detroit two weeks before Buffalo was
stricken. Conversely, the 1849 epidemic spreading northward up the Mississippi Valley—
arguably by steamboat—arrived in Buffalo at the end of May but didn't claim a victim
in Detroit until mid-August. This should not minimize the role of maritime traffic in the
transmission of disease. Certainly, the people, animals and baggage carried pathogens
and vermin of many sorts. And they, like their hosts, could travel farther faster.

42. L. N. Fuller, "Northern New York in the Patriot War," *Watertown Daily Times*,
presented in serial form in March, April, and May 1923, http://freepages.genealogy.roots
web.ancestry.com/~twigs2000/chapvii.html.

43. *Detroit Free Press*, July 14, 1847, http://images.maritimehistoryofthegreatlakes.
ca/35293/data?n=23.

Chapter 5

1. "List of Principle [*sic*] Steamboats upon the Upper Lakes in 1839," *Inland Seas*
48, no. 1 (Spring 1992): 50. My review of principal vessels on the lakes from 1839 to 1857
is based on contemporary resources, as listed later in this volume, as well as a survey
of database information through the Historical Collection of the Great Lakes and the
Labadie Collection at the Alpena Public Library. Sources generally agree on dimensional
information, but they often cite disparate figures without attribution, particularly with
regard to registered tonnage.

2. James L. Elliot, *Red Stacks over the Horizon: The Story of the Goodrich Steamboat Line* (Ellison Bay, WI: William Caxton, 1995), 16.

3. Wabash Railroad Company, "Wabash Railroad History," condensed from an article authored by the Advertising and Public Relations Department of the Wabash Railroad Company, August 1959, http://wabashrhs.org/wabhist.html.

4. H. Philip Spratt, *Transatlantic Steamers*, 2nd ed. (Glasgow: Brown and Sons, 1967), 15–19.

5. Ibid., 19–21.

6. Vernon Gibbs, *Passenger Liners of the Western Ocean* (New York: Staples Press, 1952), 29.

7. Ibid., 31.

8. Ibid., 34–36.

9. *British Whig* (Kingston, ON), May 2, 1834, 2, http://images.maritimehistoryofthegreatlakes.ca/11208/data?n=99.

10. Launch report in *Cleveland Daily Herald & Gazette*, August 9, 1838, http://images.maritimehistoryofthegreatlakes.ca/28799/data?n=1. The description of the vessel and its appointments is drawn from the *Cleveland Daily Herald & Gazette*, May 10, 1839, http://images.maritimehistoryofthegreatlakes.ca/33945/data?n=1.

11. *Chronicle & Gazette* (Kingston, ON), April 11, 1835, http://images.maritimehistoryofthegreatlakes.ca/8663/data?n=34; *Cleveland Daily Herald & Gazette*, October 11, 1837, 2, http://images.maritimehistoryofthegreatlakes.ca/31081/data?n=21; *Detroit Tribune*, quoted in the *Kingston Daily News*, February 26, 1861, 2, http://images.maritimehistoryofthegreatlakes.ca/17807/data?n=8.

12. The *Great Western* burned at a Detroit dock in September 1839, a major loss to its owner after less than fourteen months in operation. Fire report, *Detroit Free Press*, September 3, 1839, http://images.maritimehistoryofthegreatlakes.ca/3653/data?n=5.

13. Samuel Ward Stanton, in *American Steam Vessels* (New York: Smith & Stanton, 1895), 75, claimed that the vessel was the "first steamboat in the United States to measure over 1,000 tons, and when she came out was 200 tons larger than any other steam vessel in the world." Contemporary reports name it the largest steam vessel on North American freshwater. Old Measurement (OM) is a tonnage calculation. Ships have a variety of measurements—length, width (or beam), and depth being the simplest—which define how fast they can go, how much cargo they can carry, and how stable they are in a number of situations. For practical comparison of different crafts, tonnage is a volume measurement reflecting the amount of water a vessel displaces but equally defining its available interior space. One hundred cubic feet equal roughly one ton. Determining tonnage requires complicated calculations, and statutes governing that formula were updated in 1864. Any ship admeasured prior to this date is considered OM. For practicality's sake, within this volume tonnages cited for any ship built prior to 1864 are assumed to be OM, and those for ships built afterward are subject to the new calculation scheme. The designation OM has been inserted for clarification when necessary.

14. *Buffalo Daily Courier*, August 23, 1844, 2, http://images.maritimehistoryofthegreatlakes.ca/31585/data?n=60; several descriptions of the vessel on this website offer a wonderful glimpse into the amenities available to the passengers.

15. *Daily National Pilot* (Buffalo), June 5, 1845, http://images.maritimehistoryofthegreatlakes.ca/29727/data?n=2. The year 1845 also saw the launch of a *Niagara* at the yard of John Oades on Lake Ontario. Owned by Elijah Allen, and later by James Van Cleve's Ontario and St. Lawrence Steamboat Company, this 190-foot steamer maintained mail and packet routes on the eastern end of that lake until 1857. Afterward it was leased by the US Army and served as a supply vessel on the Atlantic, finally ending its career at New Orleans in 1864. TBNMS, http://www.greatlakesships.org/vesselview.aspx?id=99759. Information about Bidwell & Banta's *Niagara* may be found in John Odin

Jensen, "The History and Archeology of the Great Lakes Steamboat *Niagara*," *Wisconsin Magazine* 82, no. 3 (Spring 1999): 198–230.

16. Jensen, 218, 224. Jensen noted with respect that these milled oak beams were three inches thick, eighteen inches wide, and forty feet or more long. In 1851 published accounts described the installation of "internal arches," longitudinal supports for the middle of the vessel. Again three-inch oak planks, they stretched 118 feet starting aft at the turn of the bilge, arching to the point where the paddle axels sit, and turning again toward the chine of the framing. Thick bolts ran through the arches to each frame.

17. *Buffalo Commercial Advertiser*, April 30, 1849, 2, http://images.maritimehistoryofthegreatlakes.ca/51576/data?n=6; Walter Lewis, "Steamboat Promotion and Changing Technology: The Careers of James Sutherland and the *Magnet*," *Ontario History* 77, no. 3 (September 1985): 207–30, http://maritimehistoryoftheGreatLakes.ca/Documents/sutherlandmagnet/.

18. Jensen, 206–8.

19. Ibid., 209; *Detroit Free Press*, July 23, 1847; *Detroit Free Press*, August 5, 1847. A review of the paper over a three-month period found that it initially announced the rivalry (siding with the *Sultana*) on July 23, as the *Sultana* was returning from the Rivers and Harbors Convention. Both boats were in Buffalo by July 27, but an account of a race was not published prior to the *Niagara*'s collision soon afterward.

20. *Buffalo Morning Express*, January 11, 1856, http://images.maritimehistoryofthegreatlakes.ca/38758/data?n=2.

21. *Buffalo Daily Republic*, September 29, 1856, http://images.maritimehistoryofthegreatlakes.ca/40380/data?n=7. The next several citations come from the same website.

22. Ibid.

23. Ibid., September 30, 1856.

24. Ibid., September 29, 1856.

25. *Buffalo Daily Courier*, July 4, 1849, http://images.maritimehistoryofthegreatlakes.ca/54222/data?n=8.

26. After 1847, boats longer than 250 feet (except the *Baltic*) were built with arches.

27. Bradley A. Rodgers, *Guardian of the Great Lakes: The U.S. Paddle Frigate 'Michigan'* (Ann Arbor: University of Michigan Press, 1996), 9–10. This is a beautifully detailed thesis on the revolutionary design and long career of the USS *Michigan*. See also Arthur Woodford, *Charting the Inland Seas, Etc.* (Detroit: Wayne State University Press, 1994), 26; and Louis C. Hunter, *Steamboats on the Western Rivers: An Economic and Technological History* (Mineola, NY: Dover, 1993), 114–15.

28. Woodford, *Charting*, 25–27.

29. Rodgers, 15–34.

30. *The Argus* (Kingston, ON), November 6, 1846, http://images.maritimehistoryofthegreatlakes.ca/33165/data?n=5.

31. Lewis, "Steamboat Promotion."

32. *Peter Hogg and Cornelius H. Delamater, plaintiffs in error, v. John B. Ericsson*, 52 U.S. 587 (11 How. 587, 13 L.Ed. 824), http://www.law.cornell.edu/supremecourt/text/52/587, September 2012; H. A. Musham, "Early Great Lakes Steamboats: The First Propellers, 1841–1845," *Telescope* 6, no. 10 (October 1957): 4–6.

33. James L. Barton, *Letter to the Hon. Robert M'Clelland, Chairman of the Committee on Commerce in the U.S. House of Representatives in Relation to the Value and Importance of the Commerce of the Great Western Lakes* (Buffalo: Jewett, Thomas, 1846), 7, 19–21, Brendon Baillod Collection, Dane County, Wisconsin. The vessels ranged in size from 150 to 750 tons, with a value of 22 million dollars. By the next year, fifteen boats were leaving Buffalo weekly for Milwaukee or Chicago.

34. Lewis, "Steamboat Promotion"; Spratt, 67. As a matter of comparison, transocean fleets were quicker to abandon paddlewheels than were the East Coast and lake compa-

nies. It is notable that the venerable Cunard Steamship Company Ltd. launched nothing but propeller vessels after the *Scotia* in 1861, while the D&C of Detroit launched twin side-wheeled leviathans, the *Greater Detroit* and *Greater Buffalo*, as late as 1924.

35. Spratt, 67; *Tonnage on the Lakes* (Halton Hills, ON: Maritime History of the Great Lakes, 2004). The latter is based on the article "Tonnage on the Lakes," *The Democracy* (Buffalo), February 28, 1855, http://www.maritimehistoryofthegreatlakes.ca/Documents/ShipLists/US1855/default.asp?ID=c02.

36. Barton, *Letter*, 23.

Chapter 6

1. Thomas E. Appleton, *Usque Ad Mare: A History of the Canadian Coast Guard and Marine Services* (Ottawa: Canada Department of Transport, 1968), archived at http://www.ccg-gcc.gc.ca/eng/CCG/USQUE_Steamboat_Inspection.

2. *Black Rock Advocate*, January 27, 1837, 3, http://images.maritimehistoryoft hegreatlakes.ca/3011/data?n=15.

3. James L. Barton, *Address on the Early Reminiscences of Western New York and the Lake Region of Country* (Buffalo: Jewett, Thomas & Co., 1848), 7.

4. Ibid.

5. In *Black Rock Advocate*, February 17, 1837, quoting the *Detroit Advertiser*, http://images.maritimehistoryofthegreatlakes.ca/3009/data?n=13http://images.maritime historyofthegreatlakes.ca/3009/data?n=13.

6. *Niles' National Register* (Baltimore), June 26, 1847, vol. 72, 266, http://babel. hathitrust.org/cgi/pt?id=inu.30000117880546;view=1up;seq=271; John N. Dickenson, *To Build a Canal: Sault Ste. Marie, 1853–54 and After* (Columbus: Ohio State University Press, 1981), 15; Robert S. Cotterill, "Southern Railroads and Western Trade," *Mississippi Valley Historical Review* 3, no. 4 (March 1917): 428.

7. Robert Fergus, ed., *Chicago River and Harbor Convention: An Account of Its Origins and Proceedings* (Chicago: Fergus Printing, 1882), 11.

8. Ibid., 26.

9. *Niles' National Register* (Baltimore), June 26, 1847, vol. 72, 266.

10. Fergus, 35; J. B. Mansfield, ed., *History of the Great Lakes*, vol. 1 (Chicago: J. H. Beers, 1899); *Chicago Weekly Journal*, March 23, 1846, quoted in Betty Mendelsohn, "The Federal Hand in Urban Development: Chicago Harbor before the Civil War," *Prologue* 30, no. 4 (Winter 1998): 261.

11. Robert S. Cotterill, "Early Agitation for a Pacific Railroad, 1845–1850," *Mississippi Valley Historical Review* 5, no. 4 (March 1919): 396.

12. Ralph Gray, "A National Waterway," in *History of the Chesapeake and Delaware Canal, 1769–1965* (Urbana: University of Illinois Press, 1967); Tim McNeese, *America's Early Canals* (New York: Crestwood House, 1993); Frank N. Wilcox and William A. McGill, *The Ohio Canals* (Kent, OH: Kent State University Press, 1969); Carol Sheriff, *The Artificial River: The Erie Canal and the Paradox of Progress* (New York: Hill and Wang, 1996); John W. Larson, *Essayons: A History of the Detroit District, U.S. Army Corps of Engineers* (Detroit: US Army Corps of Engineers, Detroit District, 1981); Dickenson, 15; Martin Hershock, *The Paradox of Progress* (Athens: Ohio University Press, 2003), 1–4; John Joseph Wallis, "American Government Finance in the Long Run: 1790 to 1990," *Journal of Economic Perspectives* 14, no. 1 (Winter 2000): 62.

13. Robert H. Wiebe, *The Opening of American Society* (New York: Alfred A Knopf, 1984), 353; *Chicago Evening Journal*, July 6, 1847, quoted in Fergus, 7–13; *Southern Quarterly Review* no. 10 (October 1846): 20.

14. James K. Polk, "Veto Response to H.R. 18: An Act Making Appropriations for the Improvement of Certain Harbors and Rivers, August 3, 1846," 29th Cong., 1st sess.,

Congressional Globe (Washington, DC: US Government Printing Office, 1846), 1181–83, http://memory.loc.gov/ammem/amlaw/lwcg.html.

15. Mendelsohn, 257–65.

16. Harold M. Mayer and Richard Wade, *Chicago: Growth of a Metropolis* (Chicago: University of Chicago Press, 1969), 30. Mentor L. Williams, "The Chicago River and Harbor Convention, 1847," *Mississippi Valley Historical Review* 35, no. 4 (March 1949): 608; Joel Stone, "Survey of Detroit Taverns and Hotels," unpublished manuscript.

17. Mansfield; Emmett Dedmon, *Fabulous Chicago*, 2nd ed. (New York: Athenaeum, 1981), 17; Donald L. Mohar, "Major Economic Conventions during the Polk Administration" (MA thesis, Illinois State University, 1968), 27, 49; *Proceedings of Harbor and River Convention held in Chicago* (Chicago: R. L. Wilson, 1847), 57–66; *Commercial Review of the South and West* (New Orleans) 4, no. 1 (September 1847); *Detroit Free Press*, July 10, 1847. Various sources omit Kentucky, New Hampshire, or South Carolina, but delegates are identifiable for all nineteen.

18. Mohar, 55; Williams, "Chicago River and Harbor Convention," 623; John J. Lalor, ed., *Cyclopedia of Political Science, Political Economy, and the Political History of the United States* (New York: Maynard, Merrill, 1899), II.196.3, http://www.econlib.org/library/ydpbooks/lalor/llCy587.html.

19. Clarence M. Burton, *The City of Detroit, Michigan, 1701–1922*, 5 vols. (Detroit: S. J. Clarke, 1922), 516. It is notable that boards of trade became an institutional trend following the Chicago convention and spread from the lakes outward. In an informal survey, the term first appeared in Baltimore in 1836 and then in Toronto in 1845, predating the Harbor & Rivers Convention (H&RC). Besides the Great Lakes towns listed in the text, the following 1850 boards of trade appeared in Boston, 1855; Kansas City, 1856; St. Joseph, Missouri, 1862; New York, 1870; New Orleans, 1880; Cincinnati, 1885; and Vancouver, 1887. The search was limited to institutions with that name. There is evidence to suggest that boards of trade replaced other formal or quasi-formal organizations. New York's was formed in 1870 but grew out of the New York Cotton Exchange, which can be traced back to 1792. St. Louis had a Merchants Exchange in 1836. Memphis's Chamber of Commerce was formed in 1860 and a Cotton Exchange in 1873. At the least it might be suggested that *board of trade* was a new "buzzword" coined in Chicago and carried home with the attendees.

20. *New York Herald*, July 22, 1847; *New York Herald*, July 26, 1847.

21. Mentor L. Williams, "A Great Lakes Excursion, 1847 Style," *Inland Seas* 6, no. 3 (Fall 1950): 155.

22. Ibid., 155; Williams, "Chicago River and Harbor Convention," 623.

Chapter 7

1. John L. Sullivan, "Annexation," *United States Magazine and Democratic Review* 17, no. 1 (July–August 1845): 5–10.

2. John L. Sullivan, "The Great Nation of Futurity," *United States Democratic Review* 6, no. 23 (November 1839): 426–30.

3. Undated newspaper clipping, Great Lakes Maritime Database, http://quod.lib.umich.edu/t/tbnms1ic/x-18672.168286/*.

4. Newport survives today as Marine City, Michigan, a small, semirural river enclave generally on the fringe of the industrialization related to Detroit.

5. *Buffalo Daily Courier*, May 30, 1849, http://images.maritimehistoryofthegreat lakes.ca/33896/data?n=38. Contemporary spellings of the ship's name vary between *Mayflower* and *May Flower*. Most press accounts at the time use the traditional single-word appellation reminiscent of the Pilgrims and Plymouth Rock; indeed, the enrollment certificate is written with a lower case *f*. However, contemporary visual records—a published

illustration, a photograph, and a model ship—show the boat with the two-word name *MAY FLOWER*. This volume will use the version carried on the ship's paddle boxes: *May Flower*.

6. Artifact record of the Detroit Historical Society for the ship model *May Flower*, accession #W1959.009.006; *The Democracy* (Buffalo), November 28, 1854, http://images. maritimehistoryofthegreatlakes.ca/39717/data?n=14. For the grounding in 1853, see *Buffalo Express*, January 2, 1854, http://images.maritimehistoryofthegreatlakes.ca/39887/ data?n=12; and Bradley A. Rodgers, *Guardian of the Great Lakes: The U.S. Paddle Frigate 'Michigan'* (Ann Arbor: University of Michigan Press, 1996), 28–29, 80, 142. The story of the USS *Michigan* is beautifully detailed in this volume. The ship served many purposes on the lakes, from rescue tug to keeper of the peace. Staunchly built, the hull was one of the first ironclads in the US Navy and for many years the fastest. Its engines served for almost eighty years without a major failure.

7. *The Democracy* (Buffalo), December 8, 1854, and February 26, 1855, http://images.maritimehistoryofthegreatlakes.ca/39717/data?n=14.

8. Thunder Bay vessel database, http://www.greatlakesships.org/vesselview.aspx ?id=100763.

9. *Detroit Free Press*, April 29, 1851, http://images.maritimehistoryofthegreatlakes. ca/6391/data?n=19.

10. Carl Baehr, quoted in Valerie Van Heest, *Lost on the Lady Elgin* (Holland, MI: In-Depth Editions, 2010), 102–3.

11. *Buffalo Daily Republic*, June 17, 1852; *Buffalo Daily Republic*, December 1, 1853, both at http://images.maritimehistoryofthegreatlakes.ca/31155/data?n=94. See also *Buffalo Daily Republic*, July 3, 1854, http://images.maritimehistoryofthegreatlakes. ca/33736/data?n=128; and "Shipbuilding on the Lakes, No. 1: Buffalo and the District of Buffalo Creek, N.Y.," *Monthly Nautical Magazine and Quarterly Review* (New York), January 1855, 289–98, http://images.maritimehistoryofthegreatlakes.ca/63351/data.

12. *Detroit Free Press*, September 16, 1870, 4, http://images.maritimehistoryoft hegreatlakes.ca/3922/data?n=6. The first boat to surpass them would be the *Christopher Columbus*.

13. Figures are based on conversion calculators referencing the 1850s and 2013. The vessels' costs were slightly less than the $85,500 projected for construction of the Crystal Palace.

14. *Buffalo Daily Courier*, July 18, 1854, http://images.maritimehistoryofthegreat lakes.ca/30082/data?n=20; *Buffalo Commercial Advertiser*, April 18, 1854, http://images. maritimehistoryofthegreatlakes.ca/31157/data?n=77. The date April 11 for the *Western World*'s launch is given in Samuel Ward Stanton's *American Steam Vessels* (New York: Smith & Stanton, 1895). This work uses the date April 18, as recorded in the Buffalo paper.

15. *Buffalo Daily Courier*, February 1, 1854, http://images.maritimehistoryoft hegreatlakes.ca/30082/data?n=20.

16. *Buffalo Daily Republic*, July 3, 1854, http://images.maritimehistoryofthegreat lakes.ca/33736/data?n=128.

17. *Frank Leslie's Illustrated Newspaper* (New York), June 7, 1856, 405, http://imag es.maritimehistoryofthegreatlakes.ca/6439/data?n=78.

18. George R. Putnam, "Beacons of the Seas: Lighting the Coasts of the United States," *National Geographic* 24, no. 1 (January 1913): 19.

19. *Daily News* (Kingston, ON), January 7, 1863, http://images.maritimehistoryoft hegreatlakes.ca/18218/data?n=14.

20. *Buffalo Daily Courier*, July 18, 1854, http://images.maritimehistoryofthegreat lakes.ca/30082/data?n=5.

21. *Buffalo Daily Courier*, February 1, 1854, http://images.maritimehistoryoft

hegreatlakes.ca/30082/data?n=20; *Detroit Free Press*, January 12, 1856, http://images. maritimehistoryofthegreatlakes.ca/29567/data?n=85.

22. A full discussion of the Panic of 1857 is not warranted here. The information presented here was culled from many sources, most particularly Kenneth M. Stampp, *America in 1857: A Nation on the Brink* (New York: Oxford University Press, 1990), 213–37; and James Ford Rhodes, *History of the United States from the Compromise of 1850*, ed. Allan Nevins (Chicago: University of Chicago Press, 1966), originally published in 1904.

23. This author considers twenty-four vessels to belong in the palace steamer category (steamers over 250 feet) but is also mindful of another half dozen that were distinguished not by size but by speed or accommodations.

Chapter 8

1. Douglas North and Robert Thomas, *The Growth of the American Economy to 1860* (Columbia: University of South Carolina Press, 1968), 227–28.

2. Bern Anderson, *By Sea and by River: The Naval History of the Civil War* (New York: Alfred. A. Knopf, 1962), 7–8. The other gun, designed by Captain R. F. Stockton, exploded, killing Secretary of State Abel P. Upshur, Secretary of the Navy T. W. Gilmer, and several others. President Franklin Pierce had gone belowdecks moments before.

3. Ibid., 8–10.

4. Anderson (ibid., 12, 15), identifies Norfolk, Virginia; New Bern and Wilmington, North Carolina; Charleston, South Carolina; Savannah, Georgia; Fernandina and Pensacola, Florida; Mobile, Alabama; and New Orleans, Louisiana. Great Lakes ports handling comparable tonnage included Oswego, Rochester, Buffalo, Erie, Cleveland, Toledo, Monroe, Detroit, Port Huron, Muskegon, Grand Haven, St. Joseph, New Buffalo, Gary, South Chicago, Chicago, Waukegan, Kenosha, Racine, Milwaukee, Two Rivers, Sheboygan, Green Bay, Mackinac Island, Sault Sainte Marie, Eagle Harbor, Houghton-Hancock, Ontonagon, Duluth, Superior, and Port Edward.

5. Ibid., 6. Exemplifying the informality within the navy, Commodore Oliver H. Perry, hero of the Battle of Lake Erie in the War of 1812, was only a master commandant while aboard the *Lawrence*. As a courtesy, contemporary accounts generally refer to him as captain, a rank he received in 1814, or commodore, an honorary title conferred by President James Monroe several years later. Ranks were compiled by Edward W. Callahan in *List of Officers of the Navy of the United States and the Marine Corps from 1775 to 1900* (New York: L. R. Hamersly, 1901).

6. James Monroe to Charles Bagot, August 2, 1816, Avalon Project, http://avalon. law.yale.edu/19th_century/br1817l2.asp.

7. Bradley A. Rodgers, *Guardian of the Great Lakes: The U.S. Paddle Frigate 'Michigan'* (Ann Arbor: University of Michigan Press, 1996), 84.

8. Logbook entry, November 23, 1863, reproduced in Rodgers, 85.

9. United States War Department, *The War of the Rebellion: A Compilation of the Official Records of the Union and Confederate Armies in the War of Rebellion*, series I, vol. 43, part II (Washington, DC: US Government Printing Office, 1893), 235.

10. *Philo Parsons* data are from Great Lakes Ships, http://www.greatlakesships.org/ vesselview.aspx?id=107923; *Island Queen* data are from Great Lakes Ships, http://www. greatlakesships.org/vesselview.aspx?id=70137.

11. James L. Elliott, *Red Stacks over the Horizon: The Story of the Goodrich Steamboat Line* (Ellison Bay, WI: William Caxton, 1995), 30.

12. Carol E. Mull, *The Underground Railroad in Michigan* (Jefferson, NC: McFarland, 2010), 77–78.

Chapter 9

1. Elliott, *Red Stacks over the Horizon*, 12–16.
2. Ibid., 22–23, 26, 31, 37, 41.
3. R. G. Plumb, "The Goodrich Line," *Inland Seas* 50, no. 3 (Fall 1994), reprinted from *Inland Seas*, April 1945. The early vessels, both steamer and propeller, were markedly close in dimension and design: *Huron*, 348 tons, 165 feet long, 23.5 feet abeam, 9 feet deep; *Ogontz*, 343 tons; *Comet*, 351 tons, 158 feet long, 24.5 feet abeam, 9 feet deep; *Sunbeam*, 398 tons, 165 feet long, 23.5 feet abeam, 10.5 feet deep; and *Union*, 434 tons, 163 feet long. Figures are from HCGL; and Elliott, 35–42.
4. Elliott, 48–49, 53.
5. Ibid., 23.
6. Ibid., 41.
7. Ibid., 48–49, 53, 66–69, 71; Plumb, 204.
8. Elliott, 76–87.
9. Ibid., 50–51.
10. Ibid., 57–59, 76.
11. Ibid., 93–97.
12. Ibid., 99–102.
13. Considering the "full" careers of both lines prior to incorporation, the Goodrich interests owned thirty-eight vessels over seventy-seven years, compared to D&C's nineteen over a century.
14. George W. Hilton, *The Night Boat* (Berkeley, CA: Howell-North, 1968), 199.
15. Francis Duncan, "Story of the D&C," *Inland Seas* 7, no. 4 (Winter 1951): 222–26.
16. Francis Duncan, "Story of the D&C," *Inland Seas* 8, no. 2 (Summer 1952): 90–96.
17. Ibid., 97–98.
18. Francis Duncan, "Story of the D&C," *Inland Seas* 8, no. 3 (Fall 1952): 167–74.
19. Francis Duncan, "Story of the D&C," *Inland Seas* 8, no. 4 (Winter 1952): 268–69.
20. Ibid., 271–73; Francis Duncan, "Story of the D&C," *Inland Seas* 9, no. 1 (Spring 1953): 29. Duncan found that 60 percent of the the Mackinac Division's revenue came from tourism and 40 percent from freight; Lake Erie revenues were the opposite.
21. *Detroit News*, May 14, 1880, DGLM VF.
22. Francis Duncan, "Story of the D&C," *Inland Seas* 9, no. 1 (Spring 1953): 33.
23. Francis Duncan, "Story of the D&C," *Inland Seas* 9, no. 2 (Summer 1953): 128–29.
24. Ibid., 129; Francis Duncan, "Story of the D&C," *Inland Seas* 9, no. 3 (Fall 1953): 184–86. Carter's move was preceded in July by a roughly 20 percent cut in wages by the Lake Carriers Association, the organizations representing most American bulk carriers and managers.
25. Francis Duncan, "Story of the D&C," *Inland Seas* 9, no. 4 (Winter 1953): 283–85.
26. "General Manager's Report," found in an envelope labeled "Annual Papers 1893," D&C Papers, BHC, cited in ibid., 285.
27. Hilton, *Night Boat*, 225.
28. *Detroit City Directory* (Detroit: J. W. Weeks, 1874); *Detroit City Directory* (Detroit: J. W. Weeks, 1884); *Detroit City Directory* (Detroit: R. L. Polk, 1895).
29. H. C. Snyder, "Union Steamboat Company: Its History, in Part, with Comparison of Steamers as They Were and Are Today," *Erie Railroad Magazine, Erie Railroad Lake Line Division*, April 1914, http://freepages.genealogy.rootsweb.ancestry.com/~sponholz/erielakehistory.html. Snyder was the assistant general freight agent at Chicago. He listed the company's vessels as the *St. Louis, Toledo, Atlantic, Pacific, Arctic, Marquette, Araxes, Orontes, Evergreen City, Equinox, Dunkirk, Eclipse, Missouri, Wabash, Canisteo, Passaic, Tioga, Olean, Elmira, New York*, and a new propeller on the ways. Later operators advertised as the Erie & Western Transportation Company, with links to the New York, Lake Erie & Western Railroad. *Detroit City Directory*, various issues.

30. William Benson Wilson, *History of the Pennsylvania Railroad* (Philadelphia: Henry T. Coates, 1894), 68.

31. Maurice D. Smith. *Steamboats on the Lakes: Two Centuries of Steamboat Travel through Ontario's Waterways* (Toronto: James Lorimer & Co., 2005), 37–50.

32. "The ALGOMA of the C.P.R. Steamship Line and the First of the New Fleet to Ascend the Lakes," *Sarnia Observer*, May 16, 1884, http://www.maritimehistoryofthegreatlakes.ca/documents/scanner/08/04/default.asp?ID=c005. Electric lights were very new in large-scale maritime applications. By 1883 Siemens Brothers & Company, Ltd., a leader in the field, had fitted out only twenty steamships worldwide with a total of four thousand lights. The following year all three of the CPR liners, built in Glasgow, arrived with electric lights. By 1885 the Richelieu & Ontario line announced a complete off-season refit of its fleet with electric lighting. That same year Kirby designed the feature into the *City of Cleveland II. Marine Review*, various issues.

33. Toronto Historical Society, "The Northern Navigation Company Limited," *Scanner* 6, no. 7 (April 1974), http://www.maritimehistoryofthegreatlakes.ca/Documents/scanner/06/07/default.asp?ID=c007.

Chapter 10

1. George W. Hilton, *Lake Michigan Passenger Steamers* (Redwood City, CA: Stanford University Press, 2002), 103–36.

2. Francis Duncan, "Story of the D&C," *Inland Seas* 9, no. 3 (Fall 1953): 181–86.

3. George W. Hilton, *Great Lakes Car Ferries* (Berkeley, CA: Howell-North, 1962), 54.

4. Francis Duncan, "Story of the D&C," *Inland Seas* 8, no. 4 (Winter 1952): 272–73.

5. James L. Elliott, *Red Stacks over the Horizon: The Story of the Goodrich Steamboat Line* (Ellison Bay, WI: William Caxton, 1967), 263.

6. *Marine Review*, August 13, 1885, 1.

7. Hilton, *Lake Michigan Passenger Steamers*, 257.

Chapter 11

1. William Maybury, Letter from the Century Box opened in 2001, DHSC, accession number 2001.061.104.

2. Trucks designed by Max Grabowsky rolled out of the Rapid Motor Vehicle Company's shop in Pontiac, Michigan, in 1902. The company was absorbed by General Motors in 1909 and served as the basis of the GMC Truck division. Grabowski founded the Grabowsky Power Wagon Company soon afterward and competed successfully in the market. Augustus Fruehauf began producing trailers about 1916 for Detroit lumberman Frederick Sibley Jr. The prototype is in the collection of the Detroit Historical Society. "Problems for Package Freight Lines," *Marine Review*, January 1906, 31.

3. United States Treasury Department, *Annual Report of the Light-House Board for the Fiscal Year Ended June 30, 1903* (Washington, DC: Government Printing Office, 1903), 82, 92, 100; Minister of Marine and Fisheries of Canada, *Review of Improvements in Lighthouse and Coast Service in Canada, 1903* (Ottawa: Minister of Marine and Fisheries, 1904).

4. *Lake Carriers' Association Annual Report* (Cleveland: Lake Carriers' Association, 1913), 163–66. As of 1907, three New York–Boston steamers had adopted steam turbine technology, which was also featured on the *Lusitania* and *Mauritania*. Speeds of up to thirty-five knots were possible. Tellingly, none of the Lake boats adopted this time-saving technology. *Lake Carriers' Association Annual Report* (Cleveland: Lake Carri-

ers' Association, 1907, 78–79. The fire suppression systems on the *City of Cleveland* were emulated throughout the fleet. See *City of Cleveland*, builder's plans, Detroit Dry Dock Company, 1906, DHSC.

5. Thomas E. Appleton, *Usque Ad Mare: A History of the Canadian Coast Guard and Marine Services* (Ottawa: Canada Department of Transport, 1968), archived at http://www.ccg-gcc.gc.ca/eng/CCG/USQUE_Telegraph.

6. *Marine Review*, June 12, 1902, http://images.maritimehistoryofthegreatlakes. ca/65489/page/8?n=33&q=first-wireless&docid=MHGL.65489; *Lake Carriers' Association Annual Report* (Cleveland: Lake Carriers' Association, 1912), 81–82; *Lake Carriers' Association Annual Report* (Cleveland: Lake Carriers' Association, 1913), 108.

7. "Around the Lakes: Detroit," *Marine Record* 25, no. 8 (February 20, 1902): 6; "Around the Lakes: Detroit," *Marine Record* 25, no. 11 (March 13, 1902), 7, http://images. maritimehistoryofthegreatlakes.ca/65476/page/3?n=.

8. *Marine Record*, March 20, 1902, 3, http://images.maritimehistoryofthegreat lakes.ca/65477/page/3?n=14&q=wireless 1902&docid=MHGL.65477; *Detroit Free Press*, May 1, 1903, http://images.maritimehistoryofthegreatlakes.ca/5636/data?n=3; "Commercial Wireless Telegraph Operation Begun on the Great Lakes," *Electrical Review and Western Electrician*, September 1909, 253–54, http://earlyradiohistory.us/1909uwgl. htm. Clark is listed in the 1902 *Detroit City Directory* as general manager of the Electric Service and Appliance Company. *Detroit City Directory* (Detroit: R. L. Polk, 1902). He combined letters in his name to form the Tecla Company, which also produced equipment to his design. The first reported noncommercial ship-to-shore voice transmissions were from the yacht *Thelma* to the Fox Docks at Put-in-Bay Harbor in 1907, with reports of the annual Inter-Lakes Yachting Association (I-LYA) regatta on Lake Erie, using De-Forest equipment. *Electrical World*, August 10, 1907, 293–94, http://earlyradiohistory. us/1907yht.htm. Illustrating the growth of commercial radio, several other stations hit the airwaves in the same year. By 1924 there were around seven hundred radio stations broadcasting across the United States, including WEBC from Superior, Wisconsin, and WCCO in the Twin Cities of Minneapolis–St. Paul. There were no radio networks. There were few federal regulations. J. Zelezny, *Communications Law* (Belmont, CA: Wadsworth, 1993), 419.

9. *Marine Review*, March 13, 1902, http://images.maritimehistoryofthegreatlakes. ca/65375/page/5?n=77&q=first%20wireless&docid=MHGL.65375; "What the Wireless Telephone Is Doing for the Great Lakes," *Coos Bay Times* (Oregon), February 13, 1909, evening ed., 3, http://earlyradiohistory.us/1909gl.htm; *Marine Review* March 20, 1902, http://images.maritimehistoryofthegreatlakes.ca/65477/page/3?n=52&q=firstwire less&docid=MHGL.65477; Mark Thompson, *Steamboats and Sailors of the Great Lakes* (Detroit: Wayne State University Press, 1991), 56; United States Department of the Navy, Bureau of Equipment, *Wireless Telegraph Stations of the World* (Washington, DC: Government Printing Office, 1909), http://earlyradiohistory.us/1909stat.htm#vessels-world.

10. City of Cleveland brochure, DGLM VF.

Chapter 12

1. For further information about rail ferries of the Great Lakes, see George W. Hilton, *Great Lakes Car Ferries* (Berkeley, CA: Howell-North, 1962).

2. William Hoey, "Birth of a Lakes Leviathan: *City of Cleveland*," *Telescope* 9, no. 10 (October 1960): 175–77; Detroit & Cleveland Navigation Co., *Promotional Book for City of Cleveland (III)*, 1908, 5–12, DGLM VF; "New Steamer *City of Cleveland*," *Marine Review*, May 7, 1908, DGLM VF. The general description of the ship is based on photographs

and blueprint drawings in the DHSC, as well as information contained in the *Marine Review* article and the Detroit & Cleveland promotional book for *City of Cleveland (III)*.

3. Detroit & Cleveland Navigation Co., *Promotional Book for City of Cleveland (III)*, 1908, 6, DGLM VF.

4. Ibid.; Detroit & Cleveland Navigation Company steamer schedule, 1913. DGLM VF, accession number 2011.062.001. Median household income in Michigan in 2007–11 was $48,669 according to the US Census, http://quickfacts.census.gov/qfd/states/26000.html.

5. For watershed size, see Environmental Protection Agency, http://www.epa.gov/glnpo/factsheet.html; and State of Michigan, Department of Environmental Quality, http://www.michigan.gov/deq/0,4561,7–135–3313_3677–15926—,00.html. The total when the St. Lawrence River valley is included is 304,000 square miles per the US Army Corp of Engineers, http://www.lre.usace.army.mil/Portals/69/docs/PPPM/PlanningandStudies/johnglennbiohydrological/02-BiohydroAppA.pdf; and Wayne Grady, *The Great Lakes: The Natural History of a Changing Region* (Vancouver: Grey Stone Books, 2007), 13.

6. Grady, 21.

7. Ibid., 16.

8. National Oceanic and Atmospheric Administration, http://www.glerl.noaa.gov/pr/ourlakes/lakes.

9. Detroit & Cleveland Navigation Co., *Promotional Book for City of Cleveland (III)*.

10. E. S. Turner, *The Shocking History of Advertising* (New York: E. P. Dutton, 1953), 169–86.

11. Detroit & Cleveland Navigation Co., *Promotional Book for City of Cleveland (III)*, 1908, 42, DGLM VF.

Chapter 13

1. "Driven on Shelldrake," *Globe* (Toronto), November 12, 1913, 1–2, http://images.maritimehistoryofthegreatlakes.ca/66647/data?n=1. Figures are from George W. Hilton, *Lake Michigan Passenger Steamers* (Redwood City, CA: Stanford University Press, 2002), 147, 193.

2. Hilton, *Lake Michigan Passenger Steamers*, 147.

3. *Report of the Chief of Engineers, U.S. Army*, 1923, part 2, pp. 1011, 1050, quoted in Hilton, *Lake Michigan Passenger Steamers*, 147.

4. Hilton, *Lake Michigan Passenger Steamers*, 191.

5. Dwight Boyer, *True Tales of the Great Lakes* (New York: Dodd, Mead, 1971), 76–77.

6. Hilton, *Lake Michigan Passenger Steamers*, 147.

7. In the words of labor historian Bruce Nelson, sailors "entered the twentieth century bearing the burden of an archaic, semi-feudal tradition of the sea and a code of laws that perpetuated [their] bondage" (Bruce Nelson, *Workers on the Waterfront* [Urbana: University of Illinois Press, 1988], 11–12). Flogging was outlawed in 1850, but it did not end. The 1872 Shipping Commissioner's Act defined a sailor's legal status as that of a ward of the admiralty, prompting union activist Paul Taylor to comment, "The passage of time . . . not only failed to remove [sailors'] bondage to the vessel, but statutory enactment further stamped his status as peculiar and unfree" (Stephen Schwartz, *Brotherhood of the Sea: A History of the Sailors' Union of the Pacific, 1885–1985* [New Brunswick, NJ: Transaction Books, 1986], 4). In 1897, the Supreme Court ruling in the *Arago* case reaffirmed that the "provisions of the Thirteenth Amendment and subsequent legislation barring involuntary servitude did not apply to the seafarer" (Nelson, *Workers on the Waterfront*, 12).

8. John R. Commons, "Types of American Labor Unions: Longshoremen of the Great Lakes," *Quarterly Journal of Economics* 20, no. 1 (November 1905): 60; Francis Duncan, "The Story of the D&C," *Inland Seas* 8, no. 2 (Summer 1951): 90.

9. Henry E. Hoagland, "Wage Bargaining on the Vessels of the Great Lakes." *Studies in the Social Sciences* 6, no. 3 (1917): 104.

10. Commons, 59.

11. Francis Duncan, "The Story of the D&C," *Inland Seas* 11, no. 2 (Summer 1955): 126; Commons, 74.

12. Steve Babson, *Working Detroit* (Detroit: Wayne State University Press, 1984), 20.

13. *Machinist's Monthly Journal* 22, no. 7 (July 1910): 11–12, http://www.library.gsu.edu/dlib/iam/getBrandedPDF.asp?issue_id=208. (In the BHC, manuscripts from the early part of the decade are bound in folios by month and year and have page numbers. Manuscripts from the latter part of the decade are filed chronologically and are boxed by month and year.)

14. James L. Elliott, *Red Stacks over the Horizon: The Story of the Goodrich Steamboat Line* (Ellison Bay, WI: William Caxton, 1967), 214.

15. Stephen Schwartz, *Excerpts from "Brotherhood of the Sea: A History of the Sailors' Union of the Pacific, 1885–1985"* (San Francisco: Sailors' Union of the Pacific, 1985), 18.

16. Timothy Semenoro, "The State of Our Seafaring Nation: What Course Has Congress Laid for the U.S. Maritime Industry," *Tulane Maritime Law Journal* 25, no. 1 (Winter 2000): 335–36.

17. Augustus Schantz to T. F. Newman, May 20, 1910, James McMillan Papers, 1017, BHC.

18. A. Schantz to W. M. Brittain, October 2, 1917, James McMillan Papers, BHC. See also A. Schantz to C. L. Perkins, June 12, 1916, James McMillan Papers, BHC. For a more detailed explanation of the strategies and maneuvers employed by labor and management, see Joel Stone, "A Packet Full of Trouble: Labor Relations, Federal Legislation, and the Detroit & Cleveland Navigation Company, 1910–1920" (MA thesis, Wayne State University, 2007).

19. Elliott, 213; Francis Duncan, "The Story of the D&C," *Inland Seas* 13, no. 4 (Winter 1957): 276. Similarly, Goodrich's *Christopher Columbus*, rated to carry four thousand passengers, even as a day cruiser, could only carry twenty-two hundred.

20. A. Schantz to F. I. Collins, April 18, 1917, James McMillan Papers, BHC; Francis Duncan, "The Story of the D&C," *Inland Seas* 13 no. 4 (Winter 1957): 280.

21. Snyder's comment can be found at http://freepages.genealogy.rootsweb.ancestry.com/~sponholz/erielakeend.html. See also http://freepages.genealogy.rootsweb.ancestry.com/~sponholz/erieshippingline.html.

22. "Asserts Boats Have Polluted Detroit River," *Detroit Free Press*, February 13, 1914; "City Assailed for Polluting Detroit River," *Detroit Free Press*, September 25, 1913.

23. Hilton, *Lake Michigan Passenger Steamers*, 160–63, 306.

24. Ibid., 319.

25. Ibid., 218–35.

26. Ibid., 245–54.

27. Ibid., 267.

28. William Leonhard Taylor, *A Productive Monopoly* (Providence, RI: Brown University Press, 1970), 222–23; Alexander Crosby Brown, "Extract of the Old Bay Line of the Chesapeake, a Sketch of a Hundred Years of Steamboat Operation," *William and Mary Quarterly Historical Magazine*, ser. 2, 18, no. 4 (October 1938): 405.

29. M. Stephen Salmon, "'This Remarkable Growth': Investment in Canadian Great Lakes Shipping, 1900–1959," *Northern Mariner/Le marin du nord* 15, no. 3 (July 2005): 8, http://www.cnrs-scrn.org/northern_mariner/vol15/tnm_15_3_1-37.pdf; John Henry,

Great White Fleet: Celebrating Canada Steamship Lines Passenger Ships (Toronto: Dundurn Press, 2013), 25–26.

30. *Great Lakes Red Book* (Cleveland: Marine Review, 1916). For more information on Canadian mergers between 1900 and 1914, see Gregory Marchildon, *Profits and Politics: Beaverbrook and the Gilded Age of Canadian Finance* (Toronto: University of Toronto Press, 1996), 1–348.

Conclusion

1. Francis Duncan, "The Story of the D&C," *Inland Seas* 13 no. 4 (Winter 1957): 280.

2. Joel Stone, "A Packet Full of Trouble: Labor Relations, Federal Legislation, and the Detroit & Cleveland Navigation Company, 1910–1920" (MA thesis, Wayne State University, 2007), 59.

3. Blueprints of the conversion to aircraft carriers are held in the DHSC.

4. "D&C Plans to Buy Stock," *Detroit News*, November 30, 1949, DGLM VF.

5. Various newspaper clippings in *City of Detroit III* file, DGLM VF.

6. *Detroit News*, March 2, 1951, DGLM VF; *Detroit News*, May 9, 1951, DGLM VF.

7. *Detroit News*, October 20, 1974, DGLM VF.

8. John Henry, *Great White Fleet: Celebrating Canada Steamship Lines Passenger Ships* (Toronto: Dundurn Press, 2013), 102; "Marine Memories: Hamonic," *The Sampler* (Mooretown, ON: Moore Museum), excerpted at http://www.mooremuseum.ca/thesampler_article/marine-memories-hamonic.

9. Nancy A. Schneider, "The Magnificent *Noronic:* Absolute Queen of the Luxury Passenger Vessels on the Lakes," *Inland Seas* 52, no. 4 (Winter 1996): 241–49.

10. *Great Lakes Red Book* (Cleveland: Penton Publishing, 1965), 82, 84, 86.

11. The *North American* was launched with a single stack. A second "dummy" stack was added later.

12. Charlotte Slater, "Social Director without a Ship," *Detroit News*, October 17, 1967, D3; notes sent by Ronald Rosie to the Era of Elegance project, DGLM, in 2007.

13. Stoddard White, "Last 2 Lake Cruise Ships Up for Sale," *Detroit News*, September 30, 1962, *North American* file, DGLM VF; Bob Boelio, "Big Lakes Cruise," *Motor News* (April 1963): 22, *South American* file, DGLM VF.

14. There were several attempts to repurpose the *South American*, chronicled in the DGLM VF: (1) A group from Holland, Michigan that worked "frantically to keep afloat the last American passenger cruise ship to sail the Great Lakes"; they needed to raise $200,000 to buy the vessel and $300,000 to move it, but were only able to raise $5,000, mostly from outside the Holland area (details from a variety of articles, May 7–17, 1974); (2) a group from Duluth, headed by broadcasting executive Jack Gordon and "backed by the community," proved equally unsuccessful (*Detroit News*, Nov. 27, 1975); (3) a retired Detroit area newspaper owner proposed an entertainment complex (*Detroit News*, July 28, 1977); (4) the Mackinac Island Chamber of Commerce explored a similar concept in 1975 (*Detroit News*, August 10, 1975, C3); Chamber of Commerce member Robert Carr promoted this project until at least 1983 (*Detroit News*, July 21, 1983); (5) the City of Menominee, Wisconsin proposed utilizing the hull as a floating hotel, estimated at $5.8 million (*Marinette Eagle-Star*, August 22, 1984); (6) in 1988, the *South American* was purchased by two Detroit developers for $20,000, with restorations estimated at $8.5 million; they wanted to stage it at Mt. Elliott Park, and feature a 110-room hotel, a restaurant, and two nightclubs. Notably, the *Delta Queen* was being restored at this same time for $7 million (*Crain's Detroit Business*, December 5, 1988, p12, c1).

15. "Milwaukee Clipper: A Streamlined 106-Year-Old Steamer," *PowerShips*, Spring 2011, 30–31.

16. Unidentified 1941 news clipping, DGLM VF.

17. *Motor News*, July 1951, 16, 32–33, DGLM VF.

18. Ibid.

19. Material was drawn from various brochures in the DGLM VF. The schedules were as follows: May 26–September 25, 1961; June 11–September 7, 1965; June 9–September 5, 1967; and June 5–September 8, 1970.

20. *Milwaukee Journal Sentinel*, July 5, 1996, A8, DGLM VF.

21. "Milwaukee Clipper," 30–31.

22. *Detroit Free Press*, July 15, 1955, DGLM VF.; undated newspaper advertisement, DGLM VF.

23. Arrived Muskegon September 1953 (*Detroit News*, September 17, 1953); "Debut at Muskegon," *Detroit Free Press*, July 15, 1955, DGLM VF.

24. 1957 *Aquarama* brochure, DGLM VF; Cornelia Curtiss, "*Aquarama* Coming Here for Cruises," *Cleveland News*, June 13, 1956, 12; *Detroit Free Press*, July 15, 1955, DGLM VF.

25. Stoddard White, *Detroit News*, n.d., DGLM VF; Curtis Haseltine, "Marine Terminal to Dedicate New Offices," *Detroit Free Press*, June 19, 1961, 10, DGLM VF.

26. *Detroit Free Press*, June 22, 1957, DGLM VF; *Detroit News*, November 16, 1962, A3, DGLM VF; *Detroit Free Press*, June 22, 1957, DGLM VF; *Toledo Blade*, July 11, 1962, DGLM VF.

27. *Detroit News*, March 20, 1963, DGLM VF; *Detroit News*, December 27, 1962, DGLM VF.

28. Art O'Shea, *Detroit News*, December 27, 1981.

29. Dave LeMieux, "Tracking the Story," *Muskegon Chronicle*, April 11, 2011, http://www.mlive.com/news/muskegon/index.ssf/2011/04/looking_back_welcome_aboard_th.html.

30. For more on the Owen Sound Transportation Company, see Gordon Macaulay, "Ferries Out of Owen Sound," *Inland Seas* 21, no. 2 (Summer 1965): 92–102; and 21, no. 3 (Fall 1965): 187–209.

Bibliography

Note: Articles and other documents consulted on the Internet were accessed between 2011 and 2014.

Abbreviations

BHC—Burton Historical Collection, Detroit Public Library.
DGLM VF—Dossin Great Lakes Museum vertical files, Detroit Historical Society Collection.
DHSC—Detroit Historical Society Collection.
HCGL—Historical Collection of the Great Lakes, Bowling Green State University, Bowling Green, Ohio.
TBNMS—Labadie Collection, Thunder Bay National Marine Sanctuary Collection, Alpena Public Library, Alpena, Michigan. Since commencing this volume, the database of C. Patrick Labadie's vessel information has been moved to the University of Michigan's Bentley Historical Library online database.

Primary Sources

"The ALGOMA of the C.P.R. Steamship Line and the First of the New Fleet to Ascend the Lakes." *Sarnia Observer*, May 16, 1884. http://www.maritimehistoryofthegreat lakes.ca/documents/scanner/08/04/default.asp?ID=c005.
The Argus (Kingston, ON). November 6, 1846. http://images.maritimehistoryofthegreat lakes.ca/33165/data?n=5.
Barker, Capt. J. H. "Western World, of the Michigan Central R. R. Line, between Buffalo and Detroit." *Frank Leslie's Illustrated Newspaper* (New York). June 7, 1856. http:// images.maritimehistoryofthegreatlakes.ca/6439/data?n=78.
"BALTIC; 1847; Passenger Steamer; AMERICAN." Undated and unidentified newspa per image, University of Michigan Library Digital Collections. http://quod.lib.umich. edu/t/tbnmslic/x-18672.168286/0018672_012_f_baltic.tif.
Barton, James L. *Address on the Early Reminiscences of Western New York and the Lake Region of Country.* Buffalo: Jewett, Thomas & Co., 1848. DHSC.

Barton, James L. *Letter to the Hon. Robert M'Clelland, Chairman of the Committee on Commerce in the U.S. House of Representatives in Relation to the Value and Importance of the Commerce of the Great Western Lakes.* Buffalo: Jewett, Thomas, 1846. Brendon Baillod Collection, Dane County, Wisconsin.

Black Rock Gazette. January 13, 1827, 3. http://images.maritimehistoryofthegreatlakes. ca/2787/data?n=24.

Black Rock Advocate. January 27, 1837, 3. http://images.maritimehistoryofthegreatlakes. ca/3011/data?n=15.

Black Rock Advocate. February 17, 1837. Reprinted from the *Detroit Advertiser.* http:// images.maritimehistoryofthegreatlakes.ca/3009/data?n=13.

Boelio, Bob. "Big Lakes Cruise," *Motor News*, April 1963, 22. DGLM VF.

British Whig (Kingston, ON). May 2, 1834, 2. http://images.maritimehistoryofthegreat lakes.ca/11208/data?n=99.

Brown, Alexander Crosby. "Extract of the Old Bay Line of the Chesapeake, a Sketch of a Hundred Years of Steamboat Operation." *William and Mary Quarterly Historical Magazine*, ser. 2, 18, no. 4 (October 1938): 389–405.

Buffalo Commercial Advertiser. April 18, 1854. http://images.maritimehistoryof thegreatlakes.ca/31157/data?n=77.

Buffalo Commercial Advertiser. August 1, 1838. http://images.maritimehistoryof thegreatlakes.ca/21900/data?n=9.

Buffalo Commercial Advertiser. April 30, 1849, 2. http://images.maritimehistoryof thegreatlakes.ca/51576/data?n=6.

Buffalo Daily Courier. August 23, 1844, 2. http://images.maritimehistoryofthegreat lakes.ca/31585/data?n=60.

Buffalo Daily Courier. May 30, 1849. http://images.maritimehistoryofthegreatlakes. ca/33896/data?n=38.

Buffalo Daily Courier. July 4, 1849. http://images.maritimehistoryofthegreatlakes. ca/54222/data?n=8.

Buffalo Daily Courier. February 1, 1854. http://images.maritimehistoryofthegreatlakes. ca/30082/data?n=20.

Buffalo Daily Courier. July 18, 1854. http://images.maritimehistoryofthegreatlakes. ca/30082/data?n=20.

Buffalo Daily Republic. June 17, 1852. http://images.maritimehistoryofthegreatlakes. ca/31155/data?n=94.

Buffalo Daily Republic. December 1, 1853. http://images.maritimehistoryofthegreat lakes.ca/31155/data?n=94.

Buffalo Daily Republic. July 3, 1854. http://images.maritimehistoryofthegreatlakes. ca/33736/data?n=128.

Buffalo Daily Republic. September 30, 1856. http://images.maritimehistoryofthegreat lakes.ca/40380/data?n=7.

Buffalo Emporium. June 25, 1827. http://images.maritimehistoryofthegreatlakes.ca/re sults?q=Buffalo+Emporium%2C+June+25%2C+1827.

Buffalo Express. January 2, 1854. http://images.maritimehistoryofthegreatlakes. ca/39887/data?n=12.

Buffalo Gazette and Niagara Intelligencer. August 6, 1816. http://images.maritimehisto ryofthegreatlakes.ca/33167/data?n=17.

Buffalo Gazette. April 20, 1817. http://images.maritimehistoryofthegreatlakes.ca/33167/ data?n=1.

Buffalo Journal. Quoted in the *Cleveland Weekly Herald*, October 10, 1822. http://imag es.maritimehistoryofthegreatlakes.ca/58510/data?n=22.

Buffalo Morning Express. January 11, 1856. http://images.maritimehistoryofthegreat lakes.ca/38758/data?n=2.

Buffalo Patriot. Reprinted in the *Kingston Chronicle*, November 30, 1821. http://images. maritimehistoryofthegreatlakes.ca/8241/data?n=33.

Candidus. "Another Letter from a True Briton." *Kingston Gazette*, April 6, 1816. http:// images.maritimehistoryofthegreatlakes.ca/7845/data?n=3.

Chicago Evening Journal. July 6, 1847. Reprinted in *Chicago River and Harbor Convention: An Account of Its Origins and Proceedings*, edited by Robert Fergus, 7–13. Chicago: Fergus Printing, 1882.

Chicago Weekly Journal. March 23, 1846. Reprinted in Betty Mendelsohn, "The Federal Hand in Urban Development: Chicago Harbor before the Civil War." *Prologue* 30, no. 4 (Winter 1998): 261.

Chronicle & Gazette (Kingston, ON). April 11, 1835. http://images.maritimehistoryof thegreatlakes.ca/8663/data?n=34.

"City Assailed for Polluting Detroit River." *Detroit Free Press*, September 25, 1913.

City of Cleveland. Builder's plans, Detroit Dry Dock Company, 1906. DHSC.

Cleveland Weekly Herald. November 6, 1821. http://images.maritimehistoryofthegreat lakes.ca/47525/data?n=2.

Cleveland Weekly Herald. April 30, 1822. http://images.maritimehistoryofthegreatlakes. ca/30724/data?n=15.

Cleveland Weekly Herald. May 28, 1822. http://images.maritimehistoryofthegreatlakes. ca/33930/data?n=2.

Cleveland Daily Herald & Gazette. October 11, 1837. http://images.maritimehistoryof thegreatlakes.ca/31081/data?n=21.

Cleveland Daily Herald & Gazette. August 9, 1838. http://images.maritimehistoryof thegreatlakes.ca/28799/data?n=1.

Cleveland Daily Herald & Gazette. May 10, 1839. http://images.maritimehistoryof thegreatlakes.ca/33945/data?n=1.

Commercial Review of the South and West (New Orleans) 4, no. 1 (September 1847).

"Commercial Wireless Telegraph Operation Begun on the Great Lakes." *Electrical Review and Western Electrician*, September 1909, 253–54. http://earlyradiohistory. us/1909uwgl.htm.

Crain's Detroit Business. December 5, 1988, 12.

Curtiss, Cornelia. "Aquarama Coming Here for Cruises." *Cleveland News*, June 13, 1956, 12.

"D&C Plans to Buy Stock." *Detroit News*, November 30, 1949. DGLM VF.

Daily British Whig (Kingston, ON). August 5, 1890. http://images.maritimehistoryof thegreatlakes.ca/33167/data?n=2.

Daily National Pilot (Buffalo). June 2, 1845. http://images.maritimehistoryofthegreat lakes.ca/29727/data?n=2.

Daily News (Kingston, ON). January 7, 1863. http://images.maritimehistoryofthegreat lakes.ca/18218/data?n=14.

Darby, William. *A Tour from the City of New York to Detroit: In the Michigan Territory, Made between the 2d of May and the 22d of September, 1818* . . . New York: Kirk & Mercein, 1819.

The Democracy (Buffalo). November 28, 1854. http://images.maritimehistoryofthegreat lakes.ca/39717/data?n=14.

The Democracy. December 8, 1854, and February 26, 1855. http://images.maritimehisto ryofthegreatlakes.ca/39717/data?n=14.

The Democracy. "Tonnage on the Lakes," February 28, 1855. http://www.maritimehisto ryofthegreatlakes.ca/Documents/ShipLists/US1855/default.asp?ID=c02.

Detroit & Cleveland Navigation Company. *Promotional Book for City of Cleveland (III)*, 1908. DGLM VF.

Detroit & Cleveland Navigation Company steamer schedule, 1913. DGLM VF.

Detroit Free Press. September 3, 1839. http://images.maritimehistoryofthegreatlakes. ca/3653/data?n=5.

Detroit Free Press. July 10, 1847.

Detroit Free Press. July 14, 1847. http://images.maritimehistoryofthegreatlakes.ca/35293/ data?n=23.

Detroit Free Press. July 23, 1847.

Detroit Free Press. August 5, 1847.

Detroit Free Press. January 12, 1856. http://images.maritimehistoryofthegreatlakes. ca/29567/data?n=85.

Detroit Free Press. September 16, 1870, 4. http://images.maritimehistoryofthegreatlakes. ca/3922/data?n=6.

Detroit Free Press. May 10, 1872. http://images.maritimehistoryofthegreatlakes.ca/4054/ data?n=18.

Detroit Free Press. May 1, 1903. http://images.maritimehistoryofthegreatlakes.ca/5636/ data?n=3.

Detroit Free Press. July 15, 1955. DGLM VF.

Detroit Free Press. June 22, 1957. DGLM VF.

Detroit Free Press. "M. B.," April 29, 1851. http://images.maritimehistoryofthegreat lakes.ca/6391/data?n=19.

Detroit Gazette. August 14, 1818. http://images.maritimehistoryofthegreatlakes.ca/3228/ data?n=10.

Detroit Gazette. August 21, 1818. http://images.maritimehistoryofthegreatlakes.ca/3230/ data?n=48.

Detroit Gazette. August 28, 1818. http://images.maritimehistoryofthegreatlakes.ca/31046/ data?n=53.

Detroit Gazette. May 12, 1819. http://images.maritimehistoryofthegreatlakes.ca/4571/ data?n=27.

Detroit Gazette. June 18, 1819, 3. http://images.maritimehistoryofthegreatlakes.ca/3265/ data?n=19.

Detroit Gazette. June 25, 1819, 3. http://images.maritimehistoryofthegreatlakes.ca/3265/ data?n=20.

Detroit Gazette. July 9, 1819. http://images.maritimehistoryofthegreatlakes.ca/3267/ data?n=12.

Detroit Gazette. May 12, 1820.

Detroit Gazette. June 16, 1820, 2. http://images.maritimehistoryofthegreatlakes.ca/3295/ data?n=14.

Detroit Gazette. August 4, 1820. http://images.maritimehistoryofthegreatlakes.ca/3306/ data?n=35.

Detroit Gazette. November 17, 1820. http://images.maritimehistoryofthegreatlakes. ca/31879/data?n=9.

Detroit Gazette. April 20, 1821. http://images.maritimehistoryofthegreatlakes.ca/3320/ data?n=2.

Detroit Gazette. May 18, 1821. http://images.maritimehistoryofthegreatlakes.ca/3323/ data?n=16.

Detroit Gazette. June 26, 1821. http://images.maritimehistoryofthegreatlakes.ca/3326/ data?n=22.

Detroit Gazette. July 6, 1821. http://images.maritimehistoryofthegreatlakes.ca/3327/ data?n=40.

Detroit Gazette. July 13, 1821. http://images.maritimehistoryofthegreatlakes.ca/3328/ data?n=41.

Detroit Gazette. August 10, 1821. http://images.maritimehistoryofthegreatlakes.ca/3329/ data?n=50.

Detroit Gazette. August 17, 1821. http://images.maritimehistoryofthegreatlakes.ca/3330/data?n=42.

Detroit Gazette. January 11, 1822, 2. http://images.maritimehistoryofthegreatlakes.ca/3334/data?n=26.

Detroit Gazette. June 22, 1822. http://images.maritimehistoryofthegreatlakes.ca/3350/data?n=20.

Detroit Gazette. July 5, 1822, 2. http://images.maritimehistoryofthegreatlakes.ca/3353/data?n=3.

Detroit Gazette. July 26, 1822, 2. http://images.maritimehistoryofthegreatlakes.ca/3356/data?n=17.

Detroit Gazette. August 22, 1822, 2. http://images.maritimehistoryofthegreatlakes.ca/3360/data?n=12.

Detroit Gazette. September 27, 1822. http://images.maritimehistoryofthegreatlakes.ca/3361/data?n=32.

Detroit News. March 2, 1951. DGLM VF.

Detroit News. May 9, 1951. DGLM VF.

Detroit News. September 17, 1953. DGLM VF.

Detroit News. November 16, 1962. DGLM VF.

Detroit News. December 27, 1962. DGLM VF.

Detroit News. March 20, 1963. DGLM VF.

Detroit News. Undated, 1974. DGLM VF.

Detroit News. October 20, 1974. DGLM VF.

Detroit News. August 10, 1975, C3. DGLM VF.

Detroit News. November 27, 1975. DGLM VF.

Detroit News. July 28, 1977. DGLM VF.

Detroit News. May 14, 1880. DGLM VF.

Detroit News. December 27, 1981. DGLM VF.

Detroit News. July 21, 1983. DGLM VF.

Detroit Post and Tribune. August 17, 1881. http://images.maritimehistoryofthegreatlakes.ca/5766/data?n=1.

Detroit Post and Tribune. April 7, 1884. http://images.maritimehistoryofthegreatlakes.ca/6086/data?n=32.

Detroit Tribune. Quoted in the *Kingston Daily News*, February 26, 1861, 2. http://images.maritimehistoryofthegreatlakes.ca/17807/data?n=8.

Diaries of George W. Jonson. Vol. 1: 1833–1837. Held at Dartmouth College, Hanover, New Hampshire. http://www.buffalonian.com/diaries/dofweek.html.

Disturnell, John. *Sailing on the Great Lakes and Rivers of America.* Philadelphia: J. Disturnell, 1874.

"Driven on Shelldrake." *Globe* (Toronto), November 12, 1913, 1–2. http://images.maritimehistoryofthegreatlakes.ca/66647/data?n=1.

Electrical World. August 10, 1907, 293–94. http://earlyradiohistory.us/1907yht.htm.

Erie Gazette. December 22, 1821. http://images.maritimehistoryofthegreatlakes.ca/31879/data?n=9.

Fergus, Robert, ed. *Chicago River and Harbor Convention: An Account of Its Origins and Proceedings.* Chicago: Fergus Printing, 1882.

"Fire." *Farmer's Journal and Welland Canal Intelligencer*, September 26, 1827. Quoted in the *Cleveland Weekly Herald*, September 27, 1827, 3. http://images.maritimehistoryofthegreatlakes.ca/50737/data?n=1.

Geneva Gazette, May 12, 1819. http://images.maritimehistoryofthegreatlakes.ca/4571/data?n=1.

Great Lakes Red Book. Cleveland: Marine Review, 1916.

Great Lakes Red Book. Cleveland: Penton Publishing, 1965.

Haseltine, Curtis. "Marine Terminal to Dedicate New Offices." *Detroit Free Press*, June 19, 1961, 10. DGLM VF.

Haseltine, Curtis. "An Era Is Ended." *Detroit Free Press*, October 24, 1967.

"History of Steam Navigation on Lake Ontario." *Onondaga Standard* (New York), September 29, 1847. http://www.maritimehistoryofthegreatlakes.ca/documents/Cumber land/default.asp?ID=c008#p063.

Hoagland, Henry E. "Wage Bargaining on the Vessels of the Great Lakes." *Studies in the Social Sciences* 6, no. 3 (1917): 1–123.

Holland Sentinel. May 7, 1974. DGLM VF.

"Important Sale." *Kingston Chronicle*, December 17, 1824. http://images.maritimehisto ryofthegreatlakes.ca/33141/data?n=1.

Kingston Chronicle. January 14, 1825. http://images.maritimehistoryofthegreatlakes. ca/33141/data?n=6.

Kingston Gazette. May 24, 1817. http://images.maritimehistoryofthegreatlakes.ca/33152/ data?n=13.

Kingston Gazette. May 1, 1818. http://images.maritimehistoryofthegreatlakes.ca/57799/ data?n=2.

Kingston Gazette. September 15, 1818. http://images.maritimehistoryofthegreatlakes. ca/7941/data?n=51.

Kingston Herald. June 25, 1822. Quoted in the *Sandusky Clarion*, July 31, 1822, 2. http:// images.maritimehistoryofthegreatlakes.ca/49128/data?n=1.

Lake Carriers' Association Annual Report. Cleveland: Lake Carriers' Association, 1907.

Lake Carriers' Association Annual Report. Cleveland: Lake Carriers' Association, 1912.

Lake Carriers' Association Annual Report. Cleveland: Lake Carriers' Association, 1913.

"Launch of Steamer *Milwaukee.*" *Buffalo Daily Courier*, June 3, 1859. http://images.mar itimehistoryofthegreatlakes.ca/30725/data?n=92.

Machinist's Monthly Journal 22, no. 7 (July 1910): 11–12. http://www.library.gsu.edu/ dlib/iam/getBrandedPDF.asp?issue_id=208.

Marine Record. August 13, 1885. http://images.maritimehistoryofthegreatlakes.ca/64361/ data?n=42.

Marine Record (Cleveland). October 25, 1883. http://images.maritimehistoryofthegreat lakes.ca/47525/data?n=9.

Marine Record (Cleveland). "Around the Lakes: Detroit," February 20, 1902 (vol. 25, no. 8), 2. http://images.maritimehistoryofthegreatlakes.ca/65473/page/2?n=.

Marine Record (Cleveland). "Around the Lakes: Detroit," March 13, 1902 (vol. 25, no. 11), 3. http://images.maritimehistoryofthegreatlakes.ca/65476/page/3?n=.

Marine Record. March 20, 1902. http://images.maritimehistoryofthegreatlakes.ca/65477/ page/data?n.

Marine Review. June 14, 1894. http://images.maritimehistoryofthegreatlakes.ca/64973/ data?n.

Marine Review. March 13, 1902. http://images.maritimehistoryofthegreatlakes.ca/65375/ data?n.

Marine Review. March 20, 1902. http://images.maritimehistoryofthegreatlakes.ca/65376/ data?n.

Marine Review. June 12, 1902. http://images.maritimehistoryofthegreatlakes.ca/65389/ data?n.

Marine Review. June 12, 1902. http://images.maritimehistoryofthegreatlakes.ca/65389/ data?n.

Marinette Eagle-Star. August 22, 1984. DGLM VF.

Maybury, William. Letter from a 1901 century box, DHSC.

McMillan, Philip, to Sen. W. S. Green, May 4, 1910, James McMillan Papers, BHC.

Miller, Fred. "A Letter from Captain Miller," *Buffalo Daily Republic*, September 29, 1856. http://images.maritimehistoryofthegreatlakes.ca/40380/data?n=7.

Milwaukee Journal Sentinel. July 5, 1996, A8. DGLM VF.

Milwaukee Sentinel. August 17, 1841. http://www3.gendisasters.com/new-york/14801/ silver-creek-ny-steamer-erie-fire-aug-1841-further-particulars.

Minister of Marine and Fisheries of Canada. *Review of Improvements in Lighthouse and Coast Service in Canada, 1903.* Ottawa: Minister of Marine and Fisheries, 1904.

Monroe, James, to Charles Bagot, August 2, 1816. Avalon Project, http://avalon.law.yale. edu/19th_century/br1817I2.asp.

Motor News. July 1951. DGLM VF.

"New Lake Erie Steam-Boat *Superior.*" *Detroit Gazette,* May 15, 1822. http://images. maritimehistoryofthegreatlakes.ca/3347/data?n=11.

"New Lake Erie Steam-boat *Superior.*" *Detroit Gazette,* May 31, 1822, 3. http://images. maritimehistoryofthegreatlakes.ca/3347/data?n=11.

"The New Steam-Boat." *Detroit Gazette,* May 31, 1822, 3. http://images.maritimehistory ofthegreatlakes.ca/3346/data?n=2.

"A New Steamboat on Lake Ontario." *Kingston Gazette,* September 14, 1816, 3. http:// images.maritimehistoryofthegreatlakes.ca/7860/data?n=4.

"A New Steamboat Line." *Marine Record,* September 22, 1898, 12. http://images.mari timehistoryofthegreatlakes.ca/65195/page/4?n=.

"New Steamer *City of Cleveland.*" *Marine Review,* May 7, 1908. 1, 20-7. DGLM VF.

New York Herald. July 22, 1847.

New York Herald. July 26, 1847.

New York Mercantile Advertiser. Quoted in the *Detroit Gazette,* May 14, 1819. http:// images.maritimehistoryofthegreatlakes.ca/3256/data?n=18.

Niagara Patriot. October 6, 1818. http://images.maritimehistoryofthegreatlakes. ca/48177/data?n=52.

Niles' National Register (Baltimore). June 26, 1847, vol. 72, 266. http://babel.hathitrust. org/cgi/pt?id=inu.30000117880546;view=1up;seq=271.

Niles' Weekly Register. March 29, 1817.

O'Shea, Art. "Investors' Love Affair with Dreamboat Sours." *Detroit News,* April 27, 1981.

Oswego Palladium. April 4, 1876. http://freepages.genealogy.rootsweb.ancestry. com/~twigs2000/vancleve.html.

Oswego Palladium. July 13, 1881. http://images.maritimehistoryofthegreatlakes.ca/5265/ data?n=11.

Palmer, Mary A. Witherall. "A Letter to E. C. Walker." In *Report of the Pioneer Society of the State of Michigan,* 4:112–15. Lansing: W.S. George and Co., 1883.

Polk, James K. "Veto Response to H.R. 18: An Act Making Appropriations for the Improvement of Certain Harbors and Rivers, August 3, 1846." 29th Cong., 1st sess., *Congressional Globe.* Washington, DC: US Government Printing Office, 1846 [date], 1181–83. http://memory.loc.gov/ammem/amlaw/lwcg.html.

"Problems for Package Freight Lines." *Marine Review,* January 1906, 31. DGLM VF.

Proceedings of Harbor and Rivers Convention Held in Chicago. Chicago: R. L. Wilson, 1847.

Sacket's Harbor Gazette. Quoted in the *Buffalo Gazette,* May 20, 1817. http://images.mar itimehistoryofthegreatlakes.ca/33167/data?n=2.

Schantz, Augustus, to W. M. Brittain, October 2, 1917, James McMillan Papers, BHC.

Schantz, Augustus, to F. I. Collins, April 18, 1917, James McMillan Papers, BHC.

Schantz, Augustus, to Sen. W. S. Green, May 4, 1910, James McMillan Papers, BHC.

Schantz, Augustus, to C. L. Perkins, June 12, 1916, James McMillan Papers, BHC.

Schoolcraft, Henry Rowe. *Narrative Journal of Travels from Detroit Northwest through the Great Chain of American Lakes to the Sources of the Mississippi River Performed as a Member of the Expedition under Governor Cass in the Year 1820.* Albany: E. & E. Hosford, 1821.

"Shipbuilding on the Lakes, No. 1: Buffalo and the District of Buffalo Creek, N.Y." *Monthly Nautical Magazine and Quarterly Review* (New York), January 1855, 289–98. http://images.maritimehistoryofthegreatlakes.ca/63351/data.

Southern Quarterly Review. October 1846, n. 10, 20.

St. Catharines Journal. August 9, 1826. http://images.maritimehistoryofthegreatlakes.ca/57871/data?n=18.

"Steamboat *Frontenac.*" *Kingston Gazette*, May 31, 1817. http://images.maritimehistoryofthegreatlakes.ca/33152/data?n=2.

"Steamboat *Frontenac.*" *Kingston Gazette*, June 7, 1817. http://images.maritimehistoryofthegreatlakes.ca/7860/data?n=4.

"Steam Boat *Ontario.*" *Geneva Gazette*, July 7, 1819. http://images.maritimehistoryofthegreatlakes.ca/35718/data?n=1.

"Steam Boat *Ontario.*" *Rochester Telegraph*, July 7, 1818. http://images.maritimehistoryofthegreatlakes.ca/6612/data?n=15.

"Steam Boat *Ontario.*" *Rochester Telegraph*, August 11, 1818. http://images.maritimehistoryofthegreatlakes.ca/35912/data?n=8.

"The Steamboat *Ontario.*" *Ontario Repository* (Canandaigua, NY), August 9, 1817. http://images.maritimehistoryofthegreatlakes.ca/5084/data?n=1.

"The Steamboat *Ontario.*" *Ontario Repository*, August 18, 1818. http://images.maritimehistoryofthegreatlakes.ca/5087/data?n=12.

Sullivan, John L. "Annexation." *United States Magazine and Democratic Review* 17, no. 1 (July–August 1845): 5–10.

Sullivan, John L. "The Great Nation of Futurity," *United States Democratic Review* 6, no. 23 (November 1839): 426–30.

Tiffin, Edward, to Josiah Meigs, November 30, 1815. In *Michigan Pioneer and Historical Collections.* Lansing: Michigan Historical Commission, 1888.

Toledo Blade. July 11, 1962. DGLM VF.

Telescope 2, no. 11 (November 1953): 4–5.

Utica Sentinel. February 20, 1822. Reprinted in the *Detroit Gazette*, March 22, 1822. http://images.maritimehistoryofthegreatlakes.ca/3339/data?n=2.

"What the Wireless Telephone Is Doing for the Great Lakes." *Coos Bay Times* (Oregon), February 13, 1909, evening ed., 3. http://earlyradiohistory.us/1909gl.htm.

White, Stoddard. "Last 2 Lake Cruise Ships up for Sale." *Detroit News*, September 30, 1962. DGLM VF.

White, Stoddard. *Detroit News*, March 20, 1963. DGLM VF.

Secondary Sources

Anderson, Bern. *By Sea and by River: The Naval History of the Civil War.* New York: Alfred. A. Knopf, 1962.

Appleton, Thomas E. *Usque Ad Mare: A History of the Canadian Coast Guard and Marine Services.* Ottawa: Canada Department of Transport, 1968. Archived at http://www.ccg-gcc.gc.ca/eng/CCG/USQUE_Telegraph.

Babcock & Wilcox Company. *Steam: Its Generation and Use.* New York: Babcock & Wilcox, 1914.

Babson, Steve. *Working Detroit.* Detroit: Wayne State University Press, 1984.

Baker, Newton D. "Transportation on the Great Lakes." *Annals of the American Academy of Political and Social Science* 171 (January 1934): 204–10. http://www.jstor.org/stable/1018101.

Baker, William Avery, and Tre Tryckare. *The Engine Powered Vessel.* New York: Crescent Books, 1972.

Baldwin, Leland D. *The Keelboat Age on Western Waters*. 3rd ed. Pittsburgh: University of Pittsburgh Press, 1980.

Boyer, Dwight. *True Tales of the Great Lakes*. New York: Dodd, Mead, 1971.

Braun, Richard H. "The Georgian Bay Line." *Inland Seas* 54, no. 3 (Fall 1998): 175–83.

Brown, Grant, Jr. *Ninety Years Crossing Lake Michigan: The History of the Ann Arbor Car Ferries*. Ann Arbor: University of Michigan Press, 2008.

Burton, Clarence M. *The City of Detroit, Michigan, 1701–1922*. 5 vols. Detroit: S. J. Clarke, 1922.

Callahan, Edward W. *List of Officers of the Navy of the United States and the Marine Corps from 1775 to 1900*. New York: L. R. Hamersly, 1901.

Cameron, Scott L. *The 'Frances Smith': Palace Steamers of the Upper Great Lakes, 1867–1896*. Toronto: Natural Heritage Books, 2005.

Cantor, George. *Old Roads of the Midwest*. Ann Arbor: University of Michigan Press, 1997.

Commons, John R. "Types of American Labor Unions: Longshoremen of the Great Lakes." *Quarterly Journal of Economics* 20, no. 1 (November 1905): 59–85.

Cotterill, Robert S. "Early Agitation for a Pacific Railroad, 1845–1850." *Mississippi Valley Historical Review* 5, no. 4 (March 1919): 396–414.

Cotterill, Robert S. "Southern Railroads and Western Trade." *Mississippi Valley Historical Review* 3, no. 4 (March 1917): 427–41.

Cunningham, Barlow. *A Century of Sail and Steam on the Niagara River*. Toronto: Musson Book Company, 1911.

Dangerfield, George. "The Steamboat's Charter of Freedom." *American Heritage* 14, no. 6 (October 1963): 38–43.

Dayton, Fred Erving. *Steamboat Days*. New York: Frederick A. Stokes, 1925.

Dedmon, Emmett. *Fabulous Chicago*. 2nd ed. New York: Athenaeum, 1981.

Detroit City Directory. Detroit: J. W. Weeks, 1874.

Detroit City Directory. Detroit: J. W. Weeks, 1884.

Detroit City Directory. Detroit: R. L. Polk, 1895.

Detroit City Directory. Detroit: R. L. Polk, 1902.

Dickenson, John N. *To Build a Canal: Sault Ste. Marie, 1853–54 and After*. Columbus: Ohio State University Press, 1981.

Dixon, Michael. *Motormen and Yachting*. Grosse Pointe, MI: Mervue Publications, 2005.

Dixon, Michael. *When Detroit Rode the Waves*. Grosse Pointe, MI: Mervue Publications, 2001.

Dunbar, Willis Frederick. *Michigan through the Centuries*. New York: Lewis Historical Publishing, 1955.

Duncan, Francis. "Story of the D&C." *Inland Seas* 7, no. 4 (Winter 1951): 219–28.

Duncan, Francis. "Story of the D&C." *Inland Seas* 8, no. 2 (Summer 1952): 90–98.

Duncan, Francis. "Story of the D&C." *Inland Seas* 8, no. 3 (Fall 1952): 167–76.

Duncan, Francis. "Story of the D&C." *Inland Seas* 8, no. 4 (Winter 1952): 268–74.

Duncan, Francis. "Story of the D&C." *Inland Seas* 9, no. 1 (Spring 1953): 27–34.

Duncan, Francis. "Story of the D&C." *Inland Seas* 9, no. 2 (Summer 1953): 125–29.

Duncan, Francis. "Story of the D&C." *Inland Seas* 9, no. 3 (Fall 1953): 181–86.

Duncan, Francis. "Story of the D&C." *Inland Seas* 9, no. 4 (Winter 1953): 281–87.

Duncan, Francis. "The Story of the D&C." *Inland Seas* 11, no. 2 (Summer 1955): 126–32.

Duncan, Francis. "The Story of the D&C." *Inland Seas* 13, no. 4 (Winter 1957): 274–82.

Durham, Bill, ed. *Steamboats and Modern Steam Launches*. Burbank, CA: Howell-North Books, 1973.

Earle, Alice Morse. *Stage Coach and Tavern Days*. Detroit: Singing Tree Press, 1968. Originally published by Macmillan in 1900.

Elliott, James L. *Red Stacks over the Horizon: The Story of the Goodrich Steamboat Line*. Ellison Bay, WI: William Caxton, 1995.

Ewen, William H. *Days of the Steamboats*. New York: Parents' Magazine Press, 1967.

Fox, Celina. "The Ingenious Mr Dummer: Rationalizing the Royal Navy in Late Seventeenth-Century England." *Electronic British Library Journal*, 2007. http://www.bl.uk/eblj/2007articles/pdf/ebljarticle102007.pdf.

Fuller, George N. "Settlement of Michigan Territory." *Mississippi Valley Historical Review* 2, no. 1 (June 1915): 25–55.

Fuller, L. N. "Northern New York in the Patriot War." *Watertown Daily Times*. 25 chapters published in serial form, March–April 1923. http://freepages.genealogy.rootsweb.ancestry.com/~twigs2000/chapvii.html.

Garrity, Richard. *Canal Boatman: My Life on Upstate Waters*. Syracuse, NY: Syracuse University Press, 1977.

Gibbs, Vernon. *Passenger Liners of the Western Ocean*. New York: Staples Press, 1952.

Gillett, Mary C. *Army Medical Department, 1818–1865*. Washington, DC: US Government Printing Office, 1987.

Goode, Charles Wilson. "Recasting Michigan's Image: The Darby Treatise." In *Border Crossings: The Detroit River Region in the War of 1812*, edited by Denver Brunsman, Joel Stone, and Douglas D. Fisher, 267–80. Detroit: Detroit Historical Society, 2012.

Grady, Wayne. *The Great Lakes: The Natural History of a Changing Region*. Vancouver: Grey Stone Books, 2007.

Gray, Ralph. *A National Waterway: History of the Chesapeake and Delaware Canal, 1769–1965*. Urbana: University of Illinois Press, 1967.

Henry, John. *Great White Fleet: Celebrating Canada Steamship Lines Passenger Ships*. Toronto: Dundurn Press, 2013.

Hershock, Martin. *The Paradox of Progress*. Athens: Ohio University Press, 2003.

Heyl, Eric. *Early American Steamers*. Vols. 1–6. Buffalo: Eric Heyl, 1953–69.

Hill, Henry Wayland, ed. *Municipality of Buffalo, New York: A History, 1720–1923*. New York: Lewis Historical Publishing Company, 1923.

Hilton, George W. *Great Lakes Car Ferries*. Berkeley, CA: Howell-North, 1962.

Hilton, George W. *Lake Michigan Passenger Steamers*. Redwood City, CA: Stanford University Press, 2002.

Hilton, George W. *The Night Boat*. Berkeley, CA: Howell-North, 1968.

Hodge, William. *Papers Concerning Early Navigation on the Great Lakes*. 2 vols. Buffalo: Bigelow Bros., 1883.

Hoey, William. "Birth of a Lakes Leviathan: *City of Cleveland*." *Telescope* 9, no. 10 (October 1960): 175–77.

Hogg, Peter, and Cornelius H. Delamater, plaintiffs in error, v. John B. Ericsson. 52 U.S. 587 (11 How. 587, 13 L.Ed. 824). http://www.law.cornell.edu/supremecourt/text/52/587 September 2012.

Hunter, Louis C. *Steamboats on the Western Rivers: An Economic and Technological History*. Mineola, NY: Dover, 1993.

Jansen, Kerri. "Lydia Bacon: Army Wife, Intrepid Traveler." In *Border Crossings: The Detroit River Region in the War of 1812*, edited by Denver Brunsman, Joel Stone, and Douglas D. Fisher, 112–23. Detroit: Detroit Historical Society, 2012.

Jensen, John Odin. "The History and Archeology of the Great Lakes Steamboat Niagara." *Wisconsin Magazine* 82, no. 3 (Spring 1999): 198–230.

Jensen, Oliver. "Side-Wheels and Walking Beams." *American Heritage* 5, no. 5 (August 1961): 40–49.

Johnson, Joseph E. *Walk-in-the-Water* ship plans. Illustration, c. 1951. Ship Plans Collection. Detroit Historical Society.

Kern, Florence. *The United States Revenue Cutters in the Civil War*. Bethesda, MD: Alised Enterprises, 1976.

Klein, L. "Notes on the Steam Navigation upon the Great Northern Lakes." *Inland Seas*

48, no. 1 (Spring 1992): 54–55. Originally published in the *American Railroad Journal* in 1841.

Lalor, John J., ed. *Cyclopedia of Political Science, Political Economy, and the Political History of the United States.* New York: Maynard, Merrill, 1899.

Lane, Carl D. *American Paddle Steamboats.* New York: Coward-McCann, 1943.

Larson, John W. *Essayons: A History of the Detroit District, U.S. Army Corps of Engineers.* Detroit: US Army Corps of Engineers, Detroit District, 1981.

LeMieux, Dave. "Tracking the Story." *Muskegon Chronicle*, April 11, 2011. http://www.mlive.com/news/muskegon/index.ssf/2011/04/looking_back_welcome_aboard_th.html.

Lewis, Walter. "The *Frontenac*: A Reappraisal." *FreshWater* 2, no. 1 (Summer 1987): 28–39. http://www.maritimehistoryofthegreatlakes.ca/Documents/frontenac/default.asp?ID=ss003.

Lewis, Walter. "Steamboat Promotion and Changing Technology: The Careers of James Sutherland and the *Magnet*." *Ontario History* 77, no. 3 (September 1985): 207–30. http://maritimehistoryoftheGreatLakes.ca/Documents/sutherlandmagnet.

"List of Principle [*sic*] Steamboats upon the Upper Lakes in 1839." *Inland Seas* 48, no. 1 (Spring 1992): 50.

Macaulay, Gordon. "Ferries out of Owen Sound." *Inland Seas* 21, no. 2 (Summer 1965): 92–102.

Macaulay, Gordon. "Ferries out of Owen Sound." *Inland Seas* 21, no. 3 (Fall 1965): 187–209.

Mansfield, J. B., ed. *History of the Great Lakes.* Vol. 1. Chicago: J. H. Beers, 1899. Transcription available at http://www.maritimehistoryofthegreatlakes.ca/documents/hgl/default.asp?ID=s007.

Marchildon, Gregory. *Profits and Politics: Beaverbrook and the Gilded Age of Canadian Finance.* Toronto: University of Toronto Press, 1996.

Mayer, Harold M., and Richard Wade. *Chicago: Growth of a Metropolis.* Chicago: University of Chicago Press, 1969.

McNeese, Tim. *America's Early Canals.* New York: Crestwood House, 1993.

Mendelsohn, Betty. "The Federal Hand in Urban Development: Chicago Harbor before the Civil War." *Prologue* 30, no. 4 (Winter 1998): 257–65.

"Milwaukee Clipper: A Streamlined 106-Year-Old Steamer." *PowerShips*, no. 277 (Spring 2011): 30–31.

Mitchell, D. C. *Steamboats on the Fox River.* Oshkosh, WI: Castle-Pierce Press, 1986.

Mohar, Donald L. "Major Economic Conventions during the Polk Administration." MA thesis, Illinois State University, 1968.

Mull, Carol E. *The Underground Railroad in Michigan.* Jefferson, NC: McFarland, 2010.

Musham, H. A. "Early Great Lakes Steamboats: The First Propellers, 1841–1845." *Telescope* 6, no. 10 (October 1957): 4–6.

Nelson, Bruce. *Workers on the Waterfront.* Urbana: University of Illinois Press, 1988.

Newell, Gordon. *Pacific Steamboats.* Seattle: Superior Publishing, 1958.

North, Douglas, and Robert Thomas. *The Growth of the American Economy to 1860.* Columbia: University of South Carolina Press, 1968.

O'Brien, T. Michael. *Guardians of the Eighth Sea: a History of the U.S. Coast Guard on the Great Lakes.* Washington, DC: Government Printing Office, 1976.

Oxford, William. *The Ferry Steamers.* Toronto: Stoddard Publishing, 1992.

Palmer, Richard F. "Canadian Steamer Rescued by Woman." *Inland Seas* 54, no. 3 (Fall 1998): 189–92.

Palmer, Richard F. "The First Steamboat on the Great Lakes." *Inland Seas* 44, no. 2 (Spring 1988). http://navalmarinearchive.com/research/pdf/in_seas_xl_1–7_sm.pdf.

Palmer, Richard F. "Wreck of the Steamboat *Martha Ogden*." *Inland Seas* 55, no. 1 (Spring 1999): 5–9.

Paris, John. "Fraud on the Frontier." In *Border Crossings: The Detroit River Region in the War of 1812*, edited by Denver Brunsman, Joel Stone, and Douglas D. Fisher, 35–48. Detroit: Detroit Historical Society, 2012.

Paskoff, Paul F. *Troubled Waters: Steamboat Disasters, River Improvements, and American Public Policy, 1821–1860*. Baton Rouge: Louisiana State University Press, 2007.

Plumb, R. G. "The Goodrich Line." *Inland Seas* 50, no. 3 (Fall 1994): 202–8. Reprinted from *Inland Seas*, April 1945.

Porter, Mary. *Eliza Chappell Porter, a Memoir*. New York: Fleming H. Revell, 1892. http://openlibrary.org/books/OL7208554M/Eliza_Chappell_Porter.

Putnam, George R. "Beacons of the Seas: Lighting the Coasts of the United States." *National Geographic* 24, no. 1 (January 1913): 19.

Pyle, G. F. "The Diffusion of Cholera in the United States in the Nineteenth Century." *Geographical Analysis* 1, no. 1 (September 2010): 59–75. http://onlinelibrary.wiley.com/doi/10.1111/j.1538–4632.1969.tb00605.x/pdf.

Rhodes, James Ford. *History of the United States from the Compromise of 1850*. Edited by Allan Nevins. Chicago: University of Chicago Press, 1966. Originally published by Macmillan in 1904.

Rodgers, Bradley A. *Guardian of the Great Lakes: The U.S. Paddle Frigate 'Michigan.'* Ann Arbor: University of Michigan Press, 1996.

Rosie, Ronald. Notes submitted to the Era of Elegance project, 2007. DHSC.

Rousseau, Peter L. "A Common Currency: Early US Monetary Policy and the Transition to the Dollar." *Financial History Review* 13, no. 1 (2006): 97–122. http://www.vanderbilt.edu/econ/candidates/papers/plr/fhr06.pdf.

Salinger, Sharon V. *Taverns and Drinking in Early America*. Baltimore: Johns Hopkins University Press, 2002.

Salmon, M. Stephen. "'This Remarkable Growth': Investment in Canadian Great Lakes Shipping, 1900–1959." *Northern Mariner/Le marin du nord* 15, no. 3 (July 2005): 1–37. http://www.cnrs-scrn.org/northern_mariner/vol15/tnm_15_3_1-37.pdf.

Schmitt, Paul. "Two Sisters Tell a Story of the Remarkable Impact of the Side-Wheel Steamers." *Inland Seas* 51, no. 4 (Winter 1995): 2–10.

Schneider, Nancy A. "The Magnificent *Noronic:* Absolute Queen of the Luxury Passenger Vessels on the Lakes." *Inland Seas* 52, no. 4 (Winter 1996): 241–49.

Schwartz, Stephen. *Excerpts from "Brotherhood of the Sea: A History of the Sailors' Union of the Pacific, 1885–1985*. San Francisco: Sailors' Union of the Pacific, 1985.

Semenoro, Timothy. "The State of Our Seafaring Nation: What Course Has Congress Laid for the U.S. Maritime Industry." *Tulane Maritime Law Journal* 25, no. 1 (Winter 2000): 335–36.

Sheriff, Carol. *The Artificial River: The Erie Canal and the Paradox of Progress*. New York: Hill and Wang, 1996.

Slater, Charlotte. "Social Director without a Ship." *Detroit News*, October 17, 1967, D3.

Smith, Maurice D. *Steamboats on the Lakes: Two Centuries of Steamboat Travel through Ontario's Waterways*. Toronto: James Lorimer, 2005.

Snyder, H. C. "Union Steamboat Company: Its History, in Part, with Comparison of Steamers as They Were and Are Today." *Erie Railroad Magazine, Erie Railroad Lake Line Division*, April 1914. http://freepages.genealogy.rootsweb.ancestry.com/~sponholz/erielakehistory.html.

Spratt, H. Philip. *Transatlantic Steamers* 2nd ed. Glasgow: Brown and Sons, 1967.

St. Mane, Ted. *Lost Passenger Steamships of Lake Michigan*. Charleston, SC: History Press, 2010.

Stampp, Kenneth M. *America in 1857: A Nation on the Brink*. New York: Oxford University Press, 1990.

Stanton, Samuel Ward. *American Steam Vessels*. New York: Smith & Stanton, 1895.

Stearns, Bertha Monica. "Philadelphia Magazines for Ladies, 1830–1860." *Pennsylvania Magazine of History and Biography* 69, no. 3 (July 1945): 207–19.

Sterba, Chuck. "An Early Great Lakes Shipping Giant." *Soundings* 50, nos. 1–2 (Spring–Summer 2010): 3–5, 16–17.

Stone, Joel. "A Packet Full of Trouble: Labor Relations, Federal Legislation, and the Detroit & Cleveland Navigation Company, 1910–1920." MA thesis, Wayne State University, 2007.

Stone, Joel. "Survey of Detroit Taverns and Hotels." Unpublished manuscript.

Stonehouse, Frederick. *Wreck Ashore: The United States Life-Saving Service on the Great Lakes.* Duluth: Lake Superior Port Cities, 1994.

Symons, Thomas W., and John C. Quintus. "History of Buffalo Harbor." *Publications of the Buffalo Historical Society* 5 (January 1902): 239–85.

Taylor, Alan. *The Civil War of 1812: American Citizens, British Subjects, Irish Rebels, and Indian Allies.* New York: Alfred A. Knopf, 2010.

Taylor, William Leonhard. *A Productive Monopoly.* Providence, RI: Brown University Press, 1970.

Thompson, Mark. *Steamboats and Sailors of the Great Lakes.* Detroit: Wayne State University Press, 1991.

Tonnage on the Lakes. Halton Hills, ON: Maritime History of the Great Lakes, 2004.

Toronto Historical Society. "The Northern Navigation Company, Limited." *Scanner* 6, no. 7 (April 1974). http://www.maritimehistoryofthegreatlakes.ca/Documents/scanner/06/07/default.asp?ID=c007.

Tunell, George. "Transportation on the Great Lakes of North America." *Journal of Political Economy* 4, no. 3 (June 1896): 332–51. http://www.jstor.org/stable/1817629.

Turner, E. S. *The Shocking History of Advertising.* New York: E. P. Dutton, 1953.

United States Department of the Navy, Bureau of Equipment. *Wireless Telegraph Stations of the World.* Washington, DC: Government Printing Office, 1909. http://earlyradiohistory.us/1909stat.htm#vesselsworld.

United States Naval War Records Office. *Official Records of the Union and Confederate Armies in the War of Rebellion.* Series 1, vol. 3, pt. 2. Washington, DC: Government Printing Office, 1896.

United States Treasury Department. *Annual Report of the Light-House Board for the Fiscal Year Ended June 30, 1903.* Washington, DC: Government Printing Office, 1903.

United States War Department. *The War of Rebellion: A Compilation of the Official Records of the Union and Confederate Armies in the War of Rebellion,* Series I, Vol. 43, Part II. Washington, DC: Government Printing Office, 1893.

Van Heest, Valerie. *Lost on the Lady Elgin.* Holland, MI: In-Depth Editions, 2010.

Wabash Railroad Company. "Wabash Railroad History." Condensed from an article authored by the Advertising and Public Relations Department of the Wabash Railroad Company, August 1959. http://wabashrhs.org/wabhist.html.

Walker, Augustus. "Early Days on the Lakes, with an Account of the Cholera Visitation of 1832." *Publications of the Buffalo Historical Society* 5 (January 1902): 287–318. http://www.maritimehistoryofthegreatlakes.ca/Documents/walker/default.asp?ID=c1.

Wallis, John Joseph. "American Government Finance in the Long Run: 1790 to 1990." *Journal of Economic Perspectives* 14, no. 1 (Winter 2000): 61–82.

Warnes, Kathleen. "Steamboats and the Black Hawk War." *Inland Seas* 52, no. 3 (Fall 1998): 180–86.

Wendt, Gordon. *In the Wake of "Walk-in-the-Water."* Sandusky, OH: Commercial Printing, 1984.

Whitlark, Fred. "Sailing with the Georgian Bay Line on the Flagship *South American.*" *Inland Seas* 60, no. 4 (Winter 2004): 306–16.

Wiebe, Robert H. *The Opening of American Society.* New York: Alfred A Knopf, 1984.

Wilcox, Frank N., and William A. McGill. *The Ohio Canals*. Kent, OH: Kent State University Press, 1969.

Williams, Mentor L. "The Chicago River and Harbor Convention, 1847." *Mississippi Valley Historical Review* 35, no. 4 (March 1949): 607–28.

Williams, Mentor L. "A Great Lakes Excursion, 1847 Style." *Inland Seas* 6, no. 3 (Fall 1950): 153–45.

Wilson, William Benson. *History of the Pennsylvania Railroad*. Philadelphia: Henry T. Coates, 1894.

Woodford, Arthur. *Charting the Inland Seas, Etc.* Detroit: Wayne State University Press, 1994.

Woodford, Frank B. *Lewis Cass: The Last Jeffersonian*. New Brunswick, NJ: Rutgers University Press, 1950.

Young, Anna G. "Great beyond Knowing." Pt. 1. *Inland Seas* 21, no. 4 (Winter 1965): 267–76.

Young, Anna G. "Great Beyond Knowing." Pt. 2. *Inland Seas* 22, no. 1 (Spring 1966): 29–34.

Zelezny, J. *Communications Law*. Belmont, CA: Wadsworth, 1993.

Zimmerman, Karl. *Lake Michigan Railroad Car Ferries*. Andover, NJ: Andover Junction, 1993.

Manuscript Collections Cited

Brendon Baillod Collection, Dane County, Wisconsin.

Detroit Historical Society Collection. This includes the Dossin Great Lakes Museum Vertical Files and Ship Plans Collection.

Historical Collection of the Great Lakes, Bowling Green State University, Bowling Green, Ohio.

James McMillan Papers. Burton Historical Collection, Detroit Public Library.

Rev. Edward Dowling Collection, University of Detroit.

Ward Family Papers. Burton Historical Collection, Detroit Public Library.

Index

Note: Page locators in *italics* indicate photographs or illustrations.

134; flat-topped rail carriers, 170, 171; partnerships with, 61, 67, 68, 148, 151, 158, 160; reliance on, 160; steamers as ferry boats, 89; steamship assets, divestiture of, 223; western routes, 81, 158; year-round nature of, 150. *See also* rail ferries; railroads, regulation of
railroads, regulation of: Panama Canal Act of 1912, 218
Rand, Greenleaf, 145, 147
Ranger III, 240
Rapids King, 183, 223
Read, Nathan, 11
Red Star Line, 158
Reed, Charles Manning, 71–72, 86, 89, 121
Reed, Daniel (Master), 22
Reynolds, John (Governor), 75
Richard, Gabriel (Father), 77
Richards, Tommy (Captain), 88
Richelieu, 230
Rideau Canal, 52–53, 67
Rising Star, 82
RMS *Titanic*, 211, 215, 217
Roby, J. S., 33
Rochester, 72
Rockefeller, John D., 174
Rodgers, Jedediah (Captain), 36, 37, 39, 40, 42, 56, 57, 58, 59
Rogers, Jedediah. *See* Rodgers, Jedediah (Captain)
Roosevelt, Nicholas J., 11, 12
Roosevelt, Theodore (Vice President), 180
Royal William, 82, 83
Rumsey, James, 10
Rush-Bagot Treaty (1818), 101, 135
Ryerson, Martin, 148

Sagamo, 183
Saguenay, 183
Sailor Boy, 221
Salem Packet, 70
Sault Sainte Marie canal, 53, 111, 240
Savannah, 81–82
Schantz, Augustus, 218
Schenck, Robert, 114
Schoolcraft, Henry Rowe, 37, 50, 51, 59
Scott, Winfield (General), 76, 177
Scripps, William, 188
Sea Horse, 20
Seabird, 144, 146–47, 148
Seamen's Act, 218, 221, 227. *See also* Act to Promote the Welfare of American Seamen in the Merchant Marine of the United States (1915)
Seeandbee, 172, 183, *188*, 196, 211, 228
Sharp, George C., 234
Sheldon Thompson, 76
Shenango Furnace fleet, 189
Sherwood, Thomas, 109
ship design, twentieth-century: palace propellers, 191; palace steamers, 191
shipbuilders. *See names of specific companies or individuals*
shipbuilding: competition between US and Canada, 15–16; growth of, 121
Shipping Act of 1916, 217
shipping companies. *See names of specific companies or corporations*
shipping industry: changing trends in, 164; transportation sectors, interdependency of, 158
shipyards: Lake Ontario, expansion on, 14. *See also names of specific companies or individuals*
Simcoe & Lake Huron Rail Road, 122
Sir James Kempt, 67
Sirius, 82–83
Skylark, 147
slavery: border states' factional disputes, 118; legal slavery, 118; Underground Railroad, 141–42
Smith, Joseph: *Book of Mormon*, 68
Smith, Maurice D.: *Steamboats on the Lakes*, 160
Smith, William, 15
Sons of Liberty, 136
Soo Locks, 71. *See also* Sault Sainte Marie canal
South American, 1–3, *2*, 4, *97*, 183, 203, 214, 231, *232*, 233
Southern Michigan, 125
Southern Pacific Railroad, 158
Southerner, 151
Sport, 172
Spritalia seu Pneumatica (Heron of Alexandria), 9
St. Clair Flats: hazards of, 87–88
St. Joseph-Chicago Steamship Company, 213–14
St. Lawrence, 125, 230
St. Lawrence canals, 67, 75
St. Louis, 72, 114, 115
St. Paul, Minneapolis & Manitoba Railway, 161–62
Stackhouse, Samuel, 99

Stanard, Asa, 69
Stannard, Charles C. (Captain), 127
Star-Cole line, 158
State of New York, 156, 158
State of Ohio, 156
Ste. Claire, 183, 240
steam engines: low-pressure, twin-cylinder engine, 99–100; low-pressure lever engine, 83; quadruple expansion engine from *South American*, 97; rocker-beam engine from *Darius Cole*, 97; single-cylinder vertical-configured engine, 85; transportation, impact on, 81; twin-cylinder inclined engine, 85; types, 66; vertical or cross-head engine from *Frontenac*, 97
steam navigation, 133–76, 179–240
Steam Ship Historical Society of America, 236
steam technology, advances in, 9–12
Steamboat Act of 1838, 106
steamboat fleets: growth of, 79–81, 121
steamboat voyages: characteristics of, 61–64
steamboats. *See also* steamships: early eighteenth century, 12; eras of, 3–6
Steamboats on the Lakes (Smith), 160
steamers, Goodrich-type, 161
steamship: races, 89, 123–24
steamship companies: marketing of, 167; successful mergers of, 222–24
steamship construction: iron sheathing, 96–98; iron *vs.* wood, 98, 99
steamship design: electric lighting, 173; horizontal wheel plans, 102; internal and external arch trusses, use of, 93–94; mechanical bow rudders, 173; paddlewheel hulls, 94–95; propellers, 68, 102; Whittaker propulsion system, 175; wooden steamers, structural problems, 93
steamship industry: advertising, 208–10, *209;* business and marketing challenges, 211–12; compartmentalization of business, 161, 164; Crash of 1837, effect of, 107; customer services, 127; environmental issues, 220; federal funding, 109, 111, 112, 113; freight operations in competition with trucks and trailers, 180; Gilded Age, in the, 165–76; international publicity, 108; marketing opportunities, 108, 116; meetings, 108–12, 114; philosophical and political debates over internal

improvements, 110; political lobbying efforts, 108; professional organizations, 107; public relation advantages, 107; railroad assets, divestiture of, 218; safety technology, 184–85; US Army Corps of Engineers' report, 107–8; viability of, 72–74
steamship industry, regulation of: Act to Promote the Welfare of American Seamen in the Merchant Marine of the United States (1915), 217–18; Canadian steamship acts, 106–7; Jones Act (1920), 215; La Follette Seamen's Act (1915), 215; licensing of skilled positions, 107; Merchant Marine Act (1920), 217; Panama Canal Act of 1918, 159; Shipping Act of 1916, 217; Steamboat Act of 1838, 106; wireless equipment, 186
steamship owners' associations, 74, 107; Lake Carriers' Association (LCA), 216; Lake Steamboat Association, 109
steamship races: *Niagara vs. Empire*, 89; *Ocean vs. Empire State*, 123–24
steamships: advantages over railroads, 61; Atlantic Ocean crossings, 82–83; competition, increase in, 66; decline of, 226; era of (1861–1900), 143–63; partnerships with railroads, 61, 67, 68, 70, 148, 151, 158, 160; propeller-driven, 68, 104–5; propellers, development of, 102; speed tests, 89
steamships, passenger: Civil War role, 140; decline of, 220–25, 238–40; iron-hulled, 101; migrant trade, 164, 166, 167; physical configurations of, 168–70; trends of, 161; Underground Railroad, role in, 140–42; wireless telegraph stations, 188. *See also* palace steamers
steamships, propeller-driven, 68; efficiencies of, 104; increased use on Great Lakes, 104; on standard bulk carriers, 104; tug boats, 104–5
Stevens, John, 11
Stevens, Robert L., 11
storm of 1913, 189, 211–12
strikes, longshoremen, 218, *219*
Sullivan, John L., 117
Sultana, 72, 89, 114
Sunbeam, 144, 146, 175
Superior, 57–60, 66, 69, 76
Superior, Lake, 37, 53, 58, 79, 115, 127, 144, 161, 171, 206, 221–23, 230, 240; geological features, 205